About the Author

Guy Newmountain, a unique eccentric who defies categorisation, is a practising artist/illustrator, retired animator and occasional DJ. Most notably, however, he is a former teacher who worked in 130 different schools across the entire age-range; with a breadth of experience rare in the profession. Creator of children's fairytale *The Man with the Eye at the End of His Finger*, a short film meticulously hand-coloured pixel-by-pixel over a 27-year period and winner of multiple international awards, he is a guilty cola drinker with a fascination for contemporary fonts, TV title sequences, pioneering music videos and retro sci-fi. Parent to a wilfully muleheaded and mischievous black Labrador, he swims a mile each weekday, but never fails to visit the chip shop on a Friday night.

Guy's previous book, *"Please I Can to the Toilet Go?" (The Memoirs of a Supply Teacher)*, was published by Austin Macauley in March 2023.

GUY NEWMOUNTAIN

Funnyology
Tales Beyond Teaching

AUSTIN MACAULEY PUBLISHERS
LONDON • CAMBRIDGE • NEW YORK • SHARJAH

Copyright © Guy Newmountain 2025

The right of Guy Newmountain to be identified as author of this work has been asserted in accordance with section 77 and 78 of the Copyright, Designs and Patents Act 1988.

All rights reserved. No part of this publication may be reproduced, stored in a retrieval system, or transmitted in any form or by any means, electronic, mechanical, photocopying, recording, or otherwise, without the prior permission of the publishers.

Any person who commits any unauthorised act in relation to this publication may be liable to criminal prosecution and civil claims for damages.

All of the events in this memoir are true to the best of the author's memory. The views expressed in this memoir are solely those of the author.

A CIP catalogue record for this title is available from the British Library.

ISBN 9781035876495 (Paperback)
ISBN 9781035876501 (Hardback)
ISBN 9781035876518 (ePub e-book)

www.austinmacauley.com

First Published 2025
Austin Macauley Publishers Ltd®
1 Canada Square
Canary Wharf
London E14 5AA

Dedication

Dedicated to my beloved parents Ruth and Roger, my brother Kim and all our extended family. I am blessed with many good friends, none of whom I take for granted; a mention also to those readers struggling to know where they belong and in what vocation; you need only read the 'Jobs' section here to see how many different avenues (some of them ridiculous) I myself have explored - and I'm not done yet! All experiences for me have their own value: for even when they don't work out, they lead you somewhere and contribute to the overall person you become.

Acknowledgements

I owe inspiration for the title to former Leicester Polytechnic and De Montfort University tutor, Ian Newsham, Associate Professor of Illustration: the word was a fitting colloquialism he used to describe me! Respect also to the brilliant contemporary street artist Ben Eine for generously permitting me to use his evocative New Circus typeface in the front cover design. My gratitude to Austin Macauley Publishers for the inclusion of my own artwork and for indulging the liberties I take with English grammar. Special thanks in particular to Walter Stephenson, whose calm overseeing of the whole pre-production process over there has maintained my sanity throughout.

Contents

Formative Memories – An Introduction 10

JOBS 13

    The Artshop 14

    The Census and the Zombie 19

    The Drill Bit Snapper 20

    The Lemon Sorbet Laughter Attack 22

    The Paint Demonstrator 24

    The Window Salesman 27

    The Crisp Factory Shiftworker 30

    The Hospital Kitchen 33

    The Ghost Train Dracula 36

    Grimsby Fisheries 39

    Career Nadir 41

    AutoTrader Magazine 44

    The Prize Draw 46

    The Crooked Employer 50

    The Broken Fridge 58

    Chinese Food Delivery 60

    Pulp Media 65

    Subscription Sales Executive 67

    Royal Mail 72

    DJ Guy 81

    Author 84

PRANKS 87

    Hide and Seek 88

    The Bus Provocation 90

    An Outbreak of Spitting 93

    The Rabbit Drink 97

    An Unusually Unpleasant Proprietor 99

    The Weight-Gain Wind-up 102

    The Metal Detector 106

    Sammy Salmonella 109
    Brotherly Nemesis 112
    The Welly Prank 119

A SPECTRUM OF TRIVIA 123

    The Inept Shopper 124
    Horseflies, Rattlesnakes and the Rottweiler of Doom 126
    How Artwork Saved My Life 131
    Locked in a Skyscraper 137
    The Alternative Curriculum 143
    The Charmless Encounter 146
    A War Veteran Under the Stairs 149
    The Bedroom Flood 152
    The Traffic Warden 155
    Treviso Airport 157
    Nescafé and Webster 162
    Giraffe Epitaph 166
    Fungus the Guyman 169
    The Transformation Edit 171
    An Evening with the Freak 173
    The Alien Abduction 176
    Rough Sleeping 179
    The Rat Dissection 183
    The Whirling Dervishes 187
    Get an Eyeful 192
    Free Ads 195
    World War One in Wapping 198
    The Running Away Kit 200
    Vogon Bill 201
    Testing the Boundaries 204
    Un-Green Fingers 207
    Voluntary Service Union 210
    The Three Peaks Walk 214
    The Awkward Predicament 218
    Outdoor Antics 220
    The Cabbage Incident 225

The Have-A-Go Hero 229
The Hospital Break-In 233
Slug 236
Learning – The Roundabout Way 239
The Plaster Disaster 242
Mr B 245
The Space Invaders Machine 248
Adult Swim 251
Bungalow Cakes 256
The Brown Derby 263
The Suspicious House 265
The Furry Assailant 267
From Student Rags to a Taste of Riches 273

FORMATIVE MEMORIES
– AN INTRODUCTION

A Teaching career isn't the whole story, you know. There's more to this Guy than meets the eye.

My earliest recollection is the noxious smell of formaldehyde; and being weighed in a freezing metal scales. I could have just been born, but it was probably later; for at birth I was confined to an incubator. By five months old, though, I was fiercely independent, insisting on feeding myself. I clearly recall whilst learning to walk, making each step towards my beckoning dad look a greater struggle than it was, to receive more praise. He was away a lot, doing 100-hour weeks as a hospital houseman; and our young mum was exhausted; struggling with two tiny children. We had several au pairs: a lovely French girl danced with me in her arms to Simon & Garfunkel's "El Condor Pasa".

On my first day at kindergarten, I was so distraught at being left, I took to banging my head repeatedly on a wall. The owner, an amazing Auschwitz survivor and friend of my grandparents, simply held me by the shoulders, looking into my eyes with a "don't-be-so-daft" expression, until I turned off the waterworks. The *light* that shone from that woman... She did a puppet show every Friday as we sucked warm milk from pyramid cartons. The best thing was a sensory sunken sandpit you sat in alone, in semi-darkness. Perhaps it evoked the comfort of the womb; for I remember thinking one day, *I absolutely love it here*... But the realisation came too late – it was time for me to leave and start school.

My new teacher put me in the care of an already-established pupil: an African-Caribbean girl a full head taller than me. We became quite good classmates later, but up to then, I had never seen a person of colour before. With an iron grip and baleful stare, that child *owned* me the whole day. Not one word did she say; but the more I tried to free my hand from hers, the tighter she gripped.

The teacher herself terrified me. *"A strange, round little boy"* is how she described me in my first school report. I had never seen anyone with mirror shades: to me, she looked like a bluebottle. By home-time, I was traumatised.

"Her *eyes*..." I wailed to my busy mum.

"Tell her to take her glasses off when she talks to you," she advised – but I couldn't find the words.

"What do you want to be when you grow up?" I was asked.

"A plum," I said.

When "Away in a Manger" was the hymn in Assembly, it was assumed we all understood the words "*The little Lord Jesus, asleep on the hay.*" I didn't. I genuinely imagined a "lorjesus" to be some kind of grasshopper or cricket.

My mum taught me with flashcards at home until I could blend phonics; then the Headteacher herself tested every pupil's reading before we got a new book. You waited outside her door until a 'traffic light' changed from red to green. If you read well, you got two jellybeans from her machine. Once I was shaky and got only one – I was mortified... By the age of six, though, I had a reading age of 13, *devouring* books: it took a suitcaseful a week from the library to occupy me.

A 'difficult' child, on family holidays, I would be banished by my exasperated parents into the sea with my share of the picnic; petrified of circling wasps on the beach. Out in the water, feeling simultaneously murderous and ashamed, I would eat alone from a plastic bag: no one really 'got' the full extent of my phobia.

I was so shy at age 14 that when a colleague of my dad's dropped in, she spotted me hiding behind a tree.

I kept my first beard in a Kinder Surprise.

Just a few examples illustrating why the title (a word used by a nonplussed former college tutor mystified by my artwork) sums up both book and author perfectly. I use 'funny' here in both senses: for the quirky and odd, as well as the amusing. Hopefully at least some of the anecdotes, split into three equally ludicrous sections, make you laugh out loud: that is my mission in this edition.

JOBS

THE ARTSHOP

The gentle description people use to cover a multitude of sins within someone's job history is "Portfolio Career". The less kind one, probably closer to the truth, is of course, "Jack of all trades, master of none"; although, in my case, there are still vocations I have not explored. I've never been a barman, builder, electrician, plumber or cleaner, but I can't deny I've tried my hand at many different things. Whilst still at school, I attended a day-long test which, via responses to hundreds of multiple-choice questions, aimed to identify your ideal career. My answers indicated I should be a car mechanic – another job I never did. I barely know the first thing that's under the bonnet: if the vehicle gets my dog from A to B, that's good enough for me.

Excepting a few early bouts of babysitting, my first encounter with the world of work proper was as a school-leaver aged 18, when my brother and I went down to the Jobcentre at the start of the summer holidays. In those days, vacancies were displayed on paper cards in rows of plastic shelves along the walls and on large frames in the centre of the room. You walked around them until something of interest caught your eye, then took the card to one of the staff, who explained the details and put you in direct telephone contact with the employer. The job we'd selected was "Strawberry Picker". You had to be at a farm way out in the village of Beeby by some ridiculous time like 6.30 a.m.; and it paid just 50p per six punnets picked. We both applied, overslept the next morning – then never turned up – not the most auspicious of beginnings.

After that false start, a year or so later, having just finished Art Foundation, I was given a tip-off by a friend on the course that there was a vacancy where his dad worked at a well-known local art shop alongside the market: W. Frank Gadsby Ltd. That opportunity really *did* excite me, as wherever you looked there was a blaze of colour; and doing the job would significantly aid my own awareness of different media, card and paper types. The only advice I got was to remember to wear a tie when I went in. I did so – and the very first person I met upon entering was benevolent old Mr Gadsby senior himself, with his handlebar moustache. There was no formal interview: "You've got a friendly smile – that's enough for me," he said. I was in. It was a six-day, nine-to-five working week for which I was paid the princely sum of £1 an hour. For the first couple of months, I was more or less constantly in trouble. The manager of the Graphics department thought he might drive me out with the old "glass hammer" wind-up, but back I came. I was asked not to slouch on the counter; and, disliking business dress, came in wearing corduroys, leading to his ordering me to come in "proper" trousers – even though he himself wore cords a week later. On the shopping spree to buy them, I also took the opportunity to buy several ties, going for cut-off leathers which looked as if they had paint spattered on them by Jackson Pollock. Those were somewhat frowned upon as too zany and outrageous for a long-established firm – but in fairness, it was the era of *Miami Vice,* a popular US TV show highly influential on UK fashion at the time...

Just as in the old adage, the female of the species proved far deadlier than the male: old Mrs Gadsby, the wife of the boss, did not suffer fools lightly. One day, she took me aside; and as I gulped nervously, every word from her mouth dripping with venom, she hissed, as if it was the most horrendous sin imaginable,

"A customer... has reported to me... that *you* have been seen... *chewing gum*... and if it happens again, you know the consequences..."

On another particularly busy day, I accused a customer of not having paid for something.

"Err – I think I have," she answered.

"I think you haven't," I countered – wishing the ground would swallow me up when she produced her receipt, holding it up by the corners with the most withering curl of her lip... We had a good laugh about it later, though, when I found out she was in the year above me on my degree course!

Gradually I found my feet; and after a few early disasters, became adept at knowing just where to rip the shop's own hand-sketched paper off the roll to wrap larger items. During the Christmas rush, I was even trusted to operate an antique cash register on my own at the opposite end of the floor. It was a *monster;* no different in temperament to the famous one in *Open All Hours*: the tray would literally wind you in the stomach when it sprang open if you didn't take avoiding action. There was one frantically packed day when I took over £1000 in cash for the shop in that old till.

In the original Cockney rhyming slang used on the day, we did once did get a professional '"tea-leaf" in the shop "half-inching" stock. In his haste to get away, he was firmly brought to the ground by a rugby tackle from one of the downstairs staff; on another occasion, detectives took over the top floor for the best part of a day. The upstairs window offered a perfect view over the market; they had been given the heads-up that some illegal activity was happening down there and a wanted criminal would be passing. After hours of inactivity, they suddenly leapt to life, burst from their vantage-point and plummeted down the stairs to make the arrest... Back then, in the pre-Mac heyday of good ol' Letraset rub-down transfer lettering, a large part of the job involved stocktaking and re-ordering from the big suppliers, Daler-Rowney or Winsor & Newton. When the delivery arrived, it often fell to me to lug all the enormously heavy parcels from a shipment approaching some 30 boxes, up the stairs from the basement on my back. I would then cut the holding straps with a scalpel and meticulously tick off each item present on the invoice before labelling them all individually with a red pricing gun and replenishing the shelves.

One afternoon, I noticed all the staff behind the counter turning their backs almost as one. I wasn't fast enough to follow suit and soon found out why when I was collared by the most repellent customer, a huge man who absolutely *stank*... The poor bloke probably suffered a condition like Chron's disease or a leaking colostomy bag; but whatever it was, it was accompanied by the foulest, most demanding manner. He would insist on being physically accompanied around the entire shop floor, asking the price of virtually every item not individually labelled, such as A1 card, paintbrushes or individual tubes of artist-quality paint (which were all priced differently); meaning you would have to return to the counter repeatedly to get the relevant price lists he required. Once told, he would then invariably shout, "Orrr bloody 'ell – that's too expensive – I'm not paying that!" If helping the man had ultimately been rewarding, resulting in a decent-sized purchase for all the time invested, it may have been worthwhile; but finally – after leaving you coping with the smell for what seemed an eternity, but was probably just half an hour – he would perhaps buy *one* pencil... I know "the customer is always right", but after a couple of these encounters, it wasn't long before I too was tempted to join the back-turners; the experience was so unpleasant.

We had some very funny moments, though. One tiny boy, oblivious to all the enticing stock on sale, spent his entire time in the shop tugging on his father's sleeve, shouting repeatedly, "Daddy! Daddy! There's a *Hoover* over there!" There was also once a cameo appearance from a guest sales assistant: Legion – a giant millipede as wide as a finger, which I had purchased one lunchtime from a pet shop (for more on that horrible place, see *The Bedroom Flood* anecdote). Some of the staff had mixed feelings about the jet-black, undulating monstrosity crawling over the counter; but in any event, it was short-lived, bizarrely biting off its own head in the night.

It was a real home-spun, old-fashioned family firm from days gone by, somehow comfortingly reminiscent of Grace Brothers in *Are You Being Served?* – with its own AGM and a Christmas dinner which was very swanky indeed; and from which we were all individually driven home, a bonus in our pay-packets... Sadly, in the end, to allow sufficient time to build up a portfolio in time for upcoming art college interviews, I had to leave; but not before taking good-natured revenge on everyone, caricaturing all the events which had occurred in a full-colour, eight-page, hand-painted comic-strip, *Life at Gadsby*... Generously, the management saw the funny side of all the banter; taking a colour copy of the whole thing. Over the years, I've actually tried a couple of times to rejoin the business, the response invariably being, "I don't think we could afford you now, Guy!"

THE CENSUS AND THE ZOMBIE

The first of another two fleeting temping jobs I took in my earliest years of employment was as a Vehicle Census Operative for Leicester City Council. The vacancy was up on one of the Jobcentre cards; I don't recall the pay level, but it was high for the time. You sat on a hard chair with a clipboard and pen in this rough little wooden booth about the size of a telephone box, which was ready and waiting on the corner of a busy crossroads on London Road. I was given a specific car colour to monitor and had to record and group the number passing in the form of a 'tally' chart (four vertical lines with a diagonal strike going through them for every five), making the eventual total faster to count. It was a full day-shift, all day for a week; and I smuggled in supplies to scoff and swig. My brother passed by on a bus, leering with mirth and laughing at me in my little box. That was closely followed by a dismal graveyard shift at a City Centre plastics factory where I stood at a conveyor belt through the small hours assembling nameless vacuum-formed parts until dawn. The work was so monotonous I became a mindless automaton; fast asleep with my eyes open...

THE DRILL BIT SNAPPER

In the summer of 1987, my parents' neighbour offered me a job in his garage next door. An ingenious former engineer and lecturer who had built up a cottage industry in his retirement, he had created large energy-saving units through which any company's electricity could be channelled to cut their bills. I got trained thoroughly in constructing these from scratch. You would begin by taking one of the large, grey, electrical enclosure cabinets or steel wall-boxes, marking positions on the housing with a scribe where various components were to be added, then drill holes through the metal. Having never used a drill before, the traumatising warning posters of our school's metalwork room in the '70s came to mind: graphic, gut-churning impalements girls had suffered whilst slipping in ill-advised platform soles. Wary of injury, I wobbled nervously whilst bearing down, resulting in a fair number of drill bits snapping in the early days, much to the man's pique. True, I was clumsy, but I did okay with electric drills; it was due in part to the cordless ones being only semi-charged. The chap was patient, though; and eventually I mastered the technique.

I would then have to fix onto each casing three thyristors: black, solid-state, rectangular semi-conductors which I didn't fully understand; but which conduct, block or manage electrical currents in high-powered applications. Mine not to reason why; but to obey... Each of the thyristor bases had to be coated with this electrically conductive, tacky white gunk, then be screwed firmly onto the metal, before wires were bolted on top in correct order; a key one linking back to the side of the casing. If you put too much gloop on, the surplus all came seeping out around the blocks as the bolts were screwed in. In the workshop, Radio 1 played the entire day, which made the tasks pass a little more easily; although the Los Lobos version of "La Bamba", at Number 1, was played to saturation by every DJ. The singer would chant the first line of the chorus, then my neighbour, who always seemed to have a delayed reaction to the chorus, would suddenly burst out *"Bamba!"* several seconds late, leaving me struggling not to laugh out loud. But once I got used to the work, I found the structured routine easy; becoming good enough to be left alone at the equipment. I even went back and did a further stint ten years on before he wrapped up the business for good.

THE LEMON SORBET LAUGHTER ATTACK

In the late 1980s, during the summer break from Art college, I did a number of different short-lived temporary jobs for a local field promotions company. These positions always paid a very generous hourly rate due to the performance element required, which fostered a kind of showmanship in one's character – a skill I found fun to polish. The first job was based at a local supermarket belonging to a national chain. My task was to promote a brand-new lemon sorbet. Standing in the gap separating the front aisles from the rear, I had to offer busy shoppers free samples in mini-plastic glasses with little disposable scoops. It was a full eight-hour day and I had been given four large tubs from which to prepare trays of sorbet-filled glasses. It worked more effectively just to point at the graphics on the big container and ask the passing public if they wanted to try the product, scooping out a fresh sample in front of them and handing it over. Most were just after a refreshing freebie as they went about their shopping and had no intention of buying more; so how many sales of the full-size tubs followed is debatable.

It all began smoothly with lots of interest, the sorbet samples in the first three tubs going fast until mid-afternoon – then I began to struggle... I had not been provided with anything in which to keep the product chilled; and had zero co-operation from the supermarket staff, who, while they tolerated the promotion, certainly didn't enjoy it and regarded my presence as little more than an obstacle in the aisle. So I began the fourth tub with the sorbet, having been under the hot supermarket lights for hours, rapidly melting and becoming less and less viable. As a man who took pride in his work, however, I was obsessively determined to see every last vestige of the final container go. As the fluorescent neon lights baked down upon it, the remainder of the lemon sorbet deteriorated into a hideous green soup. My final customer was an energetic old lady pulling a shopping basket on wheels. As her curious eye fell upon me, twinkling with greed, I seized the opportunity to give away the last cupful.

"Would you like to try this delicious new lemon sorbet?" I asked.

"Ooh, go on then, duck!" she replied eagerly, as I literally *poured* the liquid into her glass. It was a stunt worthy of *Candid Camera*; pointless even offering the poor old dear a spoon. There was something maliciously enjoyable about seeing her being taken in by the alluring offer of a free taster, knowingly deceiving her as to its quality; then watching the penny drop. She put the cup to her lips and took a deep swig. A second passed; then, inevitably, I was rewarded by the hysterical reaction; as her wrinkled old mouth curved downward in a grimace of disgust.

"Oh – it's *'ORRIBLE!'*" she cried.

Faced with the bizarre spectacle of the promoter paralytic with laughter in his butcher-like, stripy apron, tears of mirth rolling down his cheeks, she flapped her hand at me in mock-indignation:

"Goo on with ya' – *goOo* away!"

THE PAINT DEMONSTRATOR

After a week giving away discount vouchers for Yorkshire tea bags, I landed my biggest promotion-based assignment of all. In 1988, a well-known firm were launching a revolutionary product to reverse their declining UK share of the white gloss paint sector in spectacular fashion: a one-coat gloss with, for the first time in history, no undercoat required. The company were going all-out to make the product launch successful; and the appointed demonstrators, one of whom was me, had to attend their national headquarters in Lancashire for a day's intensive training. An overnight stay in a nearby Town & Country house was provided the evening before, all expenses paid, so that we could wake up refreshed and reach HQ in good time for the course. One of the lads took it on himself to straighten my tie: a classic alpha-male tactic used to disempower and gain superiority over others. I was quite easy prey back then, having to fake the little confidence I had.

We were given all the blurb to say about the paint, then trained in its use on small wooden boards; the key thing being that every stroke had to be *crossed*, changing the brush's direction from vertical to horizontal. This particular paint offered outstanding coverage: when dipped into, it formed a thick, brilliant-white slab on the brush, which had to be *witnessed* by the public; as it could not fail to impress. We were taught how to remove any hair dropped in the paint, 'flicking' it back with the brush until it could be pulled away; and behind us, whilst demonstrating, we had to display a large-scale campaign ad of the new product: a photograph broken down into nine elasticated pieces, each of which had to be stretched in correct sequence over a tubular metal frame-on-legs, collapsible for transport. Once we had mastered the technique, that was it. Refilling my car on the way back, I bought a can of cola from a petrol station, making the error of opening it at the wheel. Just my luck: it must have either fallen off the shelf and been replaced, or someone had deliberately shaken it; for the flaming thing exploded, covering the curved ceiling of my Saab 96 with a myriad of glistening, sticky brown droplets which, one by one, descended on my head as I drove. Towel-less (if that's a word), there was little I could do.

A few days later, a huge lorry drew up at the house, delivering all my supplies: the point-of-sale stand and advert segments, numerous paint cans, a massive box of discount vouchers, overalls, brushes galore and a pile of wooden demo-boards; along with a month-long schedule of different DIY stores to visit all over the East Midlands. I hit it off with a gorgeous Asian assistant in one branch who wrote her name (Nada Narner) and number on a scrap of paper for me. It sounded unreal, like a wind-up, so I never rang – but I always remembered her! Coinciding with saturation-level TV advertising, the whole simultaneous campaign had been meticulously planned, one rep for every UK region. Oddly, the only thing they did forget was to send someone in-store to check the promotion was even being *conducted*, forget to standard! The whole thing was done on trust. Customers were indeed seduced by the slick marketing:

the product literally flew off the shelves — however, time-served tradesmen were less impressed, grinning and shaking their heads; saying,

"Nnnahhh — gotta be yer primer, undercoat and topcoat…"

From my own direct experience with the paint, I can tell you that while ease of use was a huge selling-point, it yellowed over the years to an *appalling* degree. The company must have done something to address that; as it is still selling both online and in DIY stores today. Not only am I proud to a rather foolish extent of playing a part in that launch, I've dined out on the experience ever since, telling anyone who needs household decorating that I am a "(company) trained painter." It may be stretching the facts rather, as it was only a day-long course — but it's still true…

THE WINDOW SALESMAN

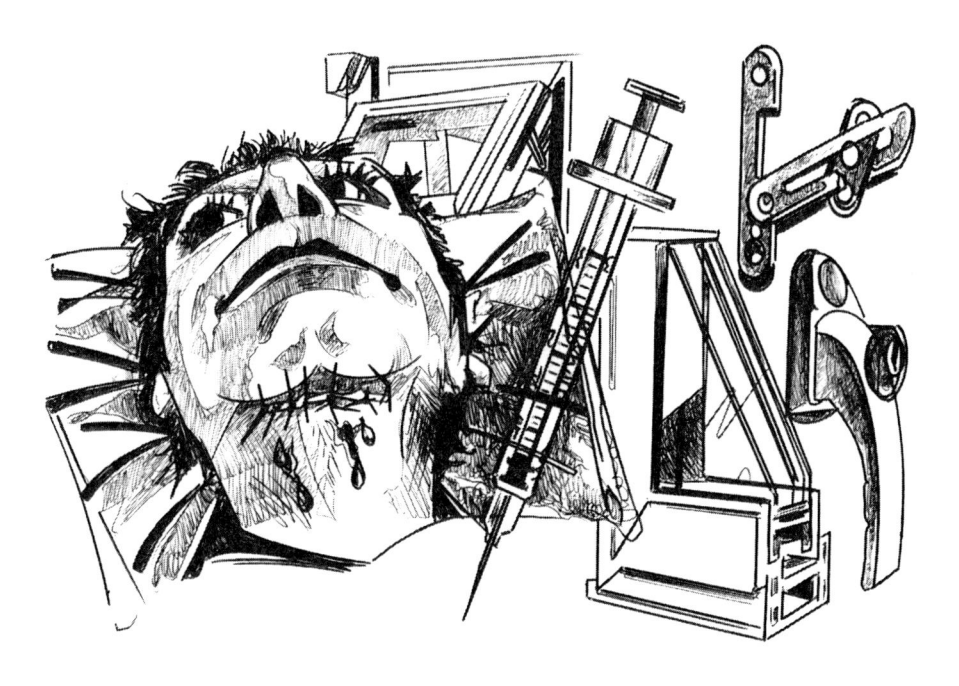

In 1989, at the end of my penultimate year as a Graphics student, I signed up to work as a door-to-door salesman for a long-since vanished UPVC window firm. The unrequited love of my life had finally left the city and returned to her own country having finished her degree; so in truth, I was just putting one foot in front of the other trying to get through each day. Perhaps this was the reason why, on the morning I was supposed to begin the new job, I didn't hear the alarm and awoke with a start, realising I had overslept and was running late. I could still salvage the situation if I was quick! Desperately multi-tasking, I ran a bath whilst simultaneously shaving and toothbrushing at breakneck speed; then rashly spent less than a minute in the hot water before leaping out. Next thing I knew, I was coming round on my parents' bathroom floor, with an agonising pain in my lower jaw... I had made the classic mistake of going from hot to cold, horizontal to vertical too fast – and blacked out, striking a small carpeted step as I fell. Instinctively, I put my hand up to the stubble under my chin, the source of the pain. To my horror, my fingers went *in*... I raised myself up then only to see the step covered in blood; threw a towel around myself and hammered on my medic brother's bedroom door.

"Wake up!" I called; "I've hurt myself badly..." To his credit, he was there for me instantly; it was a wound which you could see went way beyond skin-deep; and, with a lifelong needle-phobia, I was beginning to panic, knowing I would almost certainly require stitches.

"It does look as if you might need some sutures," my brother said tactfully, trying to spare me the fateful word. He drove me straight to A&E where I was seen by a nurse and taken into a cubicle for half a dozen of them; plus a tetanus jab not aided by my brother's involuntary sniggering at my rear end. The nurse, knowing he was a medical student, shot him a disgusted look for his inappropriate bedside manner, but in truth, adrenalin had kicked in sufficiently for it not to be as bad as I feared.

While still in the hospital, I rang the window firm to tell the manager what had happened.

"Oh, ya plonka," he said, good-naturedly. "Well, get in as quick as you can."

By 12 noon I was in his office, white bandage on my chin – not the best start to a new job. The boss was a moustachioed, overweight little man named Barry, although everyone pronounced it "Barreh" – most of the team being 16-year-old school-leavers. Barry sat slumped in a black swivel chair with his dubious "secretary" (an attractive young girl half his age) squirming brazenly on his knee in a mini-skirt and high heels. Periodically, he would grope or nuzzle at her, seeking a kiss; and she would say, "Barreh!" in a mock-scolding tone, never once moving from his lap. He was clearly exploiting his position, but it seemed to impress the school-leavers, most of whom were a horrid lot, habitually putting each other down. One of them was forever calling another "virgin;" until finally he was put in his place by an older, rather more decent team leader.

"Oi!" he said to the lad in a challenging tone. "All very well you having a go; who do you think you are – God's gift? Bet *you've* never had sex... well – *have* you?"

"Ye-aah," blustered the boy defensively, blushing to the roots of his hair.

"When?" persisted the team leader.

"In – in a hammock," the lad stuttered, "at my mate's wedding…"

"Oh yeah, right!" jeered his peers, laughing. I certainly didn't fit in; and was waiting for them to turn on me. The only other team member was a middle-aged Jehovah's Witness in a brown suit, his face bereft of expression. A little brown satchel under his arm, he walked as rigidly as a zombie.

We were driven out into a succession of small outlying villages in a transit van and dropped there, walking the streets and knocking doors trying to sell the windows until the driver chose to return for us hours later. I'd already heard horror stories from a friend who worked in a rival firm whose own office window-frames weren't even UPVC, but wood; which hardly said much for their product! As his tale went, the van driver over there had a notoriously limited vocabulary, every other word being "f*ck." His most famous sentence came following problems starting the engine:

"Which f*ckin' f*cker's f*cked this f*cker?"

The crazy thing was that we were constantly dropped in residential cul-de-sacs where all the houses already *had* UPVC doors and windows! Disillusioned, I didn't last longer than a week – the job over almost before it began. There was no basic wage at all; payment entirely on commission – no ceiling and no floor. None of the others got any business; but incredibly, I did secure one lucky lead just before leaving. A lovely African-Caribbean lady opened an upstairs window when I knocked; we had the entire conversation with her up there and me at street level. She said yes to everything, bless her – so I did at least please the boss once before throwing the towel in…

THE CRISP FACTORY SHIFTWORKER

My next job in the summer of 1989 was far more successful and lucrative. A well-known crisp firm was hiring temps to do shift work at its factory on a local industrial estate. Since its takeover by a major carbonated drinks manufacturer, it has become almost unheard of to get short-term work there now, virtually all positions are permanent; but back then, at £5.88 an hour, it was the highest-paid temping job in the UK. The factory operated 24 hours a day, 365 days a year. Shifts ran either from 2 p.m. to 10 p.m., 10 p.m. to 6 a.m. or 6 a.m. to 2 p.m.; plus overtime if required; and we "bluecoats" clocked in and out, changing into overalls, disposable hairnet and plastic overshoes, before being shunted harshly from task to task by the loathsome senior "whitecoats".

They were a good crowd, the group I was working with. One poor lad was hugely excited, having just passed his driving test the day before. He wanted to show off and got four of us to pile into his new Mini – which he promptly drove straight into a wall in front whilst attempting to reverse. We all felt really bad for him, the lads recommending various panel beaters to remove the dents. As for the work, sometimes you were sent to stand in front of a conveyor belt, sorting and removing burst packets as they passed. That was a fun novelty at first, as you were permitted to eat as many of the "reject" crisps as you liked: there was nothing actually wrong with them, so we filled our faces the first few days, but pretty soon – honestly – you never wanted to see a packet of crisps again… The worst task of all was sweeping up and adding to a "crisp mountain" of burst bags and fallen crisps. With much bending and stooping involved, you got exhausted quickly; and the whitecoat in charge was a giant of a woman who took no messing: you earned every penny…

Most days, however, we would be assigned to pack crisps into boxes as soon as they came off the production line. That was fascinating: the crisp bag plastic was one continuous "tube" of repeat-printed graphics, machine-crimped at the base, then filled with crisps from a chute above, before finally being precision-crimped again at the top to seal them in. Once cut into individual bags, they rose up separate conveyor belts to us operatives; who had to pack them 24 or 48 to a box. Now you might think it would save time to gather whole armfuls at once; then throw the whole lot in the box; but in practice, it was faster just to get into an efficient repeat-motion with individual packets. If you weren't quick enough, they began piling up in front of you, creating a bottleneck; surplus packets rising up behind to fall either side of the conveyor belt. This in turn resulted in an overload alarm going off. Your production line then ground to a halt; causing an irate whitecoat to come and scold you within seconds, before resetting the system and ordering you to speed up.

I used to get ghastly anxiety dreams about my production line overflowing with crisps. Much of the work we did back then is now fully automated; but in those days, there were four necessarily manned production lines alongside each other. The maddest day was when the management accidentally overbooked eight of us for those four machines. For some odd reason, there were no whitecoats around the whole shift. Maybe they had gone home; unlikely, but then again, it was the 10 p.m. to 6 a.m. shift... Normally you worked an hour, then got a 15-minute rest-period; but on this occasion, with twice the required number of unsupervised young rogues, we devised a system to replace each other so that we each did half an hour on, half an hour off *the whole night*. I still feel guilty about it; but at the time it was funny: in fairness, you didn't get away with much!

THE HOSPITAL KITCHEN

In the early 1990s, I signed up briefly with a temping agency based in the food sector. They took inspiration for their name from the French for "ordering individual items from a restaurant menu". The bosses were two brothers, rather decent types actually; but the telephone team, gathered around a huge table, were the vilest, solely target-driven salespeople. When I went in to register, I witnessed them first-hand in action, calling up their various employees and offering them a pitiful minimum wage for a tough physical day's work. If an assignment was refused, they would remain polite until it was clear none of their persuasive skills would result in acceptance of the job; then, the moment they hung up, each would scream "C*NT!" at the receiver at the top of their voice; along with a host of other expletives. I wouldn't be surprised if half of them had cocaine habits: there was a quivering edginess to them all, as if they lived entirely on their wits. It was all done in full earshot of the managers, who, while they didn't join in the behaviour, definitely turned a blind eye. It seemed they viewed such letting-off of steam as a regrettable, but necessary part of high-powered office culture. In the initial Food Hygiene test, I learned, among other things, that bacteria stop growing at 63 degrees Celsius – it was probably a fact I'd have known long ago in my 'O' level Biology days. I didn't score 100%, but did well enough to be accepted onto their books.

My first – and I think, only – assignment for them was as a worker in the kitchens of the Leicester Royal Infirmary. First task was to wheel all the huge metal lunch trolleys on castors up to the specified wards; each packed with freshly cooked plates of food. I had to manoeuvre each one carefully into the lift, ensuring it was delivered to the correct location; then return and whisk off with the next. You literally ran with them, because it was a vast hospital with so much to be delivered. The process was over in around an hour and a half; we were then granted a 15-minute breather before the finished dinner plates began arriving back from the wards. Now came the second, horrible, yet also weirdly fascinating task...

Given the flimsiest pair of protective blue gloves, I was told to go and stand in line with about 10 other people. Below us was a shallow trough of lukewarm water; in front of which was a moving conveyor-belt along which trays of used dishes and cutlery were passing. It's natural, of course, for bed-bound patients who feel less than 100% after operations to have little appetite – so many of these returning trays had barely been touched. There might have been the merest couple of mouthfuls attempted – but that was it. I myself was assigned soup bowls to wash. Filled with the gloopiest, brownish-green sludge which in many cases had grown a puckered, heavy skin, I had to slop each of them out with my *bare* fingers. Well okay, I had the thinnest of gloves on, but the material was still fine enough for the sickening texture of the food to be detectable through them as my fingers worked the gunge away from the sides – no implements to help you do the job, just your hands. I then had to pass each sloshed-out bowl to the woman on my left before tackling the next. On occasions when I wasn't fast enough and missed one, or hadn't cleared a bowl sufficiently for her satisfaction, without saying a word, the woman literally *threw* it back at me. It was horrific, gut-churning, visceral work; and it went on and on – and on... Standing the whole time without a stool, it wasn't long before your back began feeling the strain.

Most shocking of all, however, was what I saw happening further down the line. Once all the dishes on each tray had been "cleared" by the group of us, they and the cutlery passed steadily through an open, industrial-sized dishwasher. Although that washing unit was long and large, the trays were only in there a relatively short period – perhaps a minute in total, if that? – and on the digital temperature display on its outside, in large glowing letters, I could clearly see "63°" – the very *lowest* temperature at which bacteria stop growing – it's not until 100° that they are actually *killed*... In other words, the setting was the *barest permissible minimum*, nothing more... Worse than that, at the other end of the dishwasher were other workers taking off the stacks of washed dishes and dumping them back onto trolleys with thick crusts of gunge and dirt in the rounded corners. Small wonder people pick up hospital-acquired infections when the very kitchens had those conditions! A few years later, I had my first hernia op on the NHS. The matron refused to discharge me until I'd eaten something; but having seen first-hand what went on in the kitchens, the only thing she could persuade me to accept was a vacuum-sealed packet of cream crackers!

I seem to recall being pressurised to have hepatitis jabs in order to continue working in the kitchen; you can see why, as the risk of infection was sky-high, being in such close contact with the patients' dishes. It wasn't a step I was prepared to take; and that, plus the appalling pay, may well have been the reason why I didn't continue. A few days later, I was called up by one of the agency salespeople.

"Guy-mate!" he began chirpily, "I've got you a fantastic day's work if you want it: Wait for it: *Refuse Collector* in Market Harborough! Now ordinarily, it'd be £2.16 an hour – but seeing as it's you, I'll make it £2.30 – can't be bad, 'ey?"

"Errr, no – sorry mate, not interested," I replied, "and by the way, do feel free to scream 'C*NT!' at me after you've hung up..."

I bet he did – and worse.

THE GHOST TRAIN DRACULA

One of the most fleeting, but nonetheless entertaining jobs I ever had arose when Billy Bates & Sons Funfair set up on Leicester's Victoria Park in the late autumn of 1991. Fairgrounds have long held a magnetic allure for me with their impressive, state-of-the-art typography and beautiful airbrushed artwork intermingled with the distinctive gunpowder smell of the dodgems and delicious aromas from the various food-stalls. The lights, noises and screams of excitement and the freakish element of certain sideshows hark back nostalgically to childhood; although, while I love the fearsome Ghost Train, I only ever managed to persuade *one* girl to accompany me on it!

Wandering up to this particular example, I couldn't fail to notice a large cardboard sign off-centre in the window of the ticket booth; with crude, jumbo-markered capitals: "DRACULA WANTED". Curiosity made me go up and ask what the job entailed.

"You just have to wear a costume and stand in there," said the girl.

"Well, what's the pay like?" I asked. £5 a *night* – not even babysitter-level – but that didn't stop me going for it – it was the licence it granted to be in character and misbehave that excited me. The arrangement was a solely verbal contract agreed there and then, beginning that Monday and lasting the full two weeks the fair was scheduled to be on site. Job description: "Scaring people."

It was a freezing November evening when I turned up at 5.45 p.m. for the first day's work. I was shown inside, only to be massively disappointed by the costume. There was a just about passable Dracula mask there; but as for the rest, where was the classic long black cloak with flame-red silk lining, a frilled shirt, stylish waistcoat, Albert chains and pocket-watch? All that was provided was a pair of heavy workman's gloves and the most basic grey boiler suit lying roughly folded on the floor! It had clearly been there for days while the fair set up in its new location; and was so cold it *cracked* as I unfolded it. The budget would stretch to nothing more. Never mind. I dressed up in the outfit, looking more like Michael Myers from *Hallowe'*en than Dracula – but what could I do but work with what was given? Stepping into the darkened interior, I found this too was pretty run-down for a ghost train: a few artificial cobwebs here and there, a giant plaster-of-Paris spider with a splash of luminous green paint and a bandaged mummy was all there was. I had been given no guidance as to where to stand or what to do – the interpretation of the role was down to me. So I chose a darkened alcove in which to stand – and waited for the first punters to come through.

It didn't take me long to perfect a technique. A loud klaxon would trigger just before each buggyful of people rounded a bend of the metal tracks, alerting me that they were about to come into my area. I would stick out like a sore thumb if plainly moving about – so decided to go for the element of surprise. Folding my arms diagonally over each other, palms on chest in a 'sarcophagus' pose, I stood absolutely motionless like just another static exhibit. The riders, without exception, looked totally bored as they came into sight, visibly unimpressed with the quality of the scares. I remained completely still until they had given me a cursory glance and looked away – then suddenly came to life with the deepest, bellowing laugh, springing my arms apart in a Frankenstein-like lurch as they screamed, mouths open in genuine terror – one woman actually clutching her chest in fright as I chased the buggy all the way out into the open at the end of the ride, "nuh-hahahahaaa"-ing as I gave pursuit. Basking in the role, I got a real adrenalin-rush with each new group passing through; word must have got around, as we were busy right through until 11 p.m. every evening.

So high on the thrill was I that I rang my oldest schoolmate and insisted he came along with his girlfriend the following Friday night. They did – and through a crack in the airbrushed wooden walls I spotted the pair of them exploring the icy fairground – it was only a matter of time before they decided to take the ride. Afterwards, when the fair closed, I joined up with the pair of them. Although, quite rightly, they made disparaging comments about the standard of the exhibits, they were amused by my captive performance – but my friend did leave me with a sobering thought on which to ponder:

"You do realise that once they know you're in there, you're a sitting duck!" he warned evilly. "Anyone could come back through with a bloody knife and *stab* ya!" That did dent my enthusiasm somewhat; and I toned down the performance a little after that. The idea of a vengeful partner returning whose missus I had almost given a cardiac arrest hardly filled me with relish.

The fairground staff themselves were a friendly enough bunch: rough and ready, but welcoming and loyal to each other. On the final night, one of them called to me through the drizzle,

"Guy, mate! – you wanna run with the fair? We're going to Milton Keynes next… I know it's not much pay; you'd have to help set up and take down the rides – but we got each other's backs: anyone gives you any grief, they'll 'ave us to deal with…"

It was a tempting offer of guaranteed adventure – but the experience was just too cold and damp. Reluctantly, I declined, folded up my boiler suit and laid it with the gloves on the blackened steps; Dracula mask gazing balefully from the top of the heap as I walked away.

GRIMSBY FISHERIES

This veritable fish and chip shop *empire* in the city of Leicester is a successful business with a heritage dating as far back as 1940. When our family first moved to the area in 1975, it occupied a mere street corner; but over the years, when the next-door property became available, it expanded – then doubled again to include a full sit-down restaurant and a separate branch. Run by a warm, friendly Greek family, one of whom is a qualified biochemist who made *scientific*-level studies of the optimum conditions for chip-frying; it's now by far the biggest fish and chip shop in the East Midlands, serving simply *colossal* golden-battered cod; each of which fills two dinner plates; and for as long as I can remember, its green fluorescent tube lights, visible from half a mile away, have been a source of comfort, familiarity and enjoyable anticipation. There was a time in my teenage years when I'd barely eat at all; so no exaggeration to say those chips kept me alive...

"You *wormish* boy!" my mother would shriek; but in the end, she drove me there several nights a week. Even today, exiting their premises on a freezing winter evening with that hot packet pressed to my heart is a hugely pleasurable sensation. Such was the shop's popularity over Lockdown, the Friday queue would stretch not only to the corner, but halfway up the adjacent side-street as well.

The owner is a good friend now; I even included him, along with a 'chip' on his shoulder, in a sequence of my animated short, *The Man With The Eye At The End Of His Finger*. So key is that shop to my experience of living in Leicester, that from sheer nostalgia, I volunteered to work an evening for free behind the counter. The staff took care of me, limiting my role to less dangerous tasks; but I still picked up key facts about the cooking process. I never realised the fat in the deep fryers comes as a solid, lard-like block. When old oil must be changed, a new block is lowered into the vat, melting from the base up. And when a battered fish is dropped in to cook, it sinks down out of sight; only 'ready' once it floats back to the top... Mainly that evening, I used a metal scoop to gather cooked chips up; lifting them out of the oil, then depositing them into the serving hatch. Some were rather elusive, having to be chased across the surface until they were rounded up. The oil itself is a real hazard, reaching 400° Fahrenheit; so you do have to keep your wits about you.

True, it's a tenuous claim, as it was only one night – but I wanted to be able to list Grimsby Fisheries under the jobs I'd done. Been there, done that – and yes, I wore the T-shirt; with the GF logo picked out in blue. And of course, they never let me go home empty-handed; I left with a generous serving of their famous fish and chips.

CAREER NADIR

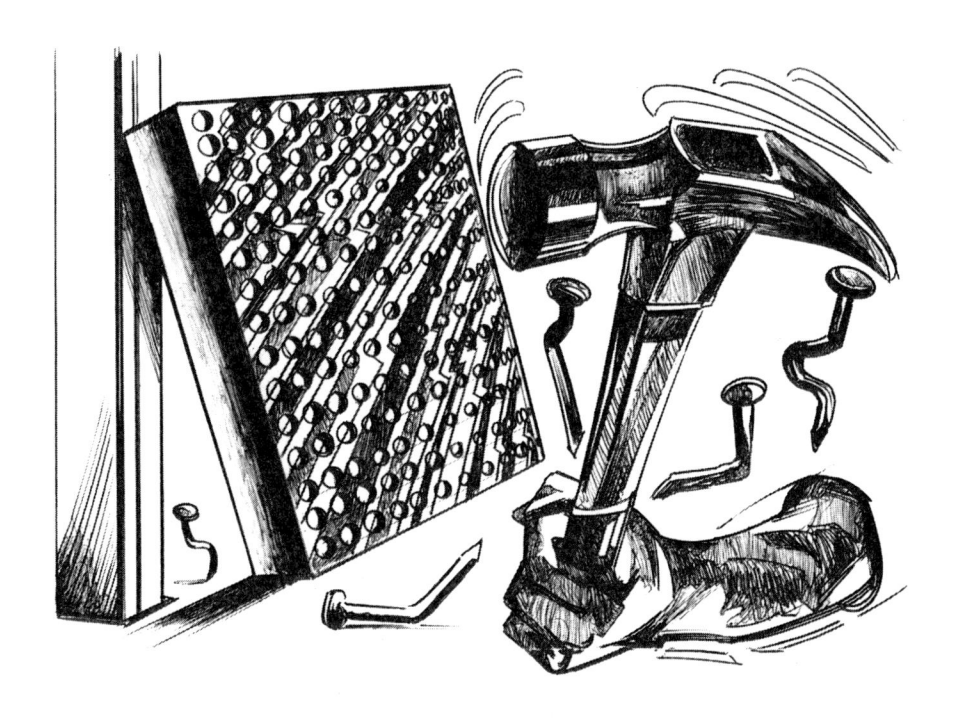

Okay – I never descended to the level of being a bog cleaner, though I do admire those who do it to bring in cash (someone's got to). I never stooped that low, but without question, the absolute *nadir* of my working life was working for minimum wage at a remote factory on the Troon Industrial Estate. I got the position via the Jobcentre, but when I arrived for the first eight-hour shift, no one was around but the site manager. He took me into a dank warehouse and picked up a heavy, hollow metre-square metal frame which he told me was perforated with 1000 pinholes. Try as I might to work out a combination of holes across and down equalling that total, I cannot; 27 across x 37 down makes 999, that's the closest I got. Anyway, he picked up a weighty metal hammer, stood the frame against a vertical girder and, as I watched, took a nail from his hand and whacked it through one of the holes, where it stuck fast.

"Now: each one of them thousand holes needs a nail stickin' out like that," he said. "You have a go." And he passed over a large pack of nails and watched me. I opened it, took a nail, placed it on one of the perforations, raised the hammer and whacked it. The nail buckled, twisted and fell.

"Nah, nah," he said. "Watch again." Taking another nail from his hand, he whacked it effortlessly through the metal, where it stuck fast, projecting firmly out of its hole.

"When you've done a whole frame, get anotha, do that the same; and so on," he said, walking off.

That was my job. It didn't make a jot of sense, no explanation given as to the purpose of the product or why I was doing it. I couldn't envisage what possible benefit it could provide to anyone.

Try as I might, I could not get one – *single* – nail through any of the holes. I lined them up carefully, whacked with all my might – but each one buckled and twisted in succession on the metal frame. Not one, not *one* solitary nail would go in! My heart sank – what kind of low-life must I be if I couldn't accomplish a task as rudimentary as this...? Even worse, there was no chair around, meaning that as you whacked, you were in a permanent stoop. Within 20 minutes my back was killing me; fingers numb with the cold. There was no one else to ask, not a living soul. It seemed as if every worker had vacated the site. I became convinced that the nails the bloke had given me were marginally wider in diameter than the ones he had in his own hand: it couldn't just be down to my own ineptitude: they were too wide to fit through those bloody holes! Paranoia consumed me: another flaming windup, ritual initiation, humiliation of the newbie for the staff's amusement.

After four hours, the light began to fail. I couldn't find a switch anywhere in the vast hangar; and so was alone in increasing darkness in which I simply couldn't work on a task requiring that degree of precision. I was hungry and cold, just standing around. I'm flaming well staying until the end of my shift, I vowed – and I did. There was no one even to check out with when I left at 9 p.m: I just got in my car and drove off, feeling an abject failure. The following morning, whole body aching, I rang the factory and told the manager I was packing it in.

"I'm sorry – but I'm just better than that," I said.

"MmYeah," he grunted moodily, "I could tell you wouldn't 'ack it. But no 'ard feelings, we'll still pay you for your time."

The next week, my cheque arrived: after deductions for tax and National Insurance, for the whole demoralising ordeal, I had made the grand total of... £11.

AUTOTRADER MAGAZINE

By 1992, in the years following our graduation, most of my peers had moved down to London in search of better Graphic Design prospects – leaving me feeling somewhat isolated in Leicester. A core group had settled at *AutoTrader Magazine* in Wimbledon when I got a tip-off from a friend that evening shifts down there were available. It wasn't exactly what you'd call "design" work, that stage was all done by Friday night: this was the rather more dogsbody task of assembling the final pages; but, with a pay-rate way more than anything the Jobcentre could offer up here, I'd have been a fool to pass it up. I took the coach down to London each Friday evening and worked a 12-hour shift through the night until the print deadline was reached and we were let go. Shattered, I then dozed all the way back to Leicester; on one occasion sleeping through my coachstop and having to take another southbound one back the other way from Derby!

As the deadline neared each week, a couple of the lads in positions of greater seniority would become increasingly heated, pressurizing us to 'up' our speed of output. There wasn't much room for humour at those times; several of us really had to bite our lips when spoken to rather roughly by those who had hitherto been no more than our contemporaries at college. Afterwards, though, we would always go for a goodwill drink together once the job was done. The only real downside to the work was that, perhaps to help them cope with stress, a couple of the group were major chain-smokers. This was long before the workplace smoking ban came into force; meaning their fumes would mix with those from the hot glue machine running continuously in close proximity. By the end of the shift, our eyes would be virtually glued shut; throats burning from the inhalation.

Although always an informal arrangement, and just one day a week, I had to give up the work in the end to train for my longest-lasting career in Education (see *"Please I Can To The Toilet Go?" (The Memoirs Of A Supply Teacher)* ISBN 9781035807987). But looking back, I'm glad I experienced that *AutoTrader* job. It was at a key time when, although the Mac was already established in Design, some old production techniques had yet to be superseded. One of these was "paste-up" – a method of laying out publication pages which pre-dated the now-standard, computerized desktop-publishing. The process was aptly named: after cutting out ads individually with a scalpel and gluing them up via the machine, we had to physically paste them down by hand into position on the master pages. The vast majority of today's generation, whilst knowing the computer command 'Paste' means moving selected photographs, artwork or text into a new document, haven't a clue where the name originated. It was the real deal we did at *AutoTrader*!

THE PRIZE DRAW

During two consecutive summers in the early 1990s, I did some promotion work for an independent financial advisor working under the umbrella of a large commercial insurance service and asset management company. In an effort to boost his own and the branches' customer traffic, this small man had devised what was meant to be an enticing prize draw to lure passers-by into divulging facts about their own savings and financial services they may potentially be interested in; such as lump-sum investments, life assurance and additional voluntary contributions (AVCs).

    He was a rather odd fella, in business dress in the office, but once I had responded to his advert and went in-branch to meet him, in charm offensive mode, he fairly quickly led me out of the premises and into a shopping mall to a chain-store's restaurant hall. I accepted his offer of a goodwill coffee, but he wouldn't leave it there.

    "Can I get you a sticky bun to go with that coffee?" I politely declined. "I'm sure you'd like a sticky bun — are you sure I can't get you a sticky bun?" he kept asking — but I was resolute. Then, once we'd sat down in one of the booths, rather than discussing the nature of the job, he launched into a relatively hard sell of his own Christianity. He played the trumpet; insisting I accept his invitation to a service at the Fellowship headquarters in Frog Island the following weekend. It was awkward: I needed the job and didn't want to offend him, so rather reluctantly, agreed to attend. The service itself was okay, the music a cheerful, lively free-for-all, with the financial advisor playing away on his trumpet now and then; although there was a very irritating man behind me who would zealously reply to everything said by the minister with "That's right... that's right..." throughout the ceremony. By the end, I suspected that even if I'd turned around and custard-pied him in the face, through the dripping crust, the man would have continued burbling, "That's right... that's right..."

At last, the following Monday morning, we got around to what the job itself entailed. The financial advisor had booked front foyer space in a local DIY store, where I was to display an enormous ghetto-blaster and boxed Black & Decker strimmer as two alluring prizes to be won by lucky participants in the draw. As the store customers passed in and out, my task was to accost each with a flyer, asking if they would like to take part. Once they were captive, I then had to ask which potential investments on the list they might be interested in; checking the relevant tick-boxes and taking contact details. If they were interested in knowing more, that counted as a 'lead,' for which I was paid £1; but if nothing on the list generated curiosity, the flyer got dropped into a reject box.

Once he had watched me approach a few customers and saw I had the knack of it, the financial advisor went on his way, leaving me alone. Almost immediately, I took liberties with the set spiel; adding a 'sensational' energy to my inflexion and using the words, "Excuse me — would you like to *win* an *exciting* prize draw?" This I found rapidly drew tickled punters in, many chuckling sardonically, "Oh yeah, I'd *love* to *win*..." although I was in danger of bursting out laughing at several as I took their names: Mr. Pratt... Mrs Liquorice... Mrs Bodycote — I found their suspicion and initial nervousness hilarious too, as well as some of their faces — it was frankly astonishing to see how easily they were lured by such scant prizes to reveal so much about their private finances!

Opposite me, on the far side of the foyer, was a very chatty middle-aged lady with a likeable, friendly nosiness about all I was doing. She herself was promoting UPVC windows for a local firm; but I could *not* understand what she kept saying to passers-by:

"Tres-chany windas? Tres-chany windas?" *Finally,* after days of hearing it, I realised it was an abbreviation of "Can I interest you in any windows?" She had done the job for so long, she had learned that such economy of speech freed her up to move on fast from uninterested customers!

"Have yer 'ad yer lunch?" she would ask me whenever I came back from my break, and when I answered in the affirmative, she would eagerly ask, "What did y'*have*?" – as if it was the most fascinating detail she *had* to know. All there was in-store really were basic sandwich selections – but I was sorely tempted to invent an outrageous three-course sci-fi-style meal to utterly shake her sensibilities. At least she wasn't nasty, though.

At the end of the first week's work, the financial advisor added up my total leads and asked me to go and sit in his car, where he wrote me a cheque. It bounced, resulting in a £30 penalty from my bank. He was profusely apologetic, asking me to go over to his house to be paid in cash. Again, it was odd. A blond-haired lad, a lot taller than he was, stood right there the whole time – a good half hour – never said a word; and was never introduced. Whether he had some disability I don't know, but it seemed like the boss got some weird ego-trip from the presence of his mute deputy!

I did the job for three weeks until the financial advisor felt he had sufficient leads and ended the arrangement. The following year, however, I worked for him again in the same capacity. I was far from impressed to see that the "prizes" looked suspiciously like the exact same ghetto-blaster and strimmer from the previous year; significantly more battered than before. Clearly, *nobody* had been selected to win the prize draw in exchange for their precious financial information. That felt fraudulent; and even though I was reunited with the same window saleswoman opposite, it wasn't the best start. But I still went for the task with all I had, determined to make the position pay. It went well enough until the Friday, when the store's security guard, an absolute behemoth of a bloke, took issue with my being there, claiming there was no booking. He asked me to leave, but I was where I'd been told to be; and stood my ground. He then returned and became confrontational to a point where I felt seriously threatened with physical violence. I had no choice but to pack up. Spurred on by the UPVC saleswoman, who was lapping up the drama, I rang my employer, who took an hour to turn up. By then, I was fuming and told him I was calling it a day.

"Look: it's clear someone's been a total a**hole to you; and now you're being one to me," he responded glibly. "We're not gonna sort this out with a slanging match. Please – come and sit in the car while I go in and sort this out." Grudgingly I agreed. As he returned and totalled up my leads from the previous four days, he admitted the slot had been double-booked; yet in just Monday to Thursday I had still secured 330 solid leads for him. With his mute friend riding pillion, he came over on a motorbike in full leathers the next weekend to pay my final wages.

"£330..." he muttered, "I've never paid *anyone* that much for a week's work... I can't persuade you to come back, can I?" But by then, I had an impending PGCE course firmly in my sights – and never saw him again. I do wonder though, if he ever *did* give away that ghetto-blaster and strimmer. Given his track record, I somehow doubt it.

THE CROOKED EMPLOYER

In 1996, after resigning from a nightmarish teaching job due to stress, I was obliged, in order to continue receiving Incapacity Benefit, to attend a Return to Work course run by the DWP in the town centre. Those completing the course automatically qualified for a forklift truck training with almost guaranteed employment at the end. I was actually quite excited by the prospect, as, despite high injury statistics, forklift work was well-paid, with no end of vacancies in the local paper: the skill was something that would have been useful to get under my belt. The tasks on the course were extremely basic: low-level Maths and English comprehension exercises; with a pot-bellied, bearded man running the course who spoke to us as if he were the oracle of all knowledge. The other participants were mostly ex-cons who could barely string a sentence of coherent English together; one boasting he'd just been released after serving years for GBH at 'The Rig' – a grim-sounding HM Prison in the North Sea. I was so bored I doodled through most of the sessions; but was singled out by the leader's assistant, a lovely, middle-aged blonde who took me to one side.

"You're wasted here: what, in an ideal world, would you like to do?" she asked. I had an immediate answer: I desperately needed to do a Mac training. Our Graphics degree had come to an end *just* as the Mac was surfacing; early models were there; but in a suite where few got to use them; and even then, only for basic typing – no image manipulation. Besides, who then could have envisaged how far the Mac would go to become the de facto standard of the design industry? Even as a qualified Graphic Designer, without those skills, most design work was a closed door. I couldn't afford to fund the training myself (around £2,500 then), no one would train me so I couldn't get work; and any design job I went for I didn't get because I hadn't the necessary training: Catch 22.

"Do you know – I'm *sure* I've heard of a completely funded course offering just that. I'll get in trouble," the lady confided, "but leave it with me." Privately, between that weekly session and the next, she looked into the matter; and sure enough, provided I remained unemployed a full six months, just such a Mac course was starting in the New Year at the National Printing Skills Centre. She made a call to the boss, who invited me down to see my portfolio. It was *that* easy: I got offered a place there and then; the only downside being that the offer was conditional, the same lady warned, on my pulling out of the Return to Work course before its end; meaning I'd lose access to the forklift truck initiation. But thousands of pounds of free Mac-training? No-brainer…

In the last week of the sessions, as we reached the final exercise, the course leader announced: "Now – if anyone wants to drop out, this is your last chance; or you'll all automatically go onto the forklift training. Speak now, or forever hold your peace." To the disbelief of the whole room, I raised my hand, gave my reasons and slunk away guiltily; yet as I went down the stairs, I heard the assistant getting an absolute *rollicking*… Clearly, the fella had twigged I must have been helped even to gain awareness of the Mac training. It must have been galling, on the last afternoon of his course, to have a 100%

pass statistic denied not just by anyone, but by the very participant who was streets ahead of the rest. It's a lasting regret of mine that I never made it back with a box of chocolates for that lady – I've long since forgotten her name, but she put her neck on the line to help someone she felt stood out; and her intervention changed the course of my life: the skills I gained on that course securing me a permanent teaching job; and as a result, my very first home.

Considering what an amazing place it was, it's surprising the National Printing Skills Centre didn't have a higher profile. Its pristine print workshop was the envy of the industry nationwide; with enormous Heidelberg offset-litho full-colour presses and even a Quantel Paintbox (a former state-of-the-art video manipulator used by the BBC and other broadcasters) gathering dust in a corner; one of just a handful in the UK. The standard of training was *remarkable*; not just in the use of Macs, but a full, hands-on, practical grounding in Electronic Pre-Press; print theory, paper sizes, desktop publishing software, imposition (the placing of all pages within a document on a single printed sheet, so that when folded, they appear in correct sequence); even redundant procedures like output to film and exposing to printing-plates, quality control checks, Health and Safety – you name it, we did it; with NVQ-level Unit Tests cementing learning at every stage. What I had really come for, though, was the Mac tuition: finally, I got the software experience I so badly needed: a full grounding in Quark XPress for desktop publishing, Illustrator and Freehand for drawing and of course, image manipulation via Adobe Photoshop. Never before had I seen my own artwork printed to such a high standard; all the secrets of the design world were now an open door to me.

We had two tutors who took different modules with us: a middle-aged bald man with a sandy moustache, who was a rough-and-ready bespectacled printworker himself; and a woman who, visually, was very striking indeed. An Asian girl, who was a good 5'10" tall, she had one of those unusual "upside-down" mouths enhanced with bright red lipstick; and was quite extraordinarily beautiful; with a cool, sophisticated London fashion-model manner complementing her stylish dress-sense. Now this girl was absolutely steeped in the print industry: her family owned a print business in the city centre, where these processes were habitually discussed over the breakfast table – all the concepts we were covering were second nature to her. It's fair to say I did have quite a crush on this tutor, as did all the lads on the course; which made me want to work hard to impress her at every stage. With my drawing ability a key advantage over most of the other students, it meant I could put into practice the skills taught; creating a higher standard of artwork that (unfortunately for me) made me stand out as a potential target...

At the end of the course, I scored very highly on the final test; and the girl was charming about it.

"No less than we expected," she said in her silky, seductive tones. "Listen: my brother runs a design studio in town. He's got a vacancy right now for new talent – you should definitely go and see him..." I was very flattered – and I wasn't going to pass up a chance like that. The property, when I found it, stood on a street corner on the edge of a busy dual-carriageway. It didn't give much away from the outside; the only sign saying "PRINTERS". The brother I had been sent to see was younger than the girl, yet had his own entire floor of the property. I was shown into this very swanky office indeed, with a rich shagpile carpet, luxury furniture, a huge television, modern 'designer' desk – and literally handfuls of club flyers spilled all over it. Now at the time, I was in the habit of collecting these very flyers from record stores and boutiques all over the city. Very suddenly, they had begun to showcase astonishing state-of-the-art 3D graphics and cutting-edge typography. I had no idea what software was generating the effects or from where the flyers themselves originated, but they were *everywhere* – becoming highly influential on youth culture. It turned out that *this* very business was where the vast majority were being produced! I guess the enthusiasm I expressed broke the ice with the brother, because after seeing my folio, he said,

"Well, Guy, I'm very impressed; the job's yours if you want it. It's only minimum wage I'm afraid, 9-5, but you'll get to use the software on those flyers..." It seemed a fair trade-off; and was also, I realised, the very first opportunity I'd had to make an income, however little, from what I'd actually *trained* for! – I'd only really ended up in Teaching owing to a lack of design opportunities.

Well, before I left, he gave me a glimpse into the room where I would be working from the following Monday on incoming design jobs; it was a pretty functional office space with swivel chairs and a desk at the far end on which there were two large Macs side by side. I did vaguely register a rather morose-looking, fed-up guy on one of them who didn't say a word; but thought nothing of it. As arranged, I turned up for work at the start of the new week and was shown into the room. The vast majority of the design tasks I was given were fairly humdrum, such as fast-food takeaway menus and a couple of club-night posters; but I didn't mind; what thrilled me was that the skills I had learned on the Mac training stood me in good stead here. With many of the jobs, I didn't have all that much creative freedom, as the brother wanted me to use his own set logos and colour-schemes. There was even a case in which one of his Asian clients literally stood over me dictating everything I did: that was a truly bespoke experience.

What *did* rankle was that unlike the experience at the NPSC, training in this job was non-existent: there were many steps in the print process I wasn't allowed involvement in. Downstairs, where the old father worked in a jam-packed office overflowing with previous jobs, was their actual printing press; much, much smaller than the Heidelbergs: there I glimpsed intriguing "knives" being created from flat metal bent around to form the outline of shapes, which, when attached to the press, would actually 'cut' certain club flyers into specific irregular forms, such as houses or pigs. I would have loved to learn that process, as well as outputting the print files to film – but they just wanted me at the desk. I only got half an hour's lunch break; the sister would drop by, but never stay more than a few minutes; and the brother himself was out most of the time: I never saw him do any design work himself. So for the vast majority of the time I was sitting there alone all day. I was eventually told where to find the software application used to create the 3D graphics on those club flyers; and in spare moments was able to experiment a little with it. While the power of the application itself was awesome, what was disappointing was how little the user really contributed beyond selecting from a library of geometric shapes, extrusions, textures and background 'weather' conditions. The whole thing then had to be left to 'render' in full resolution, which took hours – and while the results were breathtaking, they were unpredictable; with little down to the talent or creativity of the user. Most of the art was generated by the software itself; massively reducing my admiration for it.

Walking back to my bus stop one day, I happened to cross paths with a lad who'd decided to leave our Mac training after the first few sessions. He asked what I was doing now and then said,

"Oh I'm really glad you got something! – but watch out; because you know what, I tried working there, and the day before I joined, I saw the bloke before me sitting there looking very p*ssed off; then they didn't pay me for the work I did, so I left soon after!"

Alarm bells began ringing very loudly for me then: clearly there was a pattern here... Sure enough, a week later, when the final Friday of the month came and no pay was forthcoming, I raised the matter; only for the brother to say,

"Thing is Guy, I've got a bit of a *cashflow* situation at the moment – I'll pay you soon as I can..."

I thought, here we go; how long's a piece of string? I wasn't going to throw good time after bad -"as soon as" could be any time – if ever...

"No – sorry," I said. "that doesn't cut the mustard... If it's okay with you, once you've *paid* me, I'll come back. Plus I don't want to be a 'passenger' here you have to carry; if you train me up in all the processes, I'll be a lot more use." With that, I said goodnight. He wasn't happy, clearly, but I'd worked a full month; and just as with my predecessor, here he was messing me about on my pay!

After a couple of weeks, when there had still been no financial gesture, I rang the business. His mother answered and told me he wasn't there, but she'd let the young lad know I had rung. He never called me back. I tried again the next week – and the week after that. Whenever I rang, she told me he was "in a meeting" or "not here right now..."

"You bloody *sue* him!" advised my parents. I had never sued anyone. Out of curiosity, I rang the County Court to find out how much a small claims summons cost to bring. It was only £45, with the charge added to any settlement if you won; so, having kept a careful record of my hours, I had little to lose! However, there was still a certain protocol to follow: prior to issuing a summons, the claimant had to give seven days' written notice of their intention to do so – which I did, via recorded delivery. I still heard nothing. Clearly the mother was deliberately stalling contact between me and her son. I called again; and this time, when she gave me the usual excuses, I said,

"You tell him, if he doesn't come to the phone right now, I'm taking legal action..."

That finally achieved something and I gave him the total figure he owed: minimum wage multiplied by the number of hours I'd worked. "I'll pay you when I'm ready," he retorted. Using the exact spiel I'd been advised to by the court, I said,

"Okay. In accordance with Section 69 of the County Court Act, I've now given you written notice of my intention to prosecute. Take me seriously, mate; I'm not another pushover you can rip off without paying, if you call my bluff, you'll find yourself in Court."

"You do what you wanna do, Guy," he said flatly, and hung up.

So, for the first time in my life, I paid the fee, did the paperwork – and sued him.

Within 24 hours, he'd obviously been served by the bailiff, as I heard footsteps on my parents' drive. Up came the fella and rang the doorbell. I opened an upstairs window.

"What you doing takin' me to Court?" he blustered. "I've got your money here!"

"Put it through the letterbox and wait," I said.

When I came down and counted it, there was £275. I went back upstairs and called down:

"You're £100 short – it's £375 you owed me."

"I'm not paying you a penny more," he said.

"Fine. I'll see you in Court," I replied as I shut the window. Resentfully, he stalked off down the drive to his brother's car.

A few weeks later, there we were in front of the magistrate.

"He can't sue me!" said the defendant. "And they've put a hold on my credit! I know the law…"

"Listen, sonny," said the magistrate, "I think I know the law a whole lot better than you. Was the standard of his work good?"

"No – he was rubbish!" said the lad.

Calmly, I pulled out a club-night poster I had designed at the premises and found in situ pasted to a wall.

"Well, if I was so rubbish, how come I found this posted up on Mayor's Walk for all the University students?" I said. "You clearly felt it was fit enough for their purpose…" He didn't have an answer to that; and gazed sullenly at the floor in his drainpipe trousers.

"Well, was he *at* work?" asked the magistrate.

"I dunno if he was there," came the lying response. Grinning, I reeled off all the exact dates and hours I had worked, multiplied by the minimum wage to reach the total figure, minus what he had already paid.

The magistrate smiled, "If he was *there*, he gets paid…" he told the Defendant. "Now if you want that hold taking off your credit, you'll give him the rest of what you owe right now."

Which he had no choice but to do: in under 10 minutes, the Court had found in my favour.

It didn't end with that, though... Much as I admired his beautiful sister, the tutor with the upside-down mouth, I felt duty-bound to inform the National Printing Skills Centre. I was really torn about it; I liked her and didn't want to grass her up, but by the same token, couldn't just stand by and leave a load of others after me to be ripped off the same way. As course tutor, *she* was the 'honey-trap'; as culpable as her brother, if not more so; and in prime position to identify the topmost talent within each intake and repeatedly 'cream' it off; sending us one by one to her family business; our creativity then exploited for zero pay... Curiously, it turned out I wasn't the only whistle-blower: this was the *second* time staff had been made aware of the situation: they were actively monitoring what was going on; and promised, should one further incident be reported, that would be the end for the girl. I'd love to know how it panned out: whether her brother's court case proved a wake-up call, or if she carried on the scam until she herself got fired.

It's ironic that over a quarter of a century later, that fella now occasionally swims at the same pool as me. The first few times, he avoided direct eye contact; then finally came to shake my hand. While I returned the gesture, I did made the point, in full earshot of other swimmers:

"An elephant never forgets, mate: 25 years ago I had to sue you for not paying me."

"Well, all that was a long time back," he said sheepishly; then swam away; a hint of a smirk on his face. It was the personalized number plate on his fancy BMW outside that was the dead giveaway.

THE BROKEN FRIDGE

Shortly after leaving the Graphics firm, I was recontacted by the mega-prescriptive client who'd stood over me dictating each step of his menu design. It turned out his wife had been an occasional helper in one of my very first infant classes. He must have recontacted the printing firm and found out I was no longer there; for he had headhunted me to come and do some temping work directly for him. I had my reservations, but drove down to his business anyway to see what it was all about. The man, a somewhat self-aggrandizing "entrepreneur", had, like myself, done all manner of different things in his career. His current venture, for which I had done the menu, was an Italian fresh food lunchtime delivery service targeting City Centre firms. Letting it all hang out in his flip-flops, he came across as rather too chilled for the rather desperate situation he was in. A colossal industrial refrigerator housing all his ingredients had broken down and he was struggling to find a suitable engineer. With no way to keep it cold, the food he had inside the fridge had just days before it became unusable, which would lose him a huge amount of money. His only hope was to flog as much of it via orders as possible in that short time bracket. Rather than do it himself, he was seeking a general dogsbody to leaflet potential target buyers in town, ensuring that only the chief decision-maker, owner, proprietor or manager was spoken to.

If I had been him, I'd have paid for shelf space in another company's chiller until he got back on his feet; but it wasn't something he would consider; either that or the hire proved prohibitively expensive. Instead, in the hope of a big order, he got me to do the leafleting on foot for the best part of a week; which left me with some nasty blisters and the loss of a fair bit of shoe leather. After the fourth day, he asked me how I was finding the work.

"Well, to be honest, I'm flagging," I said. There didn't seem to be any takers for his Dolcellata (a blue-veined Italian soft cheese) and SDTP (sun-dried tomato paste) – key ingredients of just about every dish on his menu – so it was quite a demoralising process. In addition, most businesses I had visited cited existing arrangements they had with other firms who already brought daily basket selections into the offices for staff to select from. I think the poor bloke realised the game was up.

"Well if you're flagging, let's bring the arrangement to a close," he said, much to my relief. To his credit, he did pay me there and then for the work; although I never found out if he resurrected the fridge in time to save those expensive ingredients. He was a proud man with quite an assertive wife; so I expect he may have lost face if he told her what had happened – which I somehow doubt.

CHINESE FOOD DELIVERY

Whilst doing the six-month Mac-training, we were permitted to work a maximum 14 hours a week and still be eligible to claim benefits. Obviously any job had to be evening-orientated to fit around the course, so I found a position driving for a Chinese takeaway, The Royal Kitchen; in an area of Leicester known as the Stadium Estate. There was a big police presence there; cars whizzing up and down, sirens blaring; and a fair amount of trouble. Graffiti on the walls wasn't enough; the most inexplicable stuff could be found sprayed on the very pavement as well:

"She has pumped-up lips and silicone tits; and bleached hair and nipple care." (Whatever that is...)

A lit rocket was even thrown into the shop one bonfire night. Unaware of it, I arrived back from a delivery in time to see two figures scarpering away down the street; and entered the blackened takeaway in time to see the shaken staff climbing up from the counter they'd had to duck behind for safety; as the firework bounced terrifyingly from wall to wall, the owner refusing to call the police for fear of reprisals. Heralding from Hong Kong, he was the archetypal expressionless epitome of the stereotypically portrayed, inscrutable Chinese person, with a quiet dignity to his manner. Fearing a potential return to Communist rule once his country returned to Chinese hands in 1997 and unsure how relaxed, Westernized life might alter there, he'd decided it would be safer to start a business in the UK before he lost the freedom to leave. As it happened, life didn't actually change that much in the years immediately following; it seems he later upped sticks and returned home.

This was a man who had learned the economy of speech. The phone would ring more or less off the hook on Friday and Saturday evenings; and he would repeat each order back to the customer; "Chi-Fuy-Ruy" being "Chicken Fried Rice;" and "Addabro-ro" being "Heatherbrook Road." Aside from telling me the addresses, he would say nothing to me all night except "Some soft drink?" when I would be permitted a can of something during a lull in the orders. I was given a money pouch and a £15 float from which to buy petrol and give customers change; keeping an agreed £1 from each delivery. What was nice about the job was that you actually saw what you made accruing there and then; no waiting to be paid until the end of the month. On a good weekend, with tips, I could easily make £70 a night. Considering how little they had, the people in the area were surprisingly generous. There were some houses you delivered to where you never left without a tip; many last orders at 1 a.m. were from late-night shift-workers too tired and hungry to wait for change. If the food came to say, £6.50 and they passed me a tenner, as I fumbled for change in the pouch, they would just say, "F*ck off" and close the door – their rough-and-ready way of saying "keep it". On the downside, the speed humps in the area played havoc with my car's suspension; so most of my earnings went on vehicle maintenance. There were also some hideously run-down areas I delivered to where you wouldn't get a penny's tip and where people's priorities were hard to comprehend. One obese, barefoot lady would open the door in a flimsy nightie barely the length of a mini-skirt: no carpet on the floor, but she had Chinese *every* night...

My worst evening's work was in a dimly lit, run-down area of pebble-dashed council flats on a steep hill called Bridlespur Way. Set back from the road, there were several flights of steps to climb in order to reach the various tiers of properties, and one small area with no street lighting at all. Unbeknown to me, there was an additional step hiding in the darkness; whilst moving fast, I walked straight into it and *smashed* to the ground, the food bag bursting open with the impact. My left leg was in agony as I tried to salvage what I could of the meal into the brown paper bag. With little hope, I continued to the address, explaining what had happened to the customer and telling him if he'd accept the damaged bagful, I would give it to him for free and shoulder the cost.

"Nah, we can't 'ave it like that," he said justifiably, although showing zero concern for my injuries. The address was quite a distance from the takeaway, so it took time to limp back to the car and into the shop, leg still dripping with blood. In fairness, the shop owner, who could have demanded the whole cost of the meal from my earnings, didn't do so; I think he saw I'd been through enough. Back I went to the address in a fairly withdrawn state, saying nothing as I handed the food over.

"What the f*ck's up wi' you?" asked the customer. "You're a double-edged tosser, mate..."

It had been quite a night; and the following day, the more I thought about it, the more indignant I got about the lack of adequate street lighting where I had struck the step. I rang the Council to make a formal complaint, then drove back to the scene in broad daylight; taking a set of photos clearly showing a lamp post missing at the point of the fall. The following week, when again I delivered to Bridlespur Way, I was astonished to see a newly erected lamp post exactly there – a clear admission of guilt. So I did end up making a claim; and received £750 compensation on the understanding it was "a one-off, global settlement" covering all future issues with that leg injury.

In a top corner of the takeaway was a greasy, wall-mounted colour TV left on all night to entertain customers waiting for food. A time came when I sold a full-size Dalek through the Classified Ads of the *Leicester Mercury*. Radio Leicester got hold of the story and came over to do an interview; it wasn't long before Central TV followed suit. I'd been told the snippet was scheduled to air on the 5.45 p.m. News Update. No one believed me and there was a high chance I'd be out on a delivery when it was screened; but as luck would have it, it was a quiet spell. Suddenly, there I was on telly! The owner looked very bemused but also pleased... At this time, Hale Bopp, a record-breaking, unusually bright comet, reached its closest approach to Earth. With twin blue and white tails, it looked just like a smudge in the night sky, easily visible to the naked eye; and as I delivered to various addresses, I made a point of drawing customers' attention to it – it often got me a tip!

This was pre-Satnav; and when I began the work, I frequently had to resort to an A-Z to find the different locations. It didn't take long before I had a virtual map of the area in my head, which meant if I was handed, say, five bags of food, I could mentally sequence the destinations in an order using the minimum petrol. Many fake £20 notes were doing the rounds at the time; I nearly got fired after bringing two back to the shop – but in the darkness, struggled to tell a genuine one from a counterfeit! In the end, the owner gave me an iodine-based detector pen: the ink stayed yellow on a genuine note, but became a dark stain on imitations; so I was okay after that and never took any more dodgy ones. It was hardly going to be a job for life though; once I'd secured a new teaching post, I handed in my notice. The owner was a hard person to get to know, shaking my hand emotionlessly as I left. I knew him no better then than I had at the start 18 months earlier; but I think we had at least gained a mutual respect for each other.

On the back of that experience, the following summer holiday I found employment much closer to home at another Chinese takeaway – Ming's Kitchen; on "The Saff" – more commonly known as Saffron Lane. The telephone in there had the most maddening, piddly little ringtone; and although I never told her, in my head I named the proprietor "Thong-Toe." She wore flip-flops too narrow for the width of her feet; so one little toe was forever hanging over the side, gone red from the friction... Her little daughter would frequently appear from the back where they lived; we shared an interest in the TV show *Monkey!* and often talked about it. The takeaway's speciality was Sweet and Sour Chicken, sold in twisted paper bagfuls of battered balls – it was delicious and piping hot; so often I took some home at the end of the night. The roads branching off the Saff were even more dangerous than the Stadium Estate. You would park up and head up into these multi-storey flats stinking of urine, often with giant German Shepherd dogs behind the metal door-fronts who always seemed to bark terrifyingly loudly just a nano-second before you rang the doorbell. There were also street gangs hanging around menacingly; you sometimes doubted your car would still be there when you came back down. Luckily, my beat-up old model was hardly a target, so was never keyed or stolen. But I swear I did once hear a *real* gunshot on Neston Gardens.

PULP MEDIA

In the late 1990s, I was persuaded by a friend to "cold-call" a long list of businesses attempting to persuade them to switch their company landlines to a supposedly cheaper, long-since defunct independent competitor, for whom he himself had been working for some time. I've altered the name... Providing me with some kind of 'routing' gadget to attach to my own landline before it went into the wall socket, he categorically assured me there would be no charge added to my own bill for making these hundreds of calls a day. I was dubious, but once persuaded to come on board, was diligent about the work; learning the correct 'spiel' and ringing every number on the reams of pages provided: the idea being that, once I forwarded my friend the details of each interested party, he would make appointments with them and do the sales pitch, while his colleague performed various technical checks at the premises. I didn't warm to the other fella at all when I spoke to him; like a well-known Lord Mayor, he had this kind of sneery London accent:

"Naaah – forget abaht all that; forget abaht all that…"

My own firm belief is that to be successful in any Sales work,

1: you really have to 'know' your product inside out; and

2: You need to actually 'like' your product – for then, your own genuine passion for it is infectious.

In this case, not only did I not *know* enough about the technical side of the service to feel sufficiently articulate when dealing with the customers, I also really wasn't that *into* the product – namely the company – I was promoting! This feeling worsened when I was rung up by a smooth-talking rival in the same firm who wanted to move the established goalposts and transfer me onto his own team; talking a load of office lingo about "joined-up, blue sky thinking," with phrases like, "Do ye think ye can *run* with this, Guy?"

The final nail in the coffin though, was shortly afterwards, when I received my next itemised landline bill. *No* charge to my own provider? *ALL* the calls I had made had added to the bill; there were literally dozens of pages. Luckily, most of the conversations had been mercifully brief, lasting less than a minute (as there really wasn't a huge volume of interest in switching to this new provider) – but the mere fractions of pennies for each one still added up, resulting in a significant increase to my bill. Clearly there remained a degree of leakage from the routing gadget to the landline provider, *if* it ever indeed functioned! I didn't understand it, but in any event, had enough reservations to bring things to a halt. So – in the end, I most certainly did *"forget abaht all that…"*

SUBSCRIPTION SALES EXECUTIVE

In the autumn of 2002, I had given up permanent, full-time teaching and was exploring other options before finally settling back into supply for the next 16 years. Looking through the local newspaper, the *Leicester Mercury*, I came across a large advert from the company behind the paper itself; who were seeking to appoint several "Subscription Sales Executives" to liaise with the general public and help boost sales. Now I had been actively trying (and failing) to get into the *Leicester Mercury* for some time: they had an in-house Graphic Design department overseeing the presentation of many features; and I thought it would be fun, varied work to get into. It occurred to me that if I got another position within the company, as an insider I might find it easier to move departments. The paper itself was established in the city back in 1874, when Gladstone was Prime Minister. As a Graphics teacher, I had even taken GCSE pupils on tours of the building; seeing the print process in action really made the theory elements the students were learning fall into place. There were colossal individual floor-to-ceiling tanks of Cyan,

Magenta, Yellow and Black ink, which suddenly made CMYK make sense to them (the 'key' colour, Black, being represented by a 'K' to avoid confusion with the blue of Cyan); and suddenly, they would knuckle down, taking the subject seriously. I sent in my CV along with a covering letter; and a week later, whilst painting a friend's flat in London, I got a call during which I was asked in for initial training.

Although none of us ever met the CEO, which I think was deplorable – even the lowest bog-cleaner should get to meet their boss – we were at least introduced to other senior management in a hallowed area of the building I never saw again. At an enormous boardroom table laden with bowls of grapes and other fine-quality fruit, we were given an introductory glass of bubbly as the besuited top-brass extolled the virtues of working for the company.

"We work hard, but we also party hard," said the Circulations Manager; "and when we celebrate, we usually celebrate in *beer*..." Not sure I'm gonna fit in here, I thought, alcohol just wasn't the 'done' thing in our house. The unease grew when we were each passed a supposedly enticing full-colour review of last year's Christmas party, packed with rooftop photos in comic-strip panels of all the drunken revellers leering, cavorting on tables and snogging each others' faces off.

After telling us the origins and background history of the newspaper, the chief speaker took pains to emphasize what a pivotal role we would be playing as very much the public face of the *Mercury*. But "Subscription Sales Reps?" Rather a fancy name. It turned out we were little more than door-to-door canvassers, albeit armed with the very first hand-held PDAs (Personal Digital Assistants) in the UK. Our job was to persuade the public to take up an introductory offer to have the *Mercury* delivered every day for £1 a week; 12 weeks after which the full price would kick in... Now I had done a fair number of promotion-based jobs by then, but *never* before had I undergone a full, formal training in understanding sales techniques. This two-week-long process was *fascinating*; I realised just how adept the retail group were at profiling: the calculated classification of like-minded people by typical key interest triggers in the marketplace; how their interests fluctuate; and when to target different demographics at which times of day.

For instance, the vast majority of bungalow owners are the retired: whatever you may think of the stereotyping, "they'll often have their slippers and dressing gowns on by 5pm and won't answer the door – so you need to contact them earlier on in the day"; whereas home-owners in those areas categorised as "Thriving" were often healthy, wealthy people at the top of the social ladder in high-powered jobs, "less likely to be home until later". "Expanding" referred to business people in better-off families, paying off mortgages and bringing up children; "Settling", those who have their own homes and lead a steady lifestyle; "Rising", young professionals and executives working and studying to make their way up the career ladder; "Aspiring", those trying to better their lot, buying their council homes and pursuing goals; and "Striving": those for whom life is toughest, in the most difficult social conditions of all.

We were taken through all the basic principles of selling, the skeleton structure of a sale and the whole buying process: initial distrust, suspicion, the need for details to persuade, creating interest and desire (matching products to needs), hesitation (shall I, shan't I) and then, finally, approval. A large part of the process involved *"overcoming objections"* – and in particular, *acknowledging* the objection, before *isolating* it – citing the benefits, before again returning to "The Road" – *Close, Close, Close*. By way of a very abridged example:

Home-owner: "I think your paper's sh*t!"

Sales Executive: "Oh, I'm sorry you think that – what exactly is it that you think is sh*t?" *(Acknowledging objection/ "open-ended" question, not closed (which only gets a Yes/No answer)*

Home-owner: "It doesn't have enough jobs in it."

Sales Executive: Well, I can see how you might think that… but did you know our Wednesday edition does have a whole 'Jobsday' section… *(Matching product to needs)*

Home-owner: Oh…

Sales Executive: *(AFT)* Apart from that, is there anything you don't like? *(Isolating the objection)*

Home-owner: Well, no – I suppose not.

Sales Executive: Well look: we do have a special savings deal on right now: if you fancy trying the paper again, you can have it every day for £1 a week for 12 weeks. *(Close, close, close)*

Home-owner: Hmmm – okay. *(Approval)*

Via roleplay with each other, we practised dealing with all manner of customers, in particular, the angry. One of the other reps paired with me was rather over-zealous in his portrayal; the extent of his verbal aggression almost as harrowing as *physical*; and left me traumatised for several hours afterwards! But overall, the training and insight I gained in those two weeks is something I still value today. Each of us was given a photographic identity badge, waterproof clothing and a set of promotional discount vouchers to give to those accepting the 12-week trial. On the downside, I soon learned *no* waterproof clothing remains so when poured on for eight hours solid every day: we were drenched; many of the vouchers ending up as soaking wet pulp…

There were two already long-established sales teams within the department; and at the end of the training period, we all got assigned to one or the other team leader. Regrettably, in my case, I didn't get the cheerier, time-served veteran, but a newer, really quite sinister and lazy Turkish character who lived on a canal barge. This fella was dodgy; he had found a way to 'trip' the clock on our PDA devices to make it appear the team had worked for eight hours, when instead, they spent four of those hours down the pub each day. True, for one night in my youth, I took part in something similar at the crisp factory, however, I knew right from wrong and felt uncomfortable doing it on a daily basis, not to mention the fact I wasn't a drinker. But this team leader put me under quite threatening pressure to follow suit. As the driver who took us all out to the designated areas each day, we were under his control; I didn't like the bloke's manner at all, so took to driving out to the locations myself: I really *was* out on the street selling a full eight hours every single day.

On the opposing team was an eternally unruffled older man with a repellent collar of fatty, tadpole-like skin tags clinging like a Tudor ruff around the base of his neck as if suckling at it. When I saw the kind of places the sales teams met up and ate in regularly, I realised the probable cause. Never before had I experienced a true "truck stop". Many such places, favoured by long-distance lorry drivers, are tucked away and only entered via a discreet alley behind other buildings: giant car parks with a diner at one end; several of which were notorious for hosting live sex shows for the punters; and serving the greasiest, oil-saturated fry-ups imaginable. On my first day's work, I got no sales at all; and came home despondent, feeling it was another thing I was going to fail at. On the second day, I got three leads – and from then on, with my technique improving and confidence rising – I got *dozens*. I set myself a target of a record-breaking 100 leads a week, achieved it continuously, then, when all my efforts went unrecognised and no openings were offered from the in-house Design firm, I left in disgust, leaving a legend behind that was talked about for years. I didn't rat on my team leader, never grassed him up to our Subscription Sales Manager, but I did make her aware in no uncertain terms that the PDAs were *far* from tamper-proof; and that only honest graft secured so many leads. She went to her superior, alerted him to the fact I was going and brought me a hastily typed internal memo. But it was too little, too late.

"In my fifteen years in circulation, I do not think I have ever experienced such a result from one Subscription Sales Executive in one week..." (He should've put "*three consecutive* weeks"). "A continuation of this performance will see our sales around single-handed!"

Unexpectedly, a few months later, several of the other reps, targeting my area with the same old promotion, turned up at my house. They were astonished to see me. As my good-natured black Labrador wagged his way around them, I asked the whole lot inside and served them tea and cake, which I knew was sorely needed. They were a nice lot; and we had a great laugh reminiscing.

ROYAL MAIL

I worked for the above organisation no less than three times; the first several decades ago, sorting the Christmas Rush. Back in 2002, we had to sign the Official Secrets Act; meaning I've had to seek guidance via my MP from the Attorney General to talk about it now. Even for temps, Health and Safety training was firmly in place, with a solid Induction and video-based guidance on the safe lifting of heavy items. You might think everything would be fully automated, but the setup back then was fairly archaic: hessian sacks stretched over post-coded frames into which you directed the various letters for each UK region. The regulars were a friendly crowd who welcomed us all; there was a healthy sense of camaraderie and banter, which made the long shifts pass more easily.

Among us newbies was a very tall, elegant lady who spoke English with a strong Jamaican accent. Imagine the leggy, green Lycra-clad girl from Ottowan who sang the 1980 hit *D.I.S.C.O.* and you have it. Anyway, having taken to bringing in my own CD mixes to entertain the team, I soon found myself in direct competition with her to secure control of the music for the night. Within a couple of days, this rival was bringing in her own reggae mixes, leading to a mutual rush for the Eject button. At first she was something of a curiosity, forever announcing in a loud voice, "In Jam-ee-a-ca we do (this)...", or, "In Jam-ee-a-ca we do (that...")"; and, "Back in Jam-ee-a-ca, ma' hos-band does (this...")"; ma' hos-band does (that...)" It was refreshingly novel for the first few nights, but after days of it, I could see the patience of the regulars wearing thin; even the most mild-mannered muttering under his breath, "Who does she think she is – a flippin' ambassador for Jamaica?" I myself learned a few interesting facts from the lady, most memorable of which was a gushing description of her favourite delicacy, goat broth – a soup referred to as "Mannish Water," which had a distinct aphrodisiac reputation. The woman soon got into a clandestine plan with another postie who'd claimed he could secure her a fresh specimen. To my disbelief, the exchange occurred the very next day in the Sorting Office itself: we were party to the surreal sight of her striding through the depot with a coat-hanger on which hung a complete (albeit skinned and beheaded) goat's carcass; its rank, sour smell lingering long after it vanished into the locker room.

As soon as the shift ended at midnight on Christmas Eve, we were all out on our ear – dismissed. With it snowing hard outside, the same lady asked if she might grab a lift home. I was willing to oblige as she lived in a skyscraper next to the train station just a minute away. But no sooner had we reached her destination than she looked over at me lingeringly, eyes twinkling in a highly suggestive manner, her bright red, lipsticked sash of a mouth glowing in the dark.

"Mm-you wung come up?" she asked me. It was around 4 a.m. and I wasn't really interested in her that way, not to mention shattered; so I began spluttering excuses, trying to escape her direct gaze. "Well no – look, you told me you're married!" I ended up saying.

"Mm-so what?" was her mischievous response, licking her lips and eyeballing me with that same enticing, studied scrutiny.

"It's – it's late – I'd better get back," I stammered awkwardly.

"Mm-okay then!" she responded, shrugging indifferently as if to imply I was missing the chance of a lifetime. Proudly, she got out of the car and shimmied her way inside. I never saw her again.

With money spent on my first book's contributory contract to recoup, I rejoined Royal Mail in 2022, assuming the Christmas Sorter job would be as it was before. I couldn't have been more wrong. No Official Secrets Act, no Health & Safety training. *"There's the toilet, there's the fountain"* – and you were on the shop floor. Sorting now took place in a huge warehouse on the outskirts of the city; massive plastic doors to the outside forever opening to let in returning drivers and gusts of freezing air. Many of the temps never took off their coats. Once, there was a gas leak and the alarm went off. We all had to exit the hangar and stand in the rear car park, not for the customary 10 or 20 minutes – but for a full *hour and a half*. By the all-clear, we were virtually frozen solid…

The sorting side now involved facing a frame of letter-box-size pigeonholes, each labelled with a different local postal area. You took jammed grey tubs of letters onto the desk in front of you and tossed each into their correct slot; learning surprisingly fast where each postal area was. But the pigeonholes were labelled differently on each frame, meaning unless you got to stand in the exact same location, you had to learn the postcode whereabouts afresh each day. Other than that, it was okay, except for when a call went up: "Who's got a driving licence?" With no one else qualifying, on several occasions I was diverted from sorting to drive out and relieve postmen who'd broken down, giving them my good van so they could transfer the contents and resume their round while I stayed with the broken-down vehicle waiting for the RAC. The average wait was 240 minutes, meaning that in the cold you would end up literally busting for a wee – and if the battery was dead, there wasn't even heating. I even had to resort once to begging a nearby Halal butcher for use of his outside toilet in a beat-up wooden shack. Thereafter, I took to sneaking in a huge silver fleece given to me by a former girlfriend, to protect against being stranded again.

Just as before, all temps were ruthlessly laid off the minute the Christmas rush concluded. I lobbied my agency for weeks to get me back into Royal Mail, but so ineffectual were they that in the end, having applied for a Delivery Driver position, I rang my former manager to ask if he might at least look out for my application. My timing couldn't have been better: by coincidence, they needed a driver there and then – I had inveigled my way back in; and from that day forth, joined the Parcel Delivery team. When my agency found out, their feathers were ruffled; I had not followed "due process," the boss grumbling that: a) I'd potentially left myself open to rejection from insurers if involved in an accident; b) I was meant to have shown them a driving licence; and c) as there'd been no official interview, I might even find myself not being paid. In fact, the Christmas employment was never officially terminated by the agency via P45 – so technically, I was still on the books; besides, the Royal Mail staff had seen my driving licence back in December.

Of all three stints at the company, this one proved most exasperating of all. With a new woman boss, I was now a proper little Postman Pat for the first time, each day driving a different red van from the battered, diesel fleet of hundreds. Tracked deliveries were separated into either red-carded DPRs (Designated Parcel Route) or yellow-carded LATs (Later Acceptance Time). The process was near-relentless manual labour; and a complete lottery as to how many parcels and tracked letters you were allocated to deliver each day, piled up on one to two man-sized 'yorks' on castors, each with a mind of its own not dissimilar to a wilful supermarket trolley, save for the addition of a yellow 'brake' bar. The fewest parcels I was given was 22; but often it was many more. The hand-held PDA would calculate how long the round *should* take to complete, but took no account of prevailing weather and road conditions. Leicester was, at the time, quite literally choking on roadworks, and the SatNav repeatedly directed you into closed-off areas, meaning massive diversions to get to the required destinations. You were expected to be resourceful and find alternative routes to such locations; the whole team under pressure to bring back as few undelivered parcels as possible. Luckily, I was a time-served inhabitant of the city for almost 50 years; and knew my way around. Of all the times to join, though, it turned out to be the wettest March for over 40 years – I was drenched every day, and, rather than ruin more expensive boots, resorted to my dog-walk wellies, drawing mocking remarks of: "Ooh-arrrrr, Farmer Giles…"

With a good hour and a half's preliminary work at the depot, I found I was often dangerously exhausted before even beginning the round or setting foot in a vehicle. First, you signed in via a large book on the central stand, then went to the rear hatch to put your name down in line for a van and sign out a PDA. Invariably these gadgets were only partially charged, meaning it was wise to scrounge a second backup device from the surly manager so you could switch over its battery when the first gave out – or risk losing your entire programmed route midway. You then had to find out which yorks of parcels you'd been allocated. Less was not always more, as those destinations were often miles apart in harder-to-find areas known as the "Rurals"; whereas in a van with many parcels on a nearby, urban route, you could have several to deliver on the same road; so got through the round more quickly.

The PDA had three distinct 'modes' to program prior to leaving the depot. Formal training was non-existent; none of the managers were teachers and seemed to expect you to absorb the meaning of their jargon either by telepathy or osmosis through the skin. Determined to remember each nugget of information, I took copious notes like a policeman. Often, the gadgets, which used Wi-Fi to download required routes, encountered technical glitches between modes which were impossible to overcome unless privy to tricks guarded jealously by the managers, many of whom spent most of their time on their mobiles, walking away and disappearing for the best part of an hour in "meetings". You were left dithering like an idiot, walking endlessly up and down the labyrinth of aisles in search of them until you reached near-collapse. The best one was a good-natured fella who, while never divulging exactly how he did it, effortlessly solved any ongoing problem, handing back the PDA with a grin. But on Saturdays, he wasn't in; and none of the managers had a clue how to deal with tech problems; or, it seemed, the slightest inclination. Like Napoleon, the chief pig in Orwell's *Animal Farm,* some sat on their privileged backsides all day, snapping a mouthful of excuses that they were "too busy" to deal with the issue you had. Just when I felt like exploding, an old Indian postman sorted my PDA glitch out – he knew more than the top brass; after that degree of non-co-operation, I refused on principle to work at weekends.

Only when you had labelled all your parcels in order of delivery with a permanent black marker could you place them back onto the yorks – in *reverse* order: the earliest numbers, 1,2,3, etc. at the bottom, the last at the top. The reason was that the final numbers for delivery went on *first* at the back of the van, as they would be last to be delivered, leaving the first numbers in sequence at the front when you slid the door hatch open at the roadside: method indeed to the madness. Though the managers discouraged it, rather than using the floor, I would sneak all my parcels onto the waist-level desks by the sorting frames to number them. It was infinitely easier for your back.

What would incense me was that any time advantage you built up (either by having fewer parcels on a given day or by being more efficient with the PDA/labelling process), was utterly negated by then having to wait the best part of half an hour for a van to become available from returning postmen! *So* many man-hours were wasted. You sat twiddling your thumbs by the rear hatch, powerless to do anything, until called over to be allocated a turquoise van pouch to sign out. Each driver was meant to write the bay number in which they had parked their van into the logbook to enable it to be located easily by the next driver – but so few did. Rarely could the van managers be able to say accurately where your given van was situated: It could be on the East-side, West-side or Rear of the depot, and oft were the times they'd tell you the wrong region – little more than a guess. The place was vast, so it was no joke to be sent to the wrong part, walking around every single van in the carpark, bleeping your key and searching desperately for the matching van code emblazoned in yellow upper-case on the front. And if the van wasn't there as advised, that meant traipsing back in and doing the same search again on each of the other car park sites – often a fruitless exercise resulting in a need to return to the hatch, gain a replacement pouch for a different van and begin the process all over again.

Imagine then, having at last tracked down the right vehicle, loading your two heavy york-fuls of parcels – in *reverse* order – into its rear hold in pounding rain or a blizzard of sleet blowing directly into your face. When you had done that, you still weren't ready to go. One then had to fill in the logbook and do a detailed PDA Vehicle Check, entering the start mileage from the odometer and doing a host of indoor/outdoor checks on the working order of the steering wheel, seats, seatbelts, lights, horn, dashboard indicators, cleanliness, mirrors, windscreen wipers, number plate visibility, sensors, interior labelling, tyres and exhaust – to mention just a few. Then – provided you actually had sufficient fuel (which often you didn't, necessitating a long-winded visit to the pumps and another lengthy authorisation process I won't go into), *finally* – you could go... The PDA then did virtually everything for you. It automatically placed the deliveries in a loop, with the last few closest to the return depot; and acted as a SatNav with a rather appealing female voice telling you exactly where to turn and where to stop at the house numbers – even on which side of the road they were based. It did make mistakes, however, especially in freshly built areas such as New Lubbesthorpe, the whole of which looked like a toy scene out of Legoland or Monopoly. It once told me "Arrived at 180, Main Street", when I was in the middle of nowhere on a meadow-flanked country lane with nothing but a deserted metal hay loft in sight!

At the door of each house, you rang or knocked, then took a photo of the item in the doorway whilst handing it over to the customer. Sometimes a signature was required which the recipient would scrawl in the on-screen box with a fingernail. Failing an answer, an item could either be left in an arranged "Safe Place" – an enclosed porch, over a side gate or with an agreeable neighbour, whose own doorway the parcel would need to be photographed in and details taken. You would then fill in the requisite coloured card, pushing it through the absent addressee's letterbox to tell them where you'd left the parcel. Most of the customers were lovely. You only had a few seconds to remark on the weather or something to put them at their ease; although one sweet old lady did give me a can of cola. They liked the fact I was accepting towards their dogs, many of whom erupted into barking as soon as the doorbell rang. I always tried to prevent owners hitting their animals, reassuring them that I had a bouncy dog of my own. One or two could still be nasty, though, snatching their parcel without a word and slamming the door; others refused to take items for a neighbour, saying they weren't on speaking terms, when often I suspected a racist grudge. Or they'd shout, "Yer *not* photographing me!" (We weren't allowed to do that anyway...)

There was one very stroppy woman at an overgrown, isolated house, "The Old Rectory". Possessions were spilling out everywhere, clearly an out-of-control hoarding situation. "Leave in white cupboard" was the only Safe Place indicated on the PDA; in torrential rain, I walked around the property searching in vain for it. With no adjacent neighbour, I knocked, reluctant to take the parcel back to the depot. From deep inside, a snooty voice called, "Who is it?" but I couldn't locate from whence it emanated. Finally a door was flung open to reveal an overweight, very red lady, cream all over her face, in nothing but a large towel. "You got me out of my *bath!*" she shouted indignantly. "The other postman always puts things in the *white cupboard!*" She was quite mad... And only after visiting another beautiful, gated property in a quiet village cul-de-sac, passing the time of day with a rather serious, familiar-looking lady did it hit me that she was the mother of Madeleine McCann, the little three-year-old tragically kidnapped in Portugal... I didn't let the recognition show on my face; we had a good-natured exchange and I continued with the round.

The fleet was pretty worn; but although I did suffer one van breakdown, mostly they were reliable, sturdy little chuggers that were nice to drive. I did enjoy the freedom to park on double yellow lines; as long as you didn't blatantly take the mick and park on zig-zags, the police seemed to turn virtually a blind eye; besides, sometimes you had no choice, if delivering to a house on the edge of a dual carriageway. There were a surprising number of private 'gated' communities, which could be problematic to get into from the outside without a security guard or cleaner. They would let you in, then vanish, never considering that you would of course need to get *out* again! I got trapped inside one such complex for a good half-hour; and, with no buzzers responding, only escaped after repeatedly hammering on the glass for attention. And then there were still, I discovered, horrendous slum areas of decaying modernism I had hitherto believed no longer existed; awful, run-down, dilapidated complexes barely fit for human habitation, with flat numbers running into the hundreds: it truly made you count your blessings... Lightening the burden somewhat, I had mysteriously gained the attention of a beautiful brunette post-girl, a tall, dreamy young mum of two, who seemed fascinated by every aspect of me. Sometimes I took a couple of her packages to lighten her load; then she would ring up during my round, making my heart miss a beat whenever she suggested coming to meet me.

It's a precious thing, our Royal Mail – the public like the familiarity of the little red vans, but it's being run into the ground by Government underfunding and competition from all sides, most with more environmentally-friendly, electric vehicles. I wasn't fast enough and praise was scant; there were often quite demoralising messages left for the team by management on the group chat, one worker being told in no uncertain terms that he had to speed up;

but the final straw was when I was given 90 parcels and told I must deliver them *all*. Albeit with a total reduced to 70 after protest, with a 66-mile round trip, I was still out until 10.15 p.m. Who wants to open their door in pitch blackness? A few hours' part-time work was all I'd signed up for. Besides, hours on the clutch each day was playing havoc with some knee cartilage already damaged by someone colliding with my car; an injury which developed into a year-long limp requiring a joint injection and possible future keyhole surgery. My unfed dog was climbing the walls when I got in; and the only response from my manager was, "We do require staff to be flexible." Though I called it a day there and then, as a goodwill gesture, I agreed to complete that week's work, at the end of which she asked to me into her office.

"I want to thank you for all you've done while you've been here," she said; then, handing me a Notice of Intended Prosecution, "On a not-so-nice front, back in March, you were caught speeding doing 39 mph on a dual carriageway in a 30-mile zone."

Everyone who can should tip postal workers at Christmas; the job might be nice when the sun's shining, but they are under constant pressure, get barely more than minimum wage for driving hours in stressful, stop/go traffic; and work for hours, often in the most horrendous weather. Having been on the inside, I've gained a genuine respect for all of them.

DJ GUY

I once heard Norman Cook (a.k.a. Fatboy Slim) being interviewed about what it is exactly that makes someone a DJ. While I can't recall his exact words, the general gist as I understood it was, if you're the kind of person who listens to music on the radio, or privately through a set of headphones so you don't disturb anyone else – well, all that makes you 'normal'... But – if you're the kind of person who gets the greatest enjoyment from playing music to *others*; having *them* hear the music you play... *that* – makes you a DJ... Never was a truer word spoken. Music is such a passion of mine that being in control of what an audience hear, seeing them respond positively to tunes that mean so much to me, is one of my greatest pleasures. That doesn't mean I'm an egotistical exhibitionist who loves the sound of his own voice; and who talks a load of saccharine garbage – in fact, aside from introducing each new track, I very seldom speak myself whilst DJ-ing; I prefer just selecting and playing the music. Most professional or even semi-professional DJs would snort in derision at my set-up: I don't even have any vinyl or a turntable now; it's just me and an old .mp3 mixing deck. I used to drive my exasperated mum half mad as a teenager, playing records at full volume through just about the biggest monster ghetto blaster there ever was on the market – the Sharp VZ2000E; with its AM/FM radio, vertical twin needle integrated turntable and single cassette deck. Up the stairs she would stomp, screaming: "Turn that music *down!* Bomp, bomp, bomp – it goes through my head!" I could never help laughing, which infuriated her – but I just loved getting a reaction – even a negative one.

I've never earned a penny from my DJ-ing; it's entirely on a voluntary basis just for the joy of it; in fact I hardly consider it "work" – but I've actually done quite a lot of events now, from Jubilee street parties, friends' birthdays and College Faculty bashes to school reunions and Rotary Club Charity Fundraising Swimmarathons organised by my dad for close to ten years at the local leisure centre. The only year we had to skip was 2021 due to the Covid Lockdown... If I'm 100% honest, I think I started DJ-ing because at social events, I'm so dreadfully inept and uncomfortable: with zero rhythm or co-ordination (you're talking *three* left feet). I wouldn't be seen dead on a dancefloor – why on earth should it be required? – so being *behind* the music was a place to hide; to still be a part of the atmosphere by actually running and creating that atmosphere. It always astounds me how little confidence others have in taking on that entertainer's role when it's something that comes so naturally to me. I would hardly say I have an encyclopaedic musical knowledge, but what I am is absolutely *obsessive* about the organisation of my music and playlists. I'm massively distrustful of the long-term reliability of .mp3 as a format – I know people who have lost their entire music collections when their storage device goes down or is lost; so even though I do download music in digital form, I still write each track to physical CDs, with both a master and backup laptop, two .mp3 player copies and an external hard drive too.

Knowing what tracks to select is a key requirement: you have to be able to 'read' an audience; gauge their age and energy level and play music you believe will be up their street; whereas for the older generation, you generally have to tone it down, go lighter on the bass and select perennial, less potentially offensive classics with more of a catchy melody. In the case of the Swimmarathons, it's essential to plan quite a lot in advance, earmarking the most pumping, high-octane tracks that will motivate and speed up the swimmers. Both they and the attending lifeguards certainly react with disappointment if, say, owing to objections from an elderly participant or technical glitches, the music is temporarily interrupted. For instance, there was once a year when, as well as DJ-ing, I was required to make up team numbers in the pool for an hour. I had carefully planned for this, setting up an appropriate 70-minute playlist to run continuously until I was safely back at the helm – when, Sod's Law: one young swimmer jumped out of the pool, ran past the equipment table and inadvertently yanked the mains lead out of the iPod dock with her foot, plunging the whole place into silence. She was lucky she wasn't electrocuted – and mid-swim, there was absolutely nothing I could do; I had to complete my stint in the water.. In my absence, the other MC did his best to restore the situation, managing to get the power back on and learning how to operate the music – but what he was clueless about was *what* to play – we ended up with slow ABBA ballads cringingly out of place for that event; with him even verbalising how relieved he was when I was able to take over again...

The DJ Guy persona is also in some ways a 'mask' which grants me licence to wear outlandish costumes way larger-than-life than I am myself; from a huge rainbow cardigan bought at Camden market's Electric Ballroom, to fezzes (touchy time for them right now, though), tall Cat In The Hat-style headgear and programmable, glowing 'Funky Glasses' from Cyberdog, which allow customized, dot-matrix messages to scroll across the lenses. Music is a huge, ever-changing backdrop to all our lives; and for me, DJ-ing is just a further extension of that. I've never had so much fun at work!

AUTHOR

At the age of 18, I once had my tarot read by a mystical Italian lady I spotted crouching discreetly in a corner of a square in Florence. Her interpretation of the particular cards drawn that day was:

"You need to grasp the sceptre of your power."

Wonder of wonders, freakishness of the freakish, my readers, we finally reach the present; where – who would have thought it? – after trying the previously related cornucopia of different jobs (many of which were, admittedly, disasters), your chameleon-misfit narrator now finds himself masquerading as an author, writer, whatever you want to call it. In some ways, it's exactly where I want to be, recounting and illustrating true stories, many of which are stranger than fiction itself. Finally, the message of that long-ago reading resonates: the pen truly *is* my sword. I write – and draw – far more articulately than I ever speak. Other people *are* interested in your life experiences, you might think they won't be, but if you have valid things to say and can make your points articulately enough, that's all you need. Situations you find yourself in *are* of interest to others...

There's no particular closely-guarded secret or 'knack' to it, in case you were wondering. I simply had a headful of these tales; and followed the sage advice of an elderly uncle who once told me:

"You think you'll always remember everything that's happened in your life, but you'd be surprised how much you can forget as time goes by. So – anything that matters to you, write... it... down..."

At the start, by way of a thought trigger for each anecdote, it's enough just to make a list of a few key words, then, once you have a full list covering all the stories you intend to include, all you do is go back and put flesh on the bones of each one; expand from those key words until each full story is told. It's that simple. The modern word processor is an absolute *gift* to authors: generations born from the mid-80s onwards can never appreciate it fully, as they have not known a time when the tool didn't exist. To me, the word processor's greatest benefit is not its 'spellcheck' function, but the capacity it allows you to reposition words endlessly until you have the syntax just as you want it. Imagine *that* in the days of old typewriters: any mistake bigger than a few characters and you'd have to rip the whole page out... My degree course essays in their rough preparation stage were the most bizarre-looking things: I was trying to *be* a word processor in the days before they existed! I would quite literally 'cut' out words, sentences or whole paragraphs with scissors, repositioning those chunks earlier or later in the work using adhesive tape. The end result often stretched from floor to ceiling: a jagged, messy, irregular eccentric mass jutting wildly in and out; although once written up, each and every one resulted in an 'A' grade – so the method was certainly worth it. One housemate was so taken with the mad texture of those rough drafts that he would beg them off me to paint over and incorporate in his own illustrations!

Anyone who has ever lived has a potential book in them: to those who've thought about the idea of writing and perhaps dismissed it: just *try* it: if you speak from the heart and relate things exactly as they happened, you won't go far wrong. There's nothing whatsoever special in my own approach; but I have found the process highly cathartic; it declutters your mind and could well be the beginning of something wonderful for you.

PRANKS

HIDE AND SEEK

In 1979, we went on a family holiday to a campsite in Sarlat, a medieval town in the Dordogne region of southwest France. A seemingly never-ending summer, it was further enhanced by an added companion: the sweetest teenage girl the same age as us; whose affection my brother and I fought fiercely over. The campsite had few activities, so aside from table tennis and bombing into the swimming pool, we also resorted to Hide and Seek. One day, it was my turn to be 'it'. The deal was that you put your hands over your eyes and counted to 40; when finally I opened them, although there was no sign of the girl, I saw my brother way off in the distance, heading for refuge in the Gents on the far side of the campsite, in his conspicuous turquoise shorts. Certain I had him, I set off in pursuit towards the spacious toilet block. Now normally, this building was bustling with life, each sink occupied by holiday-makers doing their best to shave using the limited facilities – but that day, I found it silent and empty. Adopting a customary "pursuing monster" persona I had perfected since infancy, which added a delicious frisson of fear to the game, I drew my top lip over my front teeth, sawing my lower jaw up and down to the predatory vocal "*Urrr*-ah! *Urrr*-ah!" – and entered. Finding little bro was inevitable; but with every urinal vacant, where was he?

Barely able to contain my excitement at closing in on the prey, I kicked open the first door of the six toilet cubicles emphatically. It was empty; so I went on to treat the second, third, fourth and fifth doors in the same anti-social way. Still no luck. Only the final cubicle remained – but this time, the door resisted; bolted from the inside; a French *"Occupé"* sign clearly visible in red on the lock. Certain now I had my brother cornered, to a frenzied final flurry of "*Urrr*-ah! *Urrr*-ah! *Urrr*-ah! *Urrr*-ah!" I kicked the door repeatedly, relishing the assault – until finally, after a sustained attack of at least 30 seconds, I heard the chain flushing and saw the lock turn as the door started opening.

To my horror, instead of my brother, there stood this pale, bewildered, bespectacled little man in a safari jacket, matching long shorts and a pith helmet just like Don Estelle's in *It Ain't Half Hot Mum*. I must have scared him half to death. Palms upward in an attempt to placate him, I backed away, saying in my best French, "Pardon, pardon..." – until, reaching the crude stone doorway, I fled; only to find out that my brother had in fact gone around the *back* of the block to hide. That poor man in the cubicle must have had the fright of his life; he probably still wonders to this day what he'd done to deserve being so targeted while innocently going about his business in the bog!

THE BUS PROVOCATION

Without question, there is more than a little OCD in my make-up. Although that need to have things "just so" often infuriates others, I don't see it as an encumbrance; in fact, I celebrate the condition: it orders my life. I have fixed things I like to say often; for instance, "You got your hearing aid in?" when my mum sits down to watch anything. There's a real comfort in ritual. My dog loves it too. Much of the obsessiveness revolves around *numbers*; something first brought to my attention by an ex-girlfriend, when she realised in a supermarket that I was adding up the cost of the accruing groceries in my head. Most people use those trolley gadgets; but I just must do it mentally. To her astonishment, I was correct to the penny when we came to the checkout; however, I would have been upset had I *not* been... She also noticed how I position all the packet graphics in the same direction in the cupboard or freezer. The satisfaction I gain in checking *totals*, how many tablets there are in a bottle for instance (even if the number is shown on the outside) is hysterical to her. These traits aren't things you're that conscious of until someone points them out. It got me in trouble as a tiny four-year-old once, when we went to collect my grandparents from Gatwick airport. Our mum, setting off to retrieve her parked car, left me with them, but off in my own little world, I began counting the chewing gums in a packet I'd been given. When finally I looked up, they'd left me alone on a London street... Distraught, I was lucky enough to run into a policeman, who had my name called over the tannoy, reuniting us after what felt like an eternity.

 The worst my number-related OCD ever got was when my teenage brother and I, a small cousin and three family friends were on the good ol' 29 bus home after a day gallivanting in the city. A right noisy rabble of juveniles we were; the vehicle full to bursting with passengers, as we stood wobbling in the aisle on the top deck while it teetered to and fro; overgrown tree branches striking the windows as we moved along. The bell in those days wasn't a button halfway up a vertical pole as now, but a long, metal-edged rubber ceiling strip running the entire length of the bus; which you pressed before your stop. At that time, my obsession was with multiples of *three*. As we neared our road, although once would've been enough, I pressed the bell three times. *Ding, ding, ding*. Accidentally, though, I pressed it an extra time (*four*). I just couldn't have that, so had to go on to the next squared multiple of three. *Five, six, seven, eight, nine... Ding, ding, ding, ding, ding.* But the bus lurched at the wrong moment and I hit the bell a *tenth* time. I couldn't abide that; increasing the total to three *cubed: 11, 12, 13, 14, 15, 16, 17, 18, 19, 20, 21, 22, 23, 24, 25, 26, 27. Ding, ding, ding, ding, ding, ding, ding, ding, ding , ding, ding, ding, ding, ding, ding, ding, ding...*

 All of a sudden the bus driver slammed on the brakes as he reached the stop. Driven to distraction by the bell sounding right in his ear, consideration of which had never occurred to me, he must have used the glass periscope above him to identify our unsettled-looking gang in the convex mirror as the likely troublemakers. Bursting from his enclosed cabin, he tore up the stairs, roaring,

 "Which BLOODY IDIOT pressed the bell?"

You could have heard a pin drop. I went white as a sheet; spluttering inarticulately as we stumbled past him down the steps and off the bus. I was lucky not to have received a clout around the head, so incensed was the man. Someone on our deck *had* to have seen who the culprit was; but remarkably, nobody told on me – and my number-fixated OCD.

AN OUTBREAK OF SPITTING

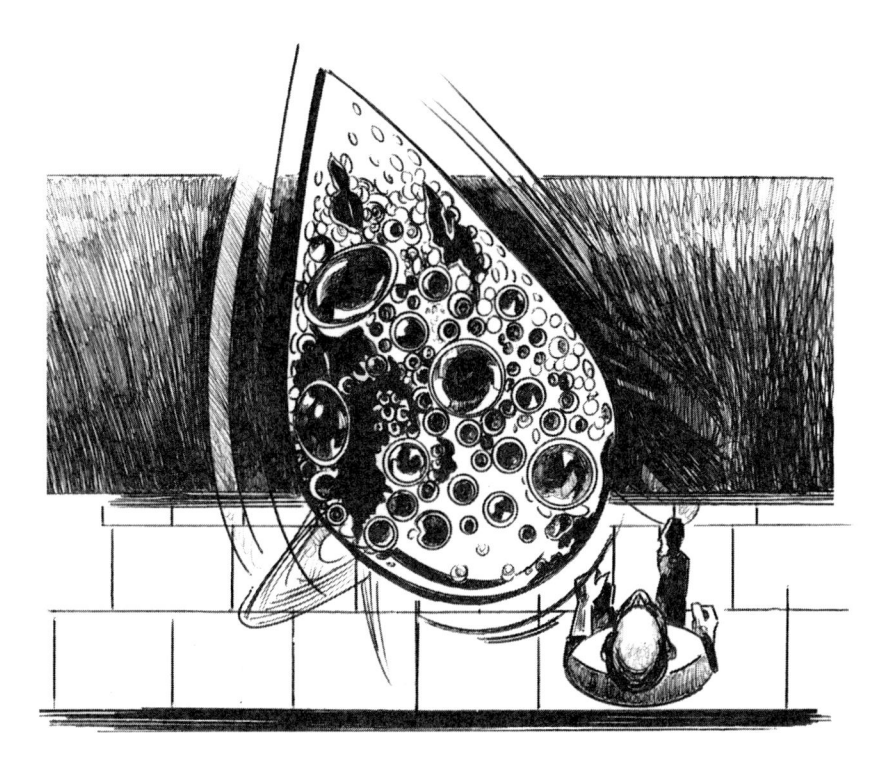

At the age of 14, my parents transferred first me, then my brother, to a private grammar school beyond the city; their aim to secure a better education for us. Whilst motivated by the best of intentions, it was a decision we didn't have a say in; and it was hard for us leaving behind our friends, who moved on by default to the local comprehensive. The school, a hallowed, long-standing establishment built in 1495 barely three years after Columbus colonised America, struck fear into us both, its battlements visible from the coach and the cane still an existing sanction. Class sizes were admittedly smaller, with the teacher/pupil ratio an undoubted advantage;

but in terms of personal/social benefits and the instilling of better values, that is harder to quantify. Any school, regardless of type, is still a standalone ecosystem, a miniature rockpool of wider society within which, as well as the noble, talented and high-achieving, less positive characters remain: the shy and withdrawn, the average and bigoted, bullies, criminals – even future murderers.

One day, at the end of Assembly, the school Bursar took to the stage to give notices in his usual manner. Glaring from his lectern onto the sea of our adolescent heads below him, he announced,

"It has come to our attention… that there has been an outbreak… of *SPITTING*… in the 'N'-block."

Under our collective breath, a discernible titter of amusement was clearly audible around the Hall.

"This will *STOP* at once," he went on, "or there will be serious consequences. Not only is spitting a revolting habit, it spreads a variety of unpleasant diseases." Then he moved on to other topics.

He wasn't misinformed about the tendency – but it had been going on for weeks. There was one short-lived, hapless new Maths teacher with no air of authority whatsoever. Barely five feet tall in his mortar-board and cloak, he hadn't the slightest sense of humour; and the bad luck to have been assigned the roughest, least able den of villains in the entire year (a group into which, having not taken the usual entry exam to assess ability level, I had been placed as a condition of being accepted). I even saw one lad position a gob of phlegm on the tip of a ruler, bend it back, then catapult it with unerring aim directly at this unfortunate teacher; where it landed, hanging pendulously, on the end of his nose. He *had* to know what it was, but was too intimidated to call it out, looking up as if it might be a drip from the ceiling. The poor man left at the end of the year.

Now the tutor group I belonged to was in the very block mentioned by the Bursar. At times, the lunch hour had become like all-out-war in the flurry of spitting; not just directly at each other, but out of windows onto passers-by; including one gowned and moustachioed teacher famously not to be messed with. Furious, he rocketed into the block in pursuit of the culprits, who fled the scene leaping like rats from a sinking ship in all directions. And woe betide anyone involved in a fight: both victor and loser ended up covered in the spectators' spit. *"Scrap! Scrap! Scrap!"* There were even *tickets* issued for one long-awaited breaktime scuffle, with bouncers assigned to the classroom door to regulate who was allowed in.

The spitting craze probably had its origins in the recent Punk Rock subculture. I myself never participated at school, but was certainly influenced by it; readily introducing my brother to the sport. He and I finally burnt out our preoccupation with spitting at each other after a frenzied battle on a Swiss holiday, forever referred to in restricted code as "The Swings at Mürren". But the most notorious incident of all was yet to come.

In Valencia, our grandparents owned a sixth-floor Spanish flat in a small municipality named Gandia. Although nice enough on the inside, it really was a perilous construction, with a filthy, yawning hole right down the centre, over which neighbours hung washing. If you were on the roof gazing at the sunbaked, whitewashed rim of that vast chasm, some primal lemming instinct would surface and almost try to pull you down to your death. There was a further hazard inside the apartment too: a balcony overlooking the street, accessed by opening a near-invisible glass panel. Tears did occur once or twice when one or other of us ran directly into it. Our bilingual cousin, brought up in Spain, was several years younger than my brother and me; so very easily influenced. When the novelty of seeing each other after years apart wore off, it would amuse us to contribute to his delinquency; introducing him to all manner of unsavoury words and skills which he inevitably tried out on his peeved parents in the days following our visit. Of course, he had to be initiated into the latest craze: spitting. And where better to demonstrate it than off the balcony?

After a few ineffective dummy runs, it was time to demonstrate to our cousin the most disgusting skill of all: "Brewing a Milky". This involved allowing saliva to build up in your mouth for a prolonged period; swilling it from cheek to cheek until it became not only pure white and aerated, but also seriously weighty. I must have spent 10 minutes building up one of these monstrosities in my mouth: it was impossible to speak in the closing stages, as your cheeks were so full. The temptation to laugh was considerable, but had to be resisted lest it all flew everywhere. When the fateful moment for the drop arrived, all I could do was make a series of guttural grunts and gestures to draw my conspirators' attention to the balcony; all three of us leaning over it to watch the colossal gob's descent. Down it plummeted, gathering momentum as it went; accompanied by our chuckles of anticipation... It was only *ever* my intention for us to watch the missile hit the ground when, at the last possible moment (the timing of such misfortune something which could only have been calculated by a master physicist's equation determining height of drop by velocity of descent times increase in mass) – a man stepped out of the building onto the pavement below...

With all the visual impact of a water droplet landing in slow motion, *SPLAT!* – right onto the top of his bald head landed the Milky, spreading out like a comic-strip bang. In a mixture of shock, guilt and surprise, we all gasped. The Spaniard looked up in time to see three juvenile, grinning heads dart back from view in unison. Enraged, he came *roaring* back upstairs like a Toro Bravo in an Iberian bullring, swearing at the top of his voice in Catalan. In cowardice, we sought hiding in the furthermost corner of the flat as he pounded on the apartment door in fury. It was left to our bewildered uncle to placate the poor man; which he managed with the aid of a 1000 peseta note.

"*WHAT*'ve you boys been doin'?" he asked irately, as we crept from our refuge feigning innocence.

A step too far, thus ended the era of spitting.

THE RABBIT DRINK

My infant brother was compelled on several occasions to drop clods of mud, water and other nameless materials into a drinking vessel. He would run inside, spilling much of it on the way; and present the filth, not dissimilar to a mud pie, to our horrified mother; before announcing proudly,

"I made a *rabbit* drink!" From whence the name came, we had no idea – but the memory stayed with us. And later, as teenagers home alone one summer's day, with our mum away and dad off at work, the devil made work for idle hands: we were seized by a desire to resurrect the tradition.

Our "rabbit drinks" now, though, were far more inventive,

elaborate and repulsive; and the game had transformed into one of direct indoor combat. The rules were, there *were* no rules – nothing was sacred; even worse, we were now armed with large projectile syringes rather than mugs; each of us hysterically trying to outdo the other with ever more revolting and slimy concoctions. Added to the mud were a cocktail of rancid foodstuffs, soap, Vaseline, salad cream, butter, pond water, cottage cheese – you name it, we squirted it all over each other at close range, with scant regard for the house: the more unpleasant the sensation for the recipient, the better. It was in our hair, on our clothes, all over the walls and landing carpet; we'd been at it most of the day – when suddenly, to our shock, we heard the sound of a car pulling up on the gravel. It was our dad!

Panicking, we ceased the confrontation, got a heap of towels and, in the time it took him to switch off the radio and come inside, did our best to rub the whole area clean. We were expecting major repercussions when he made it upstairs; but to our astonishment, preoccupied with other thoughts, he barely registered the carnage; just made a passing grumble on his way to the shower:

"What's been going on up here? Come on, lads – clean it up ..."

Which we did – very graciously. We got off incredibly lightly. Our mum would have gone ballistic!

AN UNUSUALLY UNPLEASANT PROPRIETOR

On a family holiday to Italy in our late teens, our parents gave my brother and me the freedom to leave them and go Interrailing for a couple of weeks. Even with such a ticket enabling us to go on almost any train in Europe, we stayed in the country, pigging out on pizzas and visiting the wonders of Florence and Venice; consulting a tourist guidebook on where the best, most inexpensive *pensione* boarding houses were. One kindly, elderly lady welcomed us into her hostel where we dumped our stuff and went out, only to be caught in a ferocious thunderstorm with warm, torrential rain. To our horror, when we got back, drenched, for some inexplicable reason, the woman had been in our room, turned on the light and opened the shutters wide; resulting in every mosquito in the area viewing it as a haven: it was literally *buzzing* with their high-frequency hums. The roll-on repellant that we had proved near-useless; the insects actually seemed to like it and got stuck in it, wriggling around. If we hadn't sprayed the living daylights out of the apartment, we would have been eaten alive – you could hear the creatures' kamikaze screams as one by one they plummeted from the ceiling. Worse than that, next morning, we found a yellow baby scorpion nestling in the corner wall of the bathroom – the final straw prompting us to leave.

Leafing through the guidebook in search of a new base, we came across what looked a beautiful, scenic and inexpensive option; however, there was an unsettling word of warning in the review: "*An unusually unpleasant proprietor...*" We didn't like the sound of that, but the price and location were so good we thought we'd give it a shot on the off chance that perhaps the reviewer had got it wrong, or there'd been a change of management. There hadn't. The bloke was a nasty character; fat, sweaty and humourless in off-white, stained shorts. He had dark, hostile eyes, made zero attempt to speak English and shouldn't have been within 100 miles of hospitality. He demanded payment upfront, plus our passports, which we felt uneasy with; but the custom of declaring the presence of guests to the police was initiated following a major kidnap of a local politician in 1978.

"*CAPISCE?*" he barked at us. We knew enough Italian to know he was asking if we understood. Unhappily, we exchanged glances: the fact that we didn't like him must have shown on our faces.

"*VA BENE?*" he growled menacingly; it was clearly a rhetorical question – we curtly nodded an okay.

But we didn't feel comfortable there and left to catch the midnight train without even sleeping in the single beds. However, before checking out, we left a prank to teach the undergrown little megalomaniac a lesson *real* good. Just in case we got lucky, we had each brought a packet of condoms abroad; and filled a pair of them with a bubble of soapy water to make them look used; tying them off and inserting them halfway down each bed under the sheets. We figured the owner was just the sort of lazy waster who wouldn't bother remaking either bed if they looked as if they hadn't been slept in; and that his next guests would give him an absolute rollicking upon pulling back the covers. Two wrongs may not make a right, but occasionally, it feels so damn satisfying...

Several days later, from the safety of hundreds of miles away, we sent the proprietor a postcard, with a harsh caricature of him and drawings of the condoms, along with the captions *"VA BENE?"*, *"CAPISCE?"* and *"HA-HA-HA-HAAA!"* He probably refused all British guests on principle after that.

THE WEIGHT-GAIN WIND-UP

As youngsters, my brother and I looked up considerably to our American cousins, whom we had seen very little of over the years, barring occasional trips they made over to Europe. Having grown up living largely on their wits, they were infinitely more streetwise than either of us, with a great deal more life experience. Exuding that supreme confidence instilled by the US constitution itself, both had attended the celebrated New York School of Performing Arts made famous by the hit movie and TV series *Fame*; one was now a talented musician; the other in the film business. Having not had the most stable upbringing, they valued family greatly; and one day, out of the blue, we had an unexpected telephone call from the younger of the two, saying he was on the way up to us there and then. Although he was a great chap, I always felt as if I didn't quite measure up in his eyes: that was more down to my own insecurities than anything he did – but anyway, the news made me a little jittery. Whether our folks were away just then I can't recall, but in any event, we were alone in the house; and one of us needed to go and pick him up from the train station. Suddenly it occurred to me that a practical joke might be the perfect way to break the ice.

"Hey," I said to my brother, "let's play a trick on him... Why don't we pretend I've become *really* fat... You go and collect him, that'll give me some time to pad myself out; but stop somewhere on the way back and tell him there's some serious news you have to break... Explain I haven't come to welcome him because I'm scared of his reaction; the reason being that in the years since we last met I've become absolutely huge; and I'm so self-conscious that I barely leave the house now."

"Mm-yeah," said my brother, chuckling at the prospect, "but how are you going to carry it off?"

"Leave it to me," I said. "Just go and fetch him. But remember, you *must* be serious or he won't believe it. Above all, emphasize he absolutely *cannot* laugh, or he'll give me a massive complex."

Well, the station was barely 10 minutes' drive away; so it was likely any wait, plus the return journey, only gave me a maximum 25 minutes to prepare. I took the largest pillows I could find from the airing cupboard and tied them tightly around the front of my waist with string, then arranged some smaller cushions evenly on top of the pillows. I tried to do the same on my back, but couldn't level the bulges out, so the whole thing must have looked very unbalanced and Quasimodo-like. Certainly, I'd overestimated my skills making a convincing disguise – it was hardly SFX prosthetics-level. No jumper or jacket would fit over everything, leaving the outfit looking lame in its current state; so to unify the external appearance of the different items, I layered a couple of long dressing-gowns over the lot; in a travesty of a Demis Roussos-style kaftan... Next, I raided the bathroom cabinet, finding a bag of cotton-wool balls. I shoved a load inside my cheeks until they were virtually bursting in a Don Corleone-like *Godfather* parody; and to complete the outfit, added a pair of dark metallic blue sunglasses left over from a summer holiday. Somehow being hidden behind them made me feel less inhibited, affording greater licence to be outrageous.

During this same time, my brother had already picked up our cousin; and just as instructed, pulled into a lay-by on the return journey. He turned off the engine and grimly broke the story of my colossal weight-gain; reiterating just how sensitive I was to ridicule, what the repercussions could be if anyone laughed; and that, at all costs, both of them would have to keep their expressions deadly serious around me. Clearly, he did a good job – our cousin bought the story completely…

Time seemed to fly; and before I knew it, I heard car tyres crunching on the gravel signifying their arrival at the house. A key turned in the front door lock; and I heard the footsteps of both brother and cousin climbing the stairs, deep in conversation. I couldn't just be *found*: having put in all this effort, I needed to be in utter control of the moment. Quietly, I retreated right back into the tiny walk-in closet in the furthermost corner of the bedroom and silently pulled the door to, holding my breath. The heat of the costume layers was overpowering; and it was quite a squeeze; the sink pressing into my distended belly, meaning I had to stand virtually side-on in the darkness… Distantly, I heard the strains of a familiar American accent drifting upwards:

"Oh my God – I'm gonna laugh – I just *know* I'm gonna laugh…"

The door to the bedroom swung open as both of them entered. For all parties, the air of anticipation was electric.

"Where is he? Is he hiding?" asked our cousin with intense curiosity, scanning all corners of the room. He clearly couldn't wait to witness the spectacle. It was now or never: time for my big entrance. With a loud crack, I pushed open the closet, pausing just a second to guarantee their attention would be fixed upon the doorway – then out I lurched sideways; gargantuan belly first…

"Hi-iiiiiiiii!" I said behind the shades, in a deep, stylish, benevolent voice, drawing out the vowel in what I imagined was a suave, playboy, man-of-the-world manner. My cousin's jaw dropped in utter disbelief, his face working as a multitude of expressions crossed it – my overall look bizarre in the extreme – and that was *IT*… Prone to fits of laughter at the best of times, I couldn't hold it together a moment longer. Fatally sabotaging my own performance, I lost the battle to keep a straight face and collapsed into convulsing, stifled guffaws, as the pressure in my jammed cheeks found the only possible outlet. Out of my mouth shot a pent-up blizzard of white cotton wool, just as the waist string gave out; cushions and pillows bursting their way from the makeshift kaftan. It was as if I had all-but exploded in front of him... As I stood, shaking with mirth and restored to normal size in the ruins of the fat-suit, the penny dropped and our cousin realised he'd been had.

"GUY!" he screamed in simultaneous laughter, shock and outrage; then, in mock-anger, turning to my brother: "You *B*STARD!*" We all fell about together then, any potential awkwardness between us fully dissipated – in what had to be the most memorable opening scene of all his visits.

THE METAL DETECTOR

Our next-door neighbours had a lad a couple of years younger than us with a gift for all things electronic: no exaggeration, this boy could wire a plug at the age of seven and even arranged outdoor lighting for our tents on camping sleepovers... One day, much to our envy, he was given a metal detector for his birthday. We could hear him bleeping up and down his long garden in search of valuable finds; and occasionally he would boast about all he had found. I don't think my brother and I had even heard of the gadget up until then, but once our neighbour had one, we mildly resented it, and the flimsy notion of playing a trick on him was born in our juvenile heads.

What the lad had no idea about was that I, as a child, was a veritable *magpie* drawn to anything that glittered. Christmas lights, traffic signals, chandeliers – all captivated me; and although most of mine was imitation, I even had a treasure-box full of the trinkets I had: diamonds picked out of old ladies' brooches or toy car headlights; Venetian glass and twinkling goldstone; metallic marbles, cast-off necklaces, semi-precious minerals, even a mock Fabergé egg and prismatic car stickers – all hoarded fiercely. Much as other children carry a comfort blanket or cherished teddy, I would always have a treasure in my fist, usually enclosed in a blob of Blu Tack for protection. And, of course, I would inevitably lose each one and be inconsolable until some new, better replacement seized my fancy. I had the most unusual "pink-and-white diamond" – an irregular, artificial crystal and fond link from our old home in London to the new one when we moved. One day, whilst riding a tricycle on the pavement, I hid it inside the bell for safekeeping: it fell out through a gap in the metal and was lost. I had a large, artificial emerald which one day I was washing in a sink of cold water; my brother crept up behind me and maliciously pressed the plug – why, he couldn't even explain. Down it went forever – it might still be in the pipework! One of the Blu Tack blobs containing a tiny opal triplet fell out of my pocket at school; I scoured every part of the building and, against all odds, saw it sticking to a girl's shoe in the Library. Incredibly, the opal was still there – and intact. And at one point, I somehow got possession of a *real* gold ring my dad was given by an uncle. I dropped it one evening in my grandma's loft; down it fell into the fibreglass lagging, impossible to find in the darkness. I never told anyone, so it is probably still there to this day. My treasure fascination became well-known in the family; each grandmother rifling through their jewellery to assemble bagfuls with which to keep me occupied. So within my own collection, I had more than enough material from which to fake what looked a plausible haul.

My brother and I went carefully through the lot, selecting mainly metallic, golden items which would cause the detector to react: coins, miniature goblets on saucers, a variety of pendants, scarabs and, in particular, an Egyptian-inspired belt buckle complete with relief Pharoah's head and various hieroglyphics. We added to them a selection of extra artefacts which could arguably have heralded from ancient eras harder to pinpoint: quartz crystals, opals, amethysts, rubies and sapphires. With these picked out, we took a spade from the shed and dug a shallow hole at a recognisable point in one of the back garden flower-beds; lining the pit with a worn, stained tea towel which looked as if it could have been an ancient shroud. On top of the cloth we poured in the jewellery, arranging it carefully with the gold Pharoah's head uppermost; then covered the heap with the outer edges of the frayed rag and shovelled the soil lightly back on top. We then walked around to our neighbours, rang their doorbell and invited the lad to come over and play.

"Hey – why don't you bring in your metal detector?" we asked. "You never know, you might find something in our garden!" He didn't need any persuasion – in he came. *Bleep... bleep... bleep* – we led him on a cruel and vastly entertaining wild goose chase to several different locations, all of which, of course, yielded nothing; my brother and I exchanging wicked, conniving grins behind the boy's back. Just when he'd had enough and was all but ready to give up, we said, "You know what, you haven't looked over there: why don't you try just one more spot..." – at which point, we led him over to the exact point of the burial site. As he hovered the detector's sensor over the ground, almost instantly, *"Wheee-eee-eee-eee!"* – its bleeping slid up at least two octaves into an enormously satisfying electronic howl, signifying a major find...

"Oh my God!" he exclaimed breathlessly, as we handed him a spade. No sooner had he pushed it into the ground than he felt it strike something hard – and began frantically uncovering the hidden shroud. We watched as he peeled open the edge of the cloth to reveal the unmistakable glint of gold. "Whoa!" he breathed open-mouthed – as did we all to increase his excitement. "Do you *know* what that is? Look – it's Pharoah! – this must be the lost treasure of the Ancient Egyptians!" Because we were both backing each other up, and a couple of years older, he believed us entirely.

"Ohhh-hhhhhh-hhhhhh!" he gasped, almost beside himself and literally trembling with excitement; just as we heard his mum call him back from over the fence for his tea. "Listen – don't tell anyone!" we said. "Cover it up again; let's keep it hush-hush until we've decided what to do."

It was a good week, I think, before we confessed, amid guilty sniggers, that the treasure was all fake and that we'd set him up deliberately, recovering it all immediately after he'd gone. But in any event, I have little doubt that in the intervening days, he would have spilled the secret and his parents would have chortled; firmly freeing him of any delusion he was the next Howard Carter!

SAMMY SALMONELLA

At the age of 11, even though I was unaware of the terms, I was already sampling sounds and mixing them. The freakiest thing is, *nobody* taught me – I worked out the methods myself. With new domestic VCRs still the stuff of dreams, way beyond the financial reach of most families until early in the next decade (and even then, only on a rental basis); cassette recorders with inbuilt condenser microphones were all the rage in the late 1970s. Like my whole generation, I would put ours next to the TV speaker grille and record muffled episodes of favourite sci-fi drama shows off-air, a myriad of title sequences, songs from *Top of the Pops* and the Top 40 on Radio 1 (the skill being to anticipate precisely when exactly to hit 'Pause' before the DJ began talking over the end of each track!)

Until integrated radio-cassettes came out enabling 'clean' recordings from source to recorder, you had to 'Shh!' everyone into silence, or voices would come out over what was taped! In any event, it wasn't long before I realised the technology's potential for pranks. I did some pretty crazy stuff in those days, ringing up 'Dial-A-Disc' on a rotary landline telephone, then dropping the earpiece into the goldfish bowl so that it might listen to The Members' *Sound of the Suburbs* or The Cool Notes' *In Your Car* burbling through the water. Had the phone run on electricity, both of us could've been a goner... Pity also the next user who put the receiver up to their ear: for the built-in holes would almost certainly have taken in water. But all this is to digress.

    Until we were around the ages of 13 or 14, every year in the school holidays we would meet up excitedly with cherished, now distant friends from early childhood – usually in Bournemouth, where our grandparents and their folks owned flats near the beach. Halcyon, perfect memories. A tape recorder, along with a load of mix tapes had become an essential item for any trip; my brother would bring his too; and there would usually be a third machine lying around forgotten by a cousin. I would methodically build up a soundtrack, asking my brother and the friends to chatter animatedly for a minute into the mic as if they were at some posh drinks reception – then send them on their way. Alone, I would take the cassette, play the voices in one machine, put a second alongside; and on another blank tape, record it again so I now had two copies. By winding one recording 10 seconds further on, when both were then started simultaneously and recorded onto a *third* recorder, it effectively layered and doubled the crowd. After repeating the same procedure several times, it would eventually sound as if a dense mass of people were celebrating! I would then play the multi-layered voices on one machine, some music (invariably Ron Grainer & the BBC Radiophonic Workshop's *Dr Who* theme) on another; and record the mixture onto a third cassette; so that the result now sounded like what my warped adolescent brain imagined a congenial 'party' atmosphere to be.

    It was now time to add the prank's voiceover, for which I would have to first plan and write a crude, juvenile script exposing my semi-baked knowledge of the forbidden. My voice hadn't yet broken, so the narrator's tone was a shade too high-pitched to convince anyone it was an adult's. I would distort my speech into a loathsome parody: although some four decades before his heyday, picture a highly camp, bespectacled English TV host, broadcaster, talent show judge and comedian very much in vogue in the 21st Century – and you have a dead-ringer for the sound of it. Playing the voiceover cassette simultaneously with the party soundtrack on the other, I would record the combined sound on the third tape recorder – and hey presto: party, music and announcer all on one recording! The final effort could then be presented to my astonished peers who had been busy doing what normal, non-OCD – or, almost certainly, autistic-spectrum – kids do: gossiping and playing cricket, etc. – the approval I sought coming from their raucous laughter.

Finally, it was time to subject some poor unwitting innocent to the prank. We would select a random victim from the Phone Book's residential numbers; stifling our giggles around the receiver. The moment they answered, I would hit 'Play' – and this is what the victim would hear:

"PLEASE listen carefully... This is a tape-recorded message. PLE-E-E-E-E-EASE listen carefully! This is Sammy Salmonella speaking, ladies and gentlemen; to tell you that there will be a par-ty, two houses away from you, on the same side of the road, on your left. At this par-ty, there will be records played and a disco; and you can probably hear some of the strange music behind me in the background. Well, we're looking forward to seeing you, oh – by the way, you can bring your own BOOZE if you want to... Also, there is a special rule to this: no child under 14 is allowed to come – you know why! If you don't know why, then come and see why... Well, we'll be expecting you, so see you soon – and from Sammy Salmonella, it's good-bOi!"

There would then be a pregnant pause before the music screamed in again with a loud recap...

"Oh, by the way, don't forget that it's two houses away from you, on your left. Well, we'll be expecting you; and, er, don't forget to bring some light BOOZE with you, 'cos it makes the party go better."

It's highly unlikely anyone actually listened to the whole thing, believed it, then turned up at the specified house laden with alcohol and expecting a night of revelry. Upon returning from our trip though, I did once try the recording out on our next-door neighbour one sunny afternoon. Moments later, I heard her join her husband in the garden, exclaiming in a most bewildered tone:

"Jack? I've just had the *strangest* phone call..."

BROTHERLY NEMESIS

It's fair to say I didn't cope well with my brother's arrival in the world... For the best part of a year, I'd been accustomed to being the sole focus and apple of my parents' eyes; and this huge change in the order of things wasn't handled anywhere nearly as delicately as it should have been – I was just expected to accept him and simply wasn't blessed with the requisite generosity! Reportedly, when I was first brought to see our young mum after my brother was born and she tried to kiss me, I twisted my 11-month-old head away in fury! My own earliest recollection of such murderous feelings towards my new sibling is having to sit in the pouring rain on the end of a warm pram I once inhabited; gazing in at the snug, somewhat maggot-like new occupant who'd taken my place.

To my genuine regret, I wasn't very nice to my brother for a long time, I pushed him, threw sand at him and did my best to make him laugh when he was drinking, so that he spluttered and choked. But I was intensely jealous at what I saw as a desperate loss of stature. When you don't yet have the words to articulate such emotions, they can be huge; and my feelings weren't acknowledged: the more I was reprimanded, the stronger the resentment became. It made no difference if I got *ten* times the love he did – I had, in my mind, been usurped, demoted from the main focus of attention; and my inflated baby ego simply wouldn't accept it – and never fully recovered. My brother was a very active child, almost hyperactive; and perhaps to help him expend excess energy, he was given an enormously tall inflatable punching clown for a birthday gift. I had zero interest in the thing myself, but was so envious of his delight that while he was being given a bath, I pierced it with a pencil; my vindictiveness turning to the most terrible guilt as it buckled inward; the most graphic illustration of my own malice as it sank to the floor before my eyes. I couldn't undo what I'd done; and can still see his little face falling in his pyjamas; his wailing "My punching clown!" upon discovering the act of sabotage – and the subsequent rollocking I got. Over the years, however, my feelings towards him mellowed, and the two of us became inseparable. I often gave him rides on an imaginary donkey called Peanuts – there was even a point when if anyone asked either of us who our best friend was, without hesitation, we would each answer, "My brother." Nonetheless, with my warped sense of humour, I still saw it as my prerogative to wind him up, shut him in closets and give him various malicious challenges to tackle. Looking back, I do regret a few of the meaner pranks; but provoking an irate reaction from him was such a fulfilling occupation. He learned gradually not to respond so predictably, thus denying me the satisfaction!

I told him I had written the hymn 'Morning Has Broken' – and saw him looking back over his shoulder at me with real pride the next time it was announced in our school Assembly. I 'framed' him for an outburst of hysterics I once had in the same hall when an easel was placed in front of us and we had to look at the same static canvas of Van Gogh's potatoes for what seemed an eternity (to an accompaniment of Mr Acker Bilk's 'Stranger on the Shore') – it was me that burst out laughing, but my brother that actually got hauled out and was made to stand in the aisle!

From a very early age, he had a phobia of puppets and mannequins; where it sprang from nobody knew, but even as the tiniest toddler, he would back away in floods of tears from the animatronic chefs or Santas in the Christmas window of our local bakery. Unsurprisingly, he went on to be terrified (with a capital T) of a murderous Chinese marionette named Mr Sin; who appeared in a late '70s, horror-inspired *Dr Who* story. A cyborg from the future, this Peking Homunculus had one organic component: the cerebral cortex of a pig; and, as the story went, its "swinish instinct" nearly caused World War 6. It was my brother's 10th birthday when Part 2 of that adventure, *The Talons of Weng Chiang*, screened; the Homunculus had barely been seen all episode; yet when, at the cliffhanger, Leela, the Doctor's "savage" companion heard a disturbance outside, opened the door – and in stalked Mr Sin, dagger in hand, my brother actually started to cry – on his birthday!

I was rather cruel to him in exploiting this phobia. We were both in town one dark winter's night, looking into a glittering jeweller's window, when a shockingly tiny "little person" with a box hat exactly like Mr Sin's came alongside us. Silently, I stepped away while my brother was still peering through the glass. When, finally, he looked up to where I'd been, he jumped about a foot in the air... I used to get hold of a similar hat from the coat cupboard at home and hide behind the door of his bedroom or the bathroom as he came upstairs to bed; then jump out making pig grunts. It doesn't show me in the best light, but I'd habitually lain in wait to "Ya!" him in different hiding places for years; and pretending to be Mr Sin added an extra dimension of pleasure. It got so bad that the poor lad wouldn't come upstairs without our mum holding his hand! And when we visited the *Dr Who* Exhibition on Blackpool's Golden Mile, I had to go through first to forewarn him where Mr Sin stood – ah, the joys of childhood and an education in fear! Only once did my brother ever get me back. I'd gone into the bathroom for a shower and he took the opportunity to dress up in our dad's snorkel, diving mask and flippers; curling up inside the airing cupboard until I came to get my pyjamas. Upon opening the door to see this black, alien thing coiling around, I completely freaked! No less than I deserved: it pretty much marked an end to the meaner pranks.

"The Sex Shop" was a classic among my antics. There were only a couple in our city; one of which was down by the old ABC Cinema, but until the late 1980s, the seediest was at the top of Granby Street.

As teenagers, you couldn't fail to spot it whilst travelling in or out of town on the bus; it had one of those cheap and tacky, rainbow-coloured curtains, plastic tassels hanging down over the single, narrow doorway. Off-limits to the under-18s, one could only begin to imagine the illicit, semi-naked perversions that lay behind its door; its unknown depths firing our hormone-ridden imaginations with all manner of nameless possibilities. The only slight knowledge I had in that whole sphere stemmed from an outing with our London-based cousins to Berwick Street market in Soho's red-light area; during which I had been propositioned by two blousy prostitutes calling down in pursuit of business from a floor high above the stalls. In the kind of half-knowledge you have at 14, I had assumed that, whatever the hookers' nameless acts, they always resided above sex shops. Armed with that limited, yet prized advantage, I dared my little brother one Saturday to venture into our local branch to ask the shopkeeper the exact words I gave him. He looked at me with the admiration one can only bestow on an older brother possessing infinitely greater worldly wisdom; as off he strode across the road towards the sex shop in his baggy, hooded coat, filled with missionary zeal – while I stood shaking in paroxysms of laughter… A few moments later, he reappeared through the multi-coloured tassels, red-faced and indignant at my treachery – having been given the elbow in no uncertain terms. Faced with that chubby-cheeked, bespectacled little 13-year-old asking earnestly, "Are the women working tonight?" I can only imagine the disbelief on the face of the greasy shop-owner, as he flexed the anchor tattoos on his biceps: "You *WHAT?* Sling yer hook before I *THROW* you out, you little toe-rag!" Along with the 29 bus, the shop in question is long gone. I do recall overhearing a conversation between several girls I shared a student house with, when one proudly told the rest that her Christian Union had prayed for that 'den of sin' to close. And, "Praise the Lord; Hallelujah…" A few weeks later, it had.

In our later years of boyhood, there once appeared in a shared laundry bin, a pair of used 'Y' fronts containing a truly monstrous skid mark nobody would admit responsibility for. It just so happened that we were off on holiday abroad together at the end of the week; and unbeknown to my brother, for a joke, I sneaked the offending grips into the topmost layer of his already packed suitcase, so that they would be the first thing he would discover upon arrival. We only went and got pulled over by the airport's Customs and Border

Security officials... My case was checked first and given the all-clear; then my brother's was unzipped. I will never forget the look of utter incredulity on the officer's face as he took a thin metal pole, hooked the fabric on the end of it and pulled the filthy pair of now dripping kecks into the air for closer inspection... A bottle of cream-coloured sun-tan lotion had burst all over them in transit; mixing with my 6B graphite drawing pencils to create a revolting black sludge. All it took was one glance at the look of complete disbelief on my brother's drained face for me to break down, paralytic, with laughter – leaving him to negotiate his way out of the situation amid his own sniggers! In the end, though, we were both waved through – I think the staff realised the loathsome Reg Grundies were basically harmless; they had better things to do than deal with a pair of puerile teenagers!

The toilet humour didn't end there, though. One summer, a group of us, comprised of my brother, myself and his girlfriend, plus a school pal, all went to visit our tiny grandma in Bournemouth. In fine holiday spirits, I was more than ready to commit mischief. We crowded into the lounge as my brother went to use the bathroom, locking the door behind him. Now when we were small children, one or other of us would sometimes get accidentally locked in that bathroom, due to a rather unusual button-press on the door handle. A brass skewer, not dissimilar to a tent peg, was always kept safely in the kitchen drawer; it could be inserted from the outside to unlock the door and free us. I thought it would be funny to head into the kitchen and see if the skewer was still there after all these years. Bingo! There it was. Grinning in anticipation, I took it over to the locked bathroom where my brother was enthroned. I knelt down and – although I would *never* have actually gone in – shoved the skewer suddenly through the tiny aperture. Instantly, the door popped open. "Oi – get out!" protested my brother; blocking further entry with his foot, but laughing nonetheless. It loses something in the retelling; but had you that shared memory, you'd 'get' it. Chuckling, I returned to the others. It wasn't until the couple had left that my friend said, "You should've *seen* the look on (his girlfriend's) face when you broke into the bathroom with that skewer: her mouth just *dropped* open." Our unique history wasn't always understood by others!

Now, in the earliest days of his being a medical student, my brother still lived at home. It was a tough old slog for him to become a doctor; five years of study lay ahead. Simultaneously, although I was in fact quite a tortured soul, I appeared on the surface to be a free and easy Art student; doing first a Foundation Course, then a degree in Graphic Design. All it must have seemed to him that I ever had to do was draw or paint to my heart's content. And true, with that freedom, I had plenty of time to take breaks in which to provoke him. Whenever he left his room I would turn his big medical textbooks to hideous photos (a woman whose neck was swollen up with an enormous thyroid goitre, for instance) and hide them under his pillow so he'd come across them when he got in bed. But my brother also had this little alcove in his yellow-painted bedroom in which he sat at his desk studying. It was a serious undertaking with almost endless assessments, exams and other hurdles; there wasn't much room for humour, and it didn't take a lot to arouse his temper...

While he had his head down revising or writing essays, my favourite prank would be to silently open his bedroom door enough for my fingers to pass through and reach the light switch; determine that point exactly halfway between 'on' and 'off' (which I'd discovered changed the light from its normal yellow to an uncomfortable intermediary phase) and bathe the room in an unbearable orange, making the filament inside the bulb buzz and fizz like a vibrating wasp. This was like a red rag to a bull: up he would lurch across the room and angrily make for me, but always I was too quick for him: I would retract my fingers and quickly dart back inside my room, slam the door and lock it, laughing with delight, to the sound of him growling outside "You Eun!" or some other derogatory insult; before resignedly returning to his desk. I would then let the dust settle a minute or two; then, when all was quiet, tiptoe out again, gingerly open the door, see him with his back to me studying, slip my fingers through and flicker the lights to buzzing orange again. Enraged, he would jump up and fly towards me; and I would only just get inside my room and lock it in time, before a chorus of expletives erupted outside. I might then leave it, say, 10 minutes before repeating the prank. But one day, when we happened to be alone at home, I wasn't quite fast enough... He was so furious, he burst out of his room and, like the classic pushy salesman, got his foot in the door before I could get it shut. So incandescent with rage was he, he pushed me down on the bed and began throttling me. At first, I was laughing hysterically in a mixture of fear and pleasure at his reaction, but it reached a point when I was quite literally choking to death: I couldn't breathe – and in desperation, did the only thing I could: punched my brother in the face.

It did the trick. He released his grip, rushing to the bathroom to inspect the damage I had wrought. I hadn't anticipated giving him the most enormous shiner – a black eye the likes of which I've never seen before or since; which, over the coming days, went through a myriad of different colour changes as it receded. I felt terrible; and sought escape by jumping into our shared Saab 96 and driving out for miles. It was a good two hours before I dared show my face at home, expecting severe repercussions – but astonishingly, in a major break from tradition, our mum sided with me on that occasion; and to add insult to injury, reprimanded him for giving me exactly the reaction I sought! I didn't feel good, though, for a long time afterwards: people would look at his eye in school and ask, "Who gave you that?" Imagine his having to reply, "My brother..." So thus ended that particular torment. He did get the last laugh, however, as in my mid-to-late 20s I went on to be plagued by an awful recurring headache which became known as "The Filament" – eventually necessitating an MRI scan to eliminate the chances of anything sinister. And he's a smashing chap now, respectably married with a wife and grown-up kids; and head of a GP's practice – earning infinitely more than me. So hopefully none of my antics scarred him all that badly in the long run.

THE WELLY PRANK

From the age of 14, I had a dear and loyal school friend who shared my passion for Art. Infinitely better than I ever was, with a talent for manipulating different media that I could only dream of, he was simply on fire, like a vessel for so innate a level of genius... We shared four years of largely happy school days, both eccentric misfits in a highly academic private education environment; and for the most part, we sought refuge from the school of hard knocks in the Art room; going on to do the same Foundation Course before he pursued a Fine Art degree and I diverged into Graphic Design, Illustration and Animation. For 41 years, until abruptly, he cut the friendship off without real explanation, we met up often, becoming almost as close as brothers: he was another for whom I was Best Man. But sadly, things between us descended almost to the level of a power-struggle. Just like siblings, there was a strong element of one-upmanship which did, at different times, become wearing for each of us; resulting in heated rows, which I hated – because although erupting may have cleared the air, he couldn't let go of such falling-outs easily – it took literally *hours* dissecting his grievances in meticulous detail for him to be able to do so. And life is just too short…

Over the years, however, at happier times, there were many sleepovers at each other's houses, most of them "lad's night" all-nighters, watching videos and pigging out on takeaways. But one memorable Saturday, he was being particularly obnoxious – I was fed up at his manner and had more or less had enough. The following morning, my black Labrador was due his Sunday treat as usual, the longest walk of the week out in open countryside – and at once, I knew I had the perfect vehicle for revenge. I wasn't aiming to hurt the lad physically, or do him any lasting psychological damage; but I did want to bring him down from the very superior high horse he was on just then.

Now I had noticed a discreet, barely visible, one-inch gash right through the side of a Wellington boot I owned; indeed, I'd had to buy a replacement set the previous week. The damaged pair, however, hadn't yet been thrown out. This friend, while not even remotely a dog-lover, had come to accept that walks were an inevitable part of his visits; yet had arrived unequipped for a long excursion through muddy fields. I therefore had the perfect opportunity to offer him that spare pair of wellies to borrow. Hook, line and sinker he fell for it – as I said, the hole in the boot was near-invisible; and he missed it *totally* as he slipped his big foot in. Off we drove to the remote village of Wistow; having been there numerous times, I knew that territory inside out, and was well aware that right through the centre of one particular field ran a relatively deep stream with a powerful current you had to cross in order to reach the opposite side… Wicked as I admit it was, I mentally orchestrated a route which would more or less *end* with the crossing of that stream. Eventually, the time came: into the torrent ploughed my joyful young Labrador, some distance ahead. When it came for the two of us to cross, I made sure I was several paces in front of this lad, so he couldn't see the difficulty I was having keeping my face straight. I knew the desired reaction was imminent; but the funniest, most hysterical thing was that he actually made it *two-thirds* of the way across the stream before the external pressure forced water through the boot...

All of a sudden, behind me, I heard this *unbelievably* satisfying sound – something between a scream of shock and a wail of discomfort, as his foot became soaked in freezing, muddy water. " N-YA-A-A-A-A-A-AGGH! – it's got a f*ckin' *HOLE!* A-A-A-A-ARGH!" Feigning all innocence, I composed my expression, replying "*What?*" in a surprised tone, as I turned around, frowning in mock-concern. "You must have snagged it on something, you divvy!" In his dripping wet sock, he had to 'squidge' the last few hundred yards back to the car, grumbling and swearing in extreme displeasure – unharmed, but most definitely brought down to size. It was a good month before I dared tell him I'd planned the whole thing; I picked my moment carefully – one when we were getting on okay and good-natured banter was being exchanged. To his credit, he took it well – it was, of course, very funny in hindsight and no one had suffered permanent injury. But I dined out on that story for *years*, often using it as an after-lesson filler when my school classes were waiting for the end-of-lesson bell to ring – it never failed to raise a laugh from even the most cynical of pupils.

A SPECTRUM OF TRIVIA

THE INEPT SHOPPER

Shortly after leaving home for the first time, one Saturday, whilst in the City Centre purely on a retail therapy trip, I thought, *I know: to save the hassle of having to go out again for groceries, I'll kill two birds with one stone. Get my food shopping for the week done; then catch the bus home.* Well, now: inexperienced in domestic duties, I over-estimated the strength and capacity of the single plastic carrier bag I wedged everything into. I should have got two bags and balanced things out both sides, halving the load in each – but no. Wielding heavy fruit fresh from the market, I decided to take a shortcut through W H Smith to the bus stop on the opposite side.

The late afternoon rush hour was approaching and it was a packed store, a mass of people bustling to and fro. I had barely got a third of the way through, when, with an ominous rending of polythene, my shopping burst through the base of the bag, hitting the thinly carpeted floor below with some impact. The contents went everywhere. Cans of baked beans and cola rolled their way down towards Gallowtree Gate, easily-bruised apples, bananas, tomatoes and jelly snakes sustained life-threatening injuries; worst of all, slices of supermarket's own economy brand white bread cascaded out of their sealed wrapper, surrounding the ankles of passers-by. I didn't know where to begin the damage limitation; and so resorted to my usual coping mechanism when nervous – an attack of laughter so bad I could barely retrieve anything.

"Ooya-rye!" exclaimed a helpful Leicester pensioner, picking up several slices of my bread with her fingers. "Here y' are, duck…" That only made me collapse afresh. *We've got a right one here,* said the disapproving expressions of other normal spectators. But it was either laugh or cry. With a pyramid of loose groceries stacked precariously against my chest, I lurched towards the exit, staggering into the street, arms full; a couple of replacement carriers flapping in the breeze as the bus pulled up. Still doing the balancing act, I managed to pay for a ticket and head upstairs, where, finally, I found a spare double seat on which to sit and redistribute the weight of the damaged goods. I vowed never to do any grocery shopping in the City Centre again.

HORSEFLIES, RATTLESNAKES AND THE ROTTWEILER OF DOOM

On the day my Graphic Design degree commenced back in 1986, we were all asked to gather in the large ground-floor lecture theatre for an introductory talk. There were over 60 of us on the course; and the speaker began with some thought-provoking facts and figures.

"Of all of you here today," he said, "statistically, around a quarter of you will go into something completely different; two of you will die" (he was disturbingly spot-on about that); "and the rest of you…

will walk straight into a full-time job in Graphics when you leave." On this latter point, he could not have been more wrong: by our graduation in 1990, a major recession had hit – our degree show in London's Vauxhall Gallery was attended by no one from the industry – and *none* of us got jobs... I actively recall opening *Creative Review* magazine the following year to find, on their Letters page, a plaintive appeal from a fellow student, the gist of which was:

"I sat down at my breakfast cornflakes to open my 365th rejection letter of the year... I will do *anything* to get a design job; be it charlady or whatever..." That is how bad things were: the whole lot of us were on the dole. It seemed all those years of study had been pointless; and with nothing productive in sight, a friend and I took what was left of our savings and signed up for Camp America the following summer; the real lure being the prospect of travelling once the work ended.

Assigned to be Art Director in the Deep South of Mississippi, upon stepping off the plane at Jackson Airport, the temperature, 105° Fahrenheit, hit me like a wall; heat lightning forever on the horizon. On our arrival, I was taken on a guided tour of the beautifully landscaped camp by the site foreman, a seedy character speaking with an authentic southern drawl which wouldn't have been out of place among the murderous family in *The Texas Chainsaw Massacre*. It was the *humidity,* though, I had not anticipated. Hot food was out of the question; we lived on salad and hominy grits; and you needed to shower at least twice a day, sometimes more. *My God, I'm not going to be able to stand this,* I thought; but within a few days, had acclimatised. The foreman had taken a detour on our way back to visit a local taxidermist doing a roaring trade in stuffing local creatures; including a wall-mounted wild boar's head the width of a *car.* With colossal fangs and razor-sharp, matted fur, it had the most bestial expression I had ever seen on a dead animal.

"If'n one o' them comes atcha, y'all better git up a tree, cos he'll gore ya, man..." said the owner with evident pride. Back at the camp, the gloved foreman took relish in telling me to watch out for copperheads (a venomous pit viper) in the lake and, in the undergrowth, diamondbacks (rattlesnakes with a painful bite often fatal to humans; the haemotoxin in their venom killing red blood cells and causing deadly tissue damage). He boasted how whenever he came across one whilst walking his dog, he would yank it up by the tail and swing it around to smash its head in on the nearest tree trunk. Even after he showed me a snakeskin wallet he had made for one of the young campers, the reality of the situation didn't truly sink in; so he ended up giving me a broken-off segment of rattle; a grisly souvenir I still have to this day.

Once the tour was over, I was free to explore the site on my own, ending up in a vast indoor sports hall, fully equipped with floor-to-ceiling roller-skates of all sizes. *I'd better get some practice in,* I thought, skating not being something I had even remotely mastered aside from the briefest experience at an MTV party somewhere in Bristol. It took a good 10 minutes to get into the skates, the laces taking time to get the hang of; and there being that many fasteners to loop them through. Once you were in, you were well and truly imprisoned – no getting out of those boots in a hurry... With co-ordination never having been a particularly strong skill of mine, I soon found I was hopeless. In the centre of this huge hall, there was nothing to grab hold of to stabilize myself: no sooner was I standing than the wheels slid in all directions and I fell – again and again...

All of a sudden, not one, but *two* massive horseflies flew in from outside, buzzing aggressively in figure 8s around my head. Desperately, I began flailing in all directions, in the midst of my increasing panic getting the distinct impression that the two skates had somehow become knotted together. There was no escape: the horseflies knew they were onto a winner; just a matter of time before they feasted. The most awful thing about the predicament was the sense of the inevitable, not knowing exactly when the attack was going to happen, but having no doubt it would. There I was, shouting and swearing at *flies*; all my protestations and swiping at the air a futile waste of energy. The dreaded moment could be averted no longer; one of the pair landed on my right shoulder, biting a chunk of flesh out of me before the two of them flew out, victorious.

That evening, once their younger campers were tucked up in bed, those counsellors not on babysitting duty arrived at the Art and Crafts room; a nightly occurrence during which I provided them with all the paint, brushes and paper they required to make enormous banners and signs promoting the next day's events. These students would turn up at around 10pm and be there a good few hours, many needing help with the drawing of various objects or lettering. After they had gone, there was a lot of clearing up to do, meaning I typically didn't get out of there and lock up until gone 2 a.m. Walking back alone through almost pitch blackness along the poorly lit, narrow dirt path towards my distant cabin, I became aware of a stony, disjointed and irregular shaking sound from the scrubland on my right; like a pair of dried chickpeas being repeatedly clashed together. I stopped walking and the shaking stopped. I tried taking a further step; the moment I did so, the noise returned, this time steadily rising in volume and tempo. It was very, very close. Terrified, I froze to the spot, the realisation dawning that I was just inches from a live rattlesnake poised to attack somewhere in the darkness – and already in defence mode. The increasing volume was clearly a threat; a warning the strike was imminent. I had no idea how long one's life expectancy was in the event of being bitten, or even if the camp, in so remote an area, had suitable anti-venom. Like everyone, I wore shorts due to the heat, offering no protection to my legs and ankles. I didn't dare move a muscle; scarcely dared even breathe, let alone call for help. While I knew little about the extent of a diamondback's sight, what I did know was that rattlesnakes had an exceptional sense of smell; almost a sixth sense to detect the infrared radiation of warm-blooded creatures – a form of thermal vision. An *hour* I stood there motionless in the eerie gloom before risking even the slightest movement. Having taken one excruciatingly slow step forward with no rattle, I took one more, then another before making my escape: the danger had passed; but you can bet your life I wore trousers in the evening from that day onward.

I was not out of the woods yet, however. The dirt path from the Art and Crafts room finally opened out onto the camp's main road. My log cabin was positioned close to the top of a hill on the other side; the only route to it being a further path dipping steeply downward into a valley before rising equally acutely upwards to the cabin. The way was illuminated now only by the moon. Exhausted after a long day's physical work, not to mention the trauma of a close encounter with that rattlesnake, I started on the downward slope, eager to reach the comfort of my bed. There was absolute silence, every other soul in the camp fast asleep; and the totality of that stillness seemed to heighten all my senses. In the same way one can be awoken by the force of a stare, *something* made me feel I was being watched. I shuddered inwardly, trying to shake off the notion, but try as I might, the feeling persisted; and, having reached the bottom of the slope, I couldn't resist taking a moment to look back over my shoulder in the direction from which I had come.

There, far back on the moon-drenched main road, was the

silhouette of the most *enormous* dog I had ever seen. Poised at the very top of the downward path I'd just taken, it sat upright, fully alert and focused intently on me. Now size, it's true, can distort from a distance; and dogs don't usually scare me (being an owner); but this one, evocative of Damien's canine protector in *The Omen,* was an incarnation of pure evil. Whether or not the dog belonged to the site foreman I didn't know; but the last thing I wanted was to antagonise it, given the rabies risk. So I continued the upward climb to my cabin; glancing nervously back every so often to check it hadn't moved.

There's a well-known belief that dogs can 'taste' fear; and in hindsight, my sense of foreboding was self-fulfilling. Halfway up the incline, I glanced back one final time, only to witness the creature *exploding* into action; launching itself with horrifying speed down the slope like a projectile missile. Petrified, I have never run so fast in my life. Heart pounding, I could see the rapidly pursuing dog cover the distance to the plateau of the valley in seconds; beginning the uphill leg as I made desperately for my cabin. I could hear it panting, gaining on me as I staggered the last few yards; its musty animal scent in my nostrils; paws crunching on the gravel. It must have been literally *upon* me as I yanked the door open, slamming it shut just as the dog's full weight collided with the wood, its huge limbs scrabbling violently as it tried to force its way in, slavering belligerently. Drained of every last vestige of energy, I collapsed onto the mattress, surrendering to the merciful oblivion of sleep. It seemed bad things *did* come in threes after all!

HOW ARTWORK SAVED MY LIFE

America was the one place I had always dreamed of seeing; accomplishing that goal sated the travel bug for a good decade. Once the camp ended, I had a month to explore the United States with the money I had – nowhere near sufficient to see everything, but still enough to take in a lot. I couldn't really justify the cost of either a Delta Air Pass or Amtrak Rail Pass, so went for the Greyhound option instead. In hindsight, I would recommend that choice to anyone, because apart from the downside of spending grimy days on a coach, you not only met all manner of beatniks and weirdos; especially those behind the dreaded 'line' at the rear of the coach (an area I was advised to steer clear of for my own safety); you *really* got the enormity of the country in that way, saw the landscape change as you passed from state to state; from the multicoloured strata of the Painted Desert to the glittering skyscrapers of Dallas. Just to know you were riding on the legendary New Jersey Turnpike, something I had hitherto only heard of in Simon and Garfunkel's lyrics, was thrilling. During one stop, we wound up in a tall building with what seemed like a *skyscraper*-level waterslide alongside; revellers flying down it in the sunshine – it's the briefest flash of a memory now, but I wish I knew where that was; it looked the most amazing experience.

Morgan Spurlock and his influential *Supersize Me* documentary had yet to shine a light on fast-food culture. I soon saw why there was an obesity crisis. The portions of food served wherever we stopped were *vast*. In one all-American diner, you sat on stools next to tired truckers slumped against the square, plastic bar; waitresses on the inside. I ordered some roast chicken which came in a KFC-style box with two complimentary "biscuits" – giant scones to mop up the gravy – and quite literally, a *bucket* of mashed potato. Everything was dirt-cheap; Taco Bell burritos no more than a few cents each; that was also where I found 'bottomless' refillable drinks for the first time.

Some of the Greyhound conversations I overheard and wrote down in a sketchbook left my friend and I crying with laughter. Among the best were between a pair of 80-year-old Texans, who spouted a never-ending cycle of drivel:

"Mah wife, she says 'ah like trees.' I said, 'ahh never really cared for 'em.' Now I'm livin' in a house, got trees all round it..."

"You marry a stoopid woman, y'get stupid kids... Y'don't believe me? Jus follow a stupid kid home an' see if someone dumb don't answer the door..."

"Ahh went to my doctor... he said, 'You've got the body of a twenty-year-old...' Me; I can stand 500 yards away from the target 'n' hit the bull's ahh..."

"Albuquerque? Alber cyoo-cyoo..."

"Y'wanna catcha prairie dog? You better git down his hole, 'cos that's the only way you eva gon' catch a prairie dawg..."

Not all the staff were nice; or good at their jobs. One driver changed coach without notifying us; I returned early from a scheduled break in time to spot the switchover, and transferred my luggage from the first coach onto the new one just in time. Others weren't so lucky. He took off without one poor distraught lady, who was left running down the road after us, hands waving frantically as her luggage disappeared into the distance. The driver didn't stop, sniggering,

"Didja see her face?" That's how he got his kicks – abusing the little power he had.

Another sweltering day, our driver took a wrong turn into a narrow street and had to do a *30*-point turn to get out, leaving us all nauseous. Opposite us, under a partially open concertina window sloshing back and forth with collected rainfall, sat two people of colour: a fidgeting little boy and his rather large grandmother.

"Nelson, you better behave yo'self, or I mon spank you," she warned. "On yo' black ass, y'hear?" The child stared balefully back at her with big eyes. All of a sudden, the driver took a hairpin bend; causing water to cascade inside from above – in a split second, that lady's lap, so capacious it evoked the 1950's dance move, "gathering eggs," was filled, literally, with a *lake* of water.

"Man, this is the *Lawd's* journeh!" she cried, as silent tears of mirth rolled down our faces again...

I went first to visit a cousin in Hollywood, from where we drove to the awesome Muir Woods giant redwood forest (the foreboding military prison of Alcatraz visible on its island nearby); then headed for New York and the top of the World Trade Center; meeting up with my college pal, seeing both ends of a rainbow and getting soaked like water rats at Niagara Falls. Having gone our separate ways, I next headed down to Florida, the Grand Canyon and finally Las Vegas, where another friend and I suspect we may narrowly have averted death at the hands of a serial killer, after mistaking a creepy gingerbread cottage (set back from the main strip) for a restaurant. Some sixth sense warned us to back away and decline the leering owner's invitation: "You – you come on in..."

In Arizona I had bought a large, bean-filled, tribal rainstick made from the Normata Cactus. So maddened did my friend become with its rattling whoosh that after a few days on board, he moved to the double seat in front and got lumbered with a stranger sitting next to him. I was in a very silly mood; passing a teasing note through the headrests: "How d'you like yo' beret buddy?" He got his revenge, though, when a middle-aged man with a gold Caesar's Palace medallion joined me, striking up conversation. Hours later, he was still talking. I needed matchsticks to pin my eyes open, yet on he went through the night about how he'd gambled a fortune away and lost his wife.

"I've thrown my life away," he murmured, medallion glittering in the darkness. My friend later recounted to me with amusement how he'd woken in the early hours to find the whole coach in darkness, everyone asleep – except the man next to me, our light still on as he continued talking, even though my head was nodding and I was half-asleep...

It was, however, New Orleans in Louisiana which most captivated me. Pre-Hurricane Katrina, it was the most magical place: the shuttered windows and ornate columns of the French Quarter, bars, night-life and laughing-gas of Bourbon Street, elegant plantation houses, alligator-filled bayou swamps, the evocative call of the Steamboat Natchez Calliope and the ever-present influence of Marie Laveau, the famous voodoo witch queen; not to mention a creepy waxworks museum and the original 'Streetcar Named Desire' on display. Home to Creole cooking, Gumbo and the Daiquiri (a 1940s rum and citrus cocktail I felt I must try, but found revolting), what New Orleans most definitely was *not*, though, was a place to find yourself stranded out in late at night...

There was a notorious area referred to only as "The Projects"; and the town was known to house some seriously dangerous characters. I had already had a couple of tasters of potential risk: having barely stepped off the coach, I was walking down a main road about to cross a side street at a crossroads, when from nowhere, a huge rocket, barely two feet from the ground, literally *shot* across me and vanished up the road: had I been *one* step further out, I would have lost a leg. The main road was full of slow-moving traffic, and as I reached a cyclist, a car full of young lads pulled alongside him, hurling abuse, "You faggot!" etc. I was only at walking pace, so the traffic overtook me, but a few hundred yards further on, I caught up again to find the tables turned totally; the cyclist now aiming a 45 pistol at the occupants of the car, all of whom had their hands up, terrified.

"You see, when I need to, I defend myself..." he was explaining matter-of-factly, as they fell over each other to apologise. And just as I was standing outside what was Marie Laveau's house, a giant behemoth of a man lurched around the corner, gurgling incoherently; face covered in blood.

Now the guidebook I had indicated that the one place you should not miss visiting was Tipitina's – a world-famous live music venue and former juice-bar, gambling house, gymnasium and brothel, based on the corner of Napoleon Avenue. It was named after a song performed by the forefather of Blues music – Professor Longhair – who used to be a regular there. I decided I'd better go and see what all the fuss was about; and asked for directions at my hostel.

"Get a streetcar to Napoleon Avenue, then a cab one block down to Tipitina's," advised the grizzled owner; windswept face and hooded eyelids conveying a seen-it-all-before, worldly-wise persona.

"Couldn't I just walk the last block down?" I queried.

He might just as well have spat out a slug of tobacco on the ground.

"If you walk down Napoleon Avenue at night, you'll be killed," he said flatly – a statement of fact.

I took his advice on the way there, got the tram and a taxi and entered Tipitina's. To be honest, the best thing about it was the red neon name glowing evocatively outside and the banana logo; a relic from the juice-bar days. It was barely a corner, jammed full; you couldn't move for people. While live music was blaring out, I saw no performers; whether another part was shut off I have no idea; but in any event, I didn't stay long. I had a couple of drinks, then, knowing nobody, I left.

It was dark by now; and, while I would have happily obeyed the advice and got a taxi the one block back to Napoleon Avenue, there were two reasons why I couldn't. Firstly, there were no cabs anywhere in sight. This was way before the days of mobile phones: I could have – and probably should have – gone back into the club and asked where I could pick one up, but that would have meant wading through a dense crowd to reach the bar, with no guarantee of co-operation. The second reason taking a cab was impossible was that I had overestimated the amount of cash I had on me: having paid for the streetcar, taxi and a couple of drinks, I found I only had 39 cents left until the following day, when I could change a traveller's cheque! Short of begging, I felt I had no choice but to walk it... With the hostel manager's words of warning ringing in my ears with every step, it was the scariest walk of my life. Perhaps my mind was playing tricks, but that night was absolutely *pregnant* with a sense of menace... The pavements there, known as "sidewalks", were an entirely different animal to those back home: wide as a street, they left you feeling very exposed indeed on your own – a target, no less... Periodically, a convertible with its hood down would cruise eerily past, each conveying a sense of threat. Having seen what I had earlier, I could just imagine a sawn-off shotgun suddenly pointing out and blowing my head off. Inwardly, I cursed my own thoughtlessness for bringing insufficient funds along: that walk couldn't end fast enough.

With the return ticket for the tram, I made it back as far as Bourbon Street, but knew I was still 41 cents short of the 80 I needed for a second streetcar back to my hostel. The very last bars on the strip were closing up for the night as I began hunting up and down in the gutter for dropped coins. Typical: when you actually *needed* to find coins, not a cent in sight. Seeing the shutters going down and lights going out, I was starting to feel desperate; I went to the nearest bar, explained the situation and asked if I might draw the owner's portrait for 41 cents. He shook his head. On I went to the next bar, but got the same response, just as with the following two. These were tough people. With one final bar closing on the strip, I swallowed my pride, pleading with the manager to help me. "Okay," he said at last, throwing me a lifeline: a paper napkin. On it, I did his portrait and, with a wry smile, he gave me a quarter, a dime, a nickel and a penny – *exactly* 41 cents. Added to my own 39, it made up the vital 80 I needed; and caught me that crucial streetcar out of trouble.

LOCKED IN A SKYSCRAPER

1991 had been a mixed year. I had arrived back from Camp America to find – still – no Graphics work around. Instead, I met a new London-based girlfriend and recorded a crude, stop-frame, model-animated short, *Pilgrimage of the Grison,* shot on Super 8 cine-film, with painted plasticine sets. It was my involvement in this project which led to the predicament you are about to hear...

The Grison himself was a small, biting rodent indigenous to Southern Mexico, Central and South America. As he was to be handled much more frequently than the scenery, I needed to make the figure durable. Having made an initial head and body from plasticine, I re-used a portion of a hideous blancmange-like red vinyl retained from a previous college project; which you could melt down to form a flexible mould into which could be poured liquid latex. To avoid objections from my parents, I crept downstairs in the early hours to heat it in a saucepan on the kitchen stove; pouring the red-hot liquid carefully over the plasticine parts and waiting for it to set. Having no idea the extractor fumes went up through their bedroom cupboard, inadvertently, I nearly asphyxiated both my parents, getting caught in the act when the noxious smell woke them up!

Having chosen a blue skin colour for the Grison, I put him in a red-painted kimono with swirling rainbow patterns on the back. A long robe made animating him easier: without visible legs, he could simply glide through the landscapes I created. Unlike today's digital age, where, via smartphone technology, we all have the power of movie-making at our fingertips and can see the results instantly; with old-fashioned celluloid cine-film, you had no idea of the quality of footage captured until the processed reels came back. The cine-camera was my only option: industry-level video equipment was out of reach financially. I had done my research; and not *one* domestic-level model in the UK offered the stop-frame function essential for animation. So I hired a Super 8 camera from an old, eccentric inventor advertising in the local paper. Never had I seen a place like his; the upstairs workshop of his terraced house was a chaotic mass of wires, equipment and gadgets from floor to ceiling. I truly pitied his harried wife – who looked at the end of her tether!

"What I'm really looking for is a surrogate grandson," he said, clearly with me in mind. All I wanted to do was borrow his flaming camera; but as he was doing me a favour, I was obliged to listen to him ramble on about a host of unrelated things for hours. Eventually, when his wife shouted at him for the fourth time to come down for dinner, he handed the cine-camera over to me, saying,

"Well I'm sorry to have gone on, but it's important not only to describe the camera, but also the world in which it exists…" His was a case of extreme verbal diarrhoea.

Under the floodlights I had hired, just as I was finishing filming, a sticky white gunk began seeping out of the camera's casing as it stood baking on the tripod. Panic-stricken, I cleaned it off, but more appeared. A day or so after I returned it, the old man, having inspected it for damage, rang me up to complain. I went and gave him £10, which fortunately, he accepted, having realised it was only silicone lubrication!

Once my precious Super 8 reel arrived back in the post, I had to go very much cap-in-hand back to the old Polytechnic where I was formerly a student, to ask various Audio-Visual staff for favours. First, I needed the developed film footage transferring to the U-Matic pre-digital, analogue videotape we used in those days. I had to type and record story caption-cards to go between film sequences; and, most importantly, required the use of an edit suite to combine credits, scenes and story-cards in the right order; dubbing on the calliope music I had discovered on a steamboat in New Orleans, which fitted perfectly. Considering I was now an ex-student with no right to access either premises or facilities, the staff were very obliging; letting me book a basement edit suite for a full day at the start of the new year. So it was that in early January 1992, I parked outside the long-since demolished Fletcher Building; and went in to see the 007 boys: A/V technicians nicknamed as such because they occupied a room with that distinctive code on the door. One of them took me down to the furthermost suite at the end of the basement corridor, gave me a brief refresher on the vision mixer and edit controllers; then left me to it, calling back over his shoulder,

"They lock up around 9; so expect someone to kick you out about a quarter to..."

I settled down eagerly to the work and was soon engrossed in the task, losing track of time completely. Split-second precision is required when matching changing visuals to musical rhythm; and although the work is rewarding, it is also intense, requiring a fair degree of concentration. Considering the whole film was just five minutes long, it might surprise you that I was still at it hours later. I did vaguely register distant footsteps and a clattering and clanging somewhere up the corridor, but thought nothing of it; fully expecting that when my time was up, the Premises Officer would come and tell me. I finished editing and dubbing the entire film in that one session; ejecting the chunky video-cassette with satisfaction and fitting it safely back in my rucksack with my other gear. Slinging it over one shoulder, for the first time, I glanced at my watch. 9.15 p.m. *I wonder why they didn't chuck me out?* I thought, switching off the light and pulling the door to...

I headed down the dark corridor to the large, garage door-sized opening which led to a ramp up to ground level – only to find a rusty steel roller-shutter securely down over the whole thing barring my exit. Only then, I realised the distant footsteps must have been the Premises Officer checking other rooms nearby; and the rattling, him pulling the security shutter down. He couldn't have known I was there; and finding all the other rooms uninhabited, probably just assumed the one at the far end would be too! Knowing the building well, I wasn't unduly worried. *I'll just get the lift up to a higher floor,*

I thought, then use the staircase to get down to the Ground Floor entrance. Out of sheer nostalgia, I selected the second floor, where the old A/V room was situated along with the rostrum cameras my friends and I used for two years. The lift doors opened to a pitch-black corridor, all the familiar rooms locked up; and it was freezing cold, but in the distance, a welcoming rectangle of light shone through the glass door at the end, outside which the staircase stood. I made for it, confident I'd found the way out, but as my hand made contact with the wooden frame, it met firm resistance. The door was *locked*... Only then did I consider I may be trapped. In turn, I went in the lift to all the other 10 floors, emerging, as you would expect, at the exact same place along each one – but at *every* floor's corridor exit, I met a similar locked door.

I was getting really cold now; and felt my best chance was to try the Ground Floor. I got to the Main Entrance, but it too was locked; however, at least that floor was fully lit; so not quite as creepy. There was also an enormous, wall-mounted industrial heater pumping out a reassuring gust of warmth. I slouched against it a while, but was very tired now and couldn't stay like that for long. I remembered on one of the higher floors seeing some stackable plastic chairs out in the corridor; so I travelled back up in the lift and brought three down to the Ground Floor; standing them side by side in front of the heater, to make the seat space long enough to sleep on. Using my packed rucksack as a pillow, at least that way I was off the ground. I lay down, taking stock of the situation. If the heater went out, I might be found frozen solid the next morning. There wasn't even a phone from which I could call for help. Resigned to staying the whole night in the skyscraper, I switched out as many lights as I could and shut my eyes. The chairs were hard, but I did manage to doze fitfully for a few hours; until suddenly, at around 3.15 a.m. I was woken abruptly by an alarm going off in what sounded like the vicinity of the Students' Union nearby.

This is my chance, I reasoned... *Security will have to come out and address that alarm, so they'll probably give the rest of the site the once-over too. How do I draw their attention?* I returned to the lift; and, slumped against the wall; finger pressing the red alarm button for dear life, my eyes closed through sheer exhaustion... The alert continued to ring out for what seemed an eternity – until all of a sudden, I heard approaching footsteps; then:

"What the *F*CK* are you doing here?"

The security guard actually spoke before he came into view! I was so relieved to see another human being, I didn't even mind the scolding.

"I was in one of the Edit suites working," I told him.

Which room? he demanded. I explained the situation and he shook his head incredulously.

"You'd better come along with me, mate," he said, keys rattling on his belt. "You're lucky we didn't send the dogs in. There'd have been no escape y'know – you could've run all the way up to the 10th floor and they'd still 'ave got you..." I could just envisage a colossal pair of slavering German Shepherd dogs, Doberman Pinschers or Rottweilers vaulting effortlessly up the staircase in tandem, mouths full of savage teeth as they pinned me against the wall and tore my flesh apart.

Through the falling snow, the security guard led the way down the icy street to an illuminated portable building serving as a makeshift office.

"Right," he said, "Whatever you've got in there, that rucksack stays with us."

"*Ohhh* no," I said firmly. "No can do."

"Hand it over," he said, as his colleague looked on silently; "or we'll have to call the Police."

"Call them if you must," I replied. "but I can't leave it with you... that's the master tape of my graduation showreel and first ever completed film – it's my meal ticket!"

"Look, I'll level with you," he said wearily. "If we call the Police, they'll treat this as a security breach. Someone here ain't done their job; and heads are gonna roll. You don't *really* want them losing their livelihood for one mistake, do you?"

When he put it like that, I had to concede he had a point.

"If you're prepared to leave that here *just* overnight, so we can check it over," he went on, "I give you my word we won't touch the video – you can come and pick it up first thing in the morning."

I certainly didn't want anyone fired on my account; so reluctantly agreed; provided he gave me a receipt for the contents. They were true to their promise; the handover going without a hitch next day. I had a fair bit of explaining to do to account for my whereabouts when I got home, though...

A few weeks later, I happened to call the Polytechnic about another matter.

"Heard all about your incarceration," chirped the Photography tutor who answered the phone. "It got around the whole staff, you know. Got to say, my heart went out to you: I've had a lifelong terror of *ever* getting locked in here alone overnight!"

THE ALTERNATIVE CURRICULUM

In my first year as a Secondary pupil, staff found themselves having to devise a 'holding' exercise for those remaining at the end of the Summer Term; when a major chunk of the school population was away on organised trips abroad. They decided to offer us a markedly different curriculum. The idea was a nice one, but the weather outside was distractingly beautiful, teachers were exhausted at the end of what had been a long year; and any academic structure initially in place evaporated as the week went on. No one was out on patrol to see that we were actually *in* the lessons, so sloping off from those we didn't enjoy was child's play. From a list, we were each allowed to choose three unusual subjects: I forget what the rest were, but from the options given, I picked Italian, Camping and Horseriding. The only one of the three which remotely resembled a classroom lesson was Italian. We learned a handful of phrases, but most of it was confusing, as certain words we knew in French like "il" had an altogether different usage and meaning in Italian. The other two subjects I chose were far more hands-on: for Camping, we had to pair up, learn how to pitch a tent and sleep in it overnight on the school field. We weren't trusted to cook our own food as we were still pretty young, but the whole experience was quite good fun nonetheless.

However, it was the third and final day which proved most memorable. We were driven out to a local farm where a variety of different horses were being put through their paces. I had seen the animals many times before of course, but rarely been up close to them or had much experience of riding or caring for them. First, we were given an idyllic sunshine tour around the grounds in a haycart; then each of us, with a guide, rode an individual horse on a journey of what seemed several miles through nearby country lanes. I was completely unprepared for the physical toll this motion would take: certain muscles hitherto never used were left aching for days afterwards. We were then led into a large corrugated iron hangar positioned on a steep slope. The floor was covered in a thick layer of hay; hurdles positioned at regular intervals around the periphery. This was where the farm's prime quality thoroughbreds were trained for showjumping. In a move which would be condemned in today's ultra-cautious world, having had zero training, we were each now asked to mount a horse and hang on as it did a complete circuit, jumping uphill hurdles as it went. Challenged in the co-ordination stakes, I barely managed to stay in the saddle one leap before I was thrown from the horse, landing heavily on the hay – nothing injured except my pride.

But by far the most enduring memory of the day was something the staff never intended us to witness. Making our way back to the coach, we happened to pass the stud farm area, where, as part of the selective breeding of livestock, a colossal tethered stallion was being encouraged by its keepers to mount and impregnate a mare. *Nothing* was left to the imagination. In its explicit, neighing throes of passion, bodily fluid bursting forth as if from a two-foot firehose, the whole group, eyes like saucers, burst out laughing. Our mortified teachers didn't know where to look...

"*Will* you *please* get on the coach?!" they exploded, red-faced with embarrassment... Unintentional as it was, that "alternative curriculum" certainly *did* deliver: we learned more about the birds and the bees that day than in any dry Biology lesson on Reproduction, or awkward Sex Education class!

THE CHARMLESS ENCOUNTER

In my second year at Art college, we were tasked with shadowing someone for a month; our ultimate goal being to do a 'telling' portrait of them. I chose my grandma in Bournemouth; and with her permission, went down to stay with her for a week. One evening, though, when she had gone to bed early, something in me didn't want to be alone; and I decided to go drawing in a nightclub. I wasn't a dancer; and although I would have loved to meet someone, was too shy to put myself out there; so I rather hid behind my sketchbook, which, in that setting, only made me look weird. The one nightclub nearby was on the Pier, where a couple of years earlier, my brother and I once paired up with two lovely girls on New Year's Eve and walked them back to their flat. There is a proverb warning of the folly in revisiting the scene of a good time – and never was it more true than on this occasion. In comparison to that evening, the place was dead; with the sparsest handful of revellers; leaving me feeling acutely exposed. I only did a few sketches, spending most of the evening discreetly observing the exchanges between members of the crowd from the sidelines. One poignant thing I noticed was the presence of a much older, middle-aged man with slicked-back, dyed hair: a throwback from the 1970s disco-dancing era. Dressed head-to-foot in an imitation of John Travolta's *Saturday Night Fever* outfit, right down to the nipped-in waist on the jacket, he was doing all the moves too, pointing at the ceiling and strutting around, oblivious to the snickers and whispers; and unaware how incongruous an anachronism he looked.

Finally, it came to the closing dance of the night. The DJ put on a 12" version of The Real Thing's 'You To Me Are Everything', a re-release which had been a recent hit; and I watched enviously as a few less inhibited couples paired off for a slow smooch. There was one very pretty brunette in a figure-hugging black skirt; and the lucky fella who had won her attention was as besotted with her as she was with him. It wasn't long before they were kissing passionately, totally wrapped up in each other. The girl had happened to arrive with a rather unpleasant companion: a rough-voiced, squat-and-dumpy, frizzy-haired blonde with glasses, a mouthful of jutting teeth and simply rolls of fat squeezed into a way-too-tight, white dress. Given her unappealing physique and battle-axe personality, clearly her mama had taught her to be a go-getter and to make her *own* luck. Determined not to miss a slice of the action, she located the only available bloke in sight, stomped over – and before I knew it, grabbed my hand, dragging me forcefully onto the dance floor. I didn't find her remotely attractive and certainly didn't want to dance – but I had no say in the matter…

"What's yer name?" she barked, pulling me close to her. I told her, but if I did ask hers in return, I've long-since forgotten it.

"Where ya from?" she yelled above the music.

"Leicester," I answered. "You?"

"WATFORD!" she spat, with no femininity at all; her inflexion evocative of the noise a weightlifter makes when hoisting barbells into the air. It was a totally charmless encounter, made worse by the fact that now she began *grinding* her thigh up and down my inner leg in a *Dirty Dancing* stylee. As the music reached a crescendo,

she began moving in greedily for a kiss – and I could take no more. Tearing myself away, I made an ungentlemanly exit from the dance floor, grabbing my sketchbook and heading for the door just as the lights came on. Looking back, the last thing I saw was the same big girl stalking up behind the still-snogging couple and savagely pinching the poor lad's behind until he broke apart from her friend – whom she dragged off in pursuit of a taxi home.

A WAR VETERAN UNDER THE STAIRS

One afternoon in my late 20s, whilst house-sitting for my parents as I often did when they were away, the doorbell rang unexpectedly. I opened it to see a smartly dressed old man and his wife.

"Believe it or not, we were the first owners of this house when it was originally built!" the man said in an American drawl. I was intrigued. "Would you mind if we came in for a couple of minutes and took a look round?"

Ordinarily, that might have been a rather strange request, but I was happy to oblige. It turned out to be a mutually rewarding decision. Obviously, the place had altered considerably since their ownership; but I could see how nostalgic the experience still was for the pair. As we went from room to room, one or other of them would remark on different features. I don't recall all they pointed out, but there were some things which did stick in my mind.

"Over there, there used to be a dumbwaiter in the wall to deliver food from one floor to another," the old lady said; "and see that bell system behind the door? We used that to summon maids from different rooms." The wooden, wall-mounted box filled with circular white and red signals was long-disused; it sounded like a scene right out of *Upstairs, Downstairs!* But the most amazing revelation was yet to come. To our family, the sloping, cobwebby, wood-fronted cupboard under the hall stairs was just a convenient place in which to hide a multitude of clutter like the vacuum cleaner, spare plastic chairs and cushions for outdoor furniture; with the hooks on the inside weighed down with coats and scarves. Yet upon seeing it, the man made for it with excitement...

"Now see here?" he went on. "This used to be our air raid shelter during World War Two! We happened to have our good friend Douglas Bader visiting us at the time..."

"What?" I exclaimed, incredulous. A legendary figure to the British public, Douglas Bader was, of course, a celebrated hero of the Battle of Britain and possibly the most internationally famous of all war veterans; immortalised both in books and in the film *Reach For the Sky*...

"Yes, yes," the old man continued. "He was here with us one summer, when all of a sudden, there was an air raid. Bombers were flying over and the three of us took refuge in here together. As you can imagine, it was quite a squeeze; Douglas had to take off his prosthetic legs and leave them outside the door until we got the all-clear: it was the only way we could get the door shut..."

What an unbelievable story!

"Please come back anytime – I'm sure my folks would love to meet you," I said, as they left. But they never did return – and sadly, I found out that both have since passed away... If the Douglas Bader story could be proved as more than just hearsay, what remarkable provenance that connection could add value-wise to the property. I did do a little research; and quite aside from his reputation as an intrepid R.A.F flying ace, Bader was made both an OBE and Knight Bachelor for his services to disabled people. He championed the establishment of rehabilitation services for amputees and those with physical disabilities nationwide; and, although it was sold via auction for redevelopment in late 2014, there did once exist a Douglas Bader Day Centre in the St Matthews area of Leicester. While, arguably, the building may just have been named after him, it is certainly possible that the great man himself played a campaigning role in founding it; and so definitely not out of the question that he might have visited local friends whilst up in our region!

THE BEDROOM FLOOD

At the tail-end of the 1970s, there was a comedy drama named *Turtle's Progress* running at night on ITV. An impressionable age when this serial went out, I recall little about it now; except that it concerned the exploits of a petty criminal similar to loveable rogue Arthur Daley in *Minder*. But what fascinated me most about it was that in the thieves' den, the villain had an aquarium of massive goldfish passing over the screen behind him. The visual clash of complementary colours, orange against blue, seemed the height of cool; and having seen a few episodes, I decided my own street cred would be equally enhanced if I were to create the same scenario in my bedroom.

So one Saturday, I gathered up all my pocket money and caught the bus into town. Below ground level, there was a horrid, run-down pet shop in Cank Street back then, manned by a rough local family; there were always forlorn-looking puppies standing on their hind legs crying plaintively from the cages... Anyway, I went in and spent a considerable time looking in all the fish tanks. The goldfish were only 30p each then; and aside from my bus fare, I had exactly £3 to spend. So, when I finally got the attention of the shopkeeper, I selected the ten largest, most perfect goldfish I could. I must have been a right pain to deal with, making her chase around inside the tanks with her little green net until she captured the exact ones I wanted; because I wouldn't settle for any with as much as a scale missing, I was going for a uniform look across them all; and nothing less would suffice. They weren't as big as Turtle's goldfish, nor were there as many as he had – but I had done what I could and couldn't wait to get them home and set up their new environment. Thrilled, I watched them all mingle around in their bulging plastic bags on the top deck of the bus.

Once back, I headed straight for our garden, where on the wall stood a large, grimy aquarium my brother and I had used in our younger days to contain a succession of frogs and toads: Hazel, Warty, Green Beauty, Superfrog, Massive, Massiver, Blackavar and Beelzebub to name but a few. I lugged the heavy tank over to the garden tap and hosed it out until it was perfect; dried it, then carried it upstairs to the bedroom; setting it up on the desk surface opposite my bed. That way I could watch the fish swimming as I fell asleep. It took many buckets to fill the tank, but eventually I watched the last gap above the surface disappear under the black plastic rim. Now to add the fish themselves. With the bags bobbing up and down in the water, I took the blade of a pair of scissors and popped them; looking on, wonderstruck, as each of the inhabitants found their way out of the holes and into their infinitely more spacious new life. Pleased with the result, I called every member of the family in to see the tank; each of them making encouraging remarks about how nice it all looked; and giving me helpful tips on the things I should do to take care of the fish.

It was a relaxing thing to look at, my new display; and as I lay there marvelling at it that night, I felt real satisfaction with the job I had done. Switching off the bedside light, eventually I fell asleep.

All of a sudden, I was awoken by a bone-jarring *crack*... What on earth was that? I sat up, disorientated, only to hear an even louder noise follow it. Turning on the light, I looked across to the aquarium only to spot, with alarm, a visible fissure in the glass; With each sound, it grew longer and more substantial, until, with an awful splintering, the crack burst outwards from the front face of the tank and a mini *waterfall* began cascading out onto the bedroom carpet below... Of course, there must have been a good reason why the tank had been left outside and replaced by a new tropical fish tank downstairs. It was structurally compromised in some way – and I, with my latest hare-brained scheme, had overloaded it to the point of no return... I leapt out of bed and ran across the landing in my pyjamas, hammering on my sleeping parents' door and rousing them abruptly from their slumber. My dad just muttered something restlessly, rolled over and went back to sleep – leaving it to my poor mum to throw on her dressing gown and take control. Most crucial of all was of course to save the lives of the goldfish, none of which, fortunately, had yet slipped out of the crack along with the water: they had simply continued to sink down the tank as it emptied. But with less and less liquid remaining for them to survive in, it was still a crisis and must have been hugely traumatic for them, With the aid of an old tropical fish net from downstairs, I managed to retrieve all ten from the last few inches of water; transferring them temporarily into a green plastic bucket. But they couldn't stay in that all night. There was only one thing for it: I had to stagger into the pitch 3 a.m. blackness outside with the bucket and a torch; emptying all my costly purchases into the garden pond. Then, with the aid of a heap of towels, we soaked up all the water as best we could from the drenched carpet before it made its way into the perilously close mains socket nearby.

Thus it was that my meticulously crafted career as a master criminal was over before it began.

THE TRAFFIC WARDEN

There was once, from the late 1970s to mid-'80s, a nasty old Traffic Warden in Leicester with a major chip on his shoulder, perhaps due to his limp. He was *huge*, almost certainly around six foot four inches tall, with a massive club foot covered by an enormous, outsize black boot. If you got caught by him, there was no humouring or reasoning with him; you took the usual chances anyone did with those of his ilk; in the same never-ending cycle of pursuit, near-capture and escape... There weren't that many ATMs around back then, but one was in the wall of the bank facing the Town Hall Square. The City Centre wasn't pedestrianised then as it is now; you could drive through most of it, the only problem being that all roads leading to the cashpoint had single or double yellow lines throughout. One drizzly evening, I found myself short of money; and took the risk of parking on a single yellow on Bishop Street, just around the corner from the 'No Entry' road on which the ATM was situated. Running to the cashpoint and back, I could not have been longer than 90 seconds in total – yet as if out of nowhere, I found the Traffic Warden at my car, writing out one of his sopping wet tickets and inserting it into an adhesive, plastic-covered yellow sleeve.

"Uhh – come on mate – please," I pleaded with him. "I've been no more than a minute and a half..."

"You know the regulations," he answered monotonously, ripping the completed ticket off his pad. "I'm only doing my job..."

I could see it was futile – he was so self-righteous and full of himself, it made me lose my temper.

"You've just *got* to exercise your little bit of power, haven't you?" I shouted. "You *love* it! You're not a policeman, you know... "

That clearly hit a nerve, for the man drew himself up to his full height, puffed out his chest and bellowed pompously,

"*Oi*... am part of the *BRITISH CONSTABULARY* – and as such, a member of this *FORCE!*"

"Oh yeah? And what's to stop me driving off?" I taunted, getting in the car and starting the engine.

Determined to achieve his aim, the Warden stepped into the road, just as I began to pull out. So focused was he on his objective that, in the same movement he slapped the ticket successfully onto my windscreen, out came his *tongue*. I can still see it now, slithering from his cheek, dripping with cords of ropy saliva; and the triumphant, ugly expression in his eye. As I drove away in disgust, I caught a last sight of the Traffic Warden in my rear-view mirror. Dressed from head to foot in his black oilskins, he blended with the bars of the rain like a gigantic, predatory bat – and was gone.

TREVISO AIRPORT

I was invited by a close friend to be Best Man at his wedding in Venice back in 1999; the second of three such duties. It was always the greatest honour to be asked; and a responsibility I took seriously. The date was tricky, however, as I was teaching just then in a particularly high-powered community college; and the wedding was scheduled in the middle of term-time. I had to go cap-in-hand to the formidable Principal to request a special dispensation allowing me to miss that Friday's work. A day off in lieu was granted on two provisos: firstly, that I made up for the absence in the summer holiday by attending for free on GCSE Results Day; and secondly, that I gave her a *cast-iron* guarantee that, without fail, I would be at my desk as usual the following Monday. Still new to the staff, I accepted her terms, confident I would prove myself reliable and trustworthy.

The wedding itself was a beautiful, intimate affair with just 14 people, including bride and groom, an event organiser and a tour guide. I ensured my friend was woken early, immaculately turned out in his suit and (after snapping a final, commemorative photo of him as a single man) that he was at the church when he needed to be. With the power having gone to my head somewhat, I even took it on myself to firmly eject a handful of casual tourists who had wandered in before the ceremony began. Passing the ring to the groom right on cue, I translated the key paragraph of my speech into phonetically learned Serbo-Croat, much to the delight of the bride's family, who heralded from the former Yugoslavia, and after dinner, the happy couple sailed off into the sunset on a gondola. It couldn't have been a more perfect, fairy-tale experience. Aside from a tiny gnat becoming trapped in my eye for what seemed like an eternity, everything went exactly as planned.

With all my duties performed, still high on the success, admiration and gratitude from all quarters, I had allowed plenty of time on the Sunday afternoon to say my farewells and reach the evening plane. Taking detailed instructions from my host on how best to reach the airport, I set off from his base in Lido, took the required water taxi and arrived at the bus station well ahead of time. I was surprised, however, to find no building there at all; just a vast square of tarmac as far as the eye could see; no labelled bays or even posts to give you a clue where you had to stand. With only occasional vehicles pulling in and out from the furthermost periphery, there were no staff anywhere; and I spoke only the fewest words of Italian. I did, though, at least know the name of the airport I had to reach – Treviso – and decided, the area to traverse being huge, that I'd better ensure I was in the right place for the bus when it did finally arrive. So I took the long walk across the square to a friendly group of passengers queuing on the far side; and with the resourceful use of gesture, plus the name of the airport, managed to make my needs understood. In a flurry of incomprehensible Italian, they pointed to the middle right edge of the square; and with hands clasped together and an obsequious "*grazie mille*", I made my way to the spot they had indicated.

Time had been ticking away without a sign of the bus anywhere in sight and I was becoming decidedly twitchy: if many more minutes elapsed, I would have no choice but to reach the airport by other means. Just when I was on the point of despair, in pulled a bus, heading directly to where I was standing. To my vast relief, I saw on the front the word 'TREVISO' emblazoned against the black route indicator in large, white, uppercase letters. I was going to be okay after all. Gratefully, I showed the driver my ticket, clambered aboard and headed straight for the back seat, so that I could easily retrieve from my rucksack the things I needed on the plane. Always inclined to travel light, I foolishly had my passport and ticket bundled together in a flimsy, knotted plastic bag, in which also lay a messy collection of crumpled banknotes and coins: this was the dual circulation period when both the Italian Lira and Euro had legal tender status, prior to the former being abolished. I knew I had more than enough left to travel in comfort, buy a few drinks and snacks on board and a UK paper for the flight; pay Stansted airport's 72-hour fee to retrieve my car and fill it with petrol for the return journey home. Relaxing, I lay back, congratulating myself for planning and budgeting so thoroughly. But as the famous saying warns, pride comes before a fall...

There was still around an hour left before take-off at this point, less margin than I had anticipated, but nonetheless sufficient for a rapid check-in; and my thoughts began to drift. Playing Devil's Advocate to my brother, close family and friends was a lifelong pleasure of mine. I had even created a game called "Situations" – effectively, "what-would-you-do-if"s – and took the most ridiculous amusement in making my poor victim pick between two equally unpalatable fictional scenarios; for example, "Which would you prefer: being stung to death by a swarm of wasps, or being eaten by a shark?" Now I was all-but nodding off when this tiny kernel of a thought began to form in my head. It began like the flimsiest of cobwebs, but every time I pushed it to one side, back it came, increasing in urgency. What this nagging little inner voice kept whispering, was, *"Imagine if you had got on the wrong bus..."* Don't be daft, I told myself, that queue knew where the stop was; and the bus said Treviso. "*Yeah, but it didn't actually say Airport, did it?*" Well, no; but obviously that's the destination. Still, the journey did seem to be taking rather long; and try as I might, I just couldn't dispel a sense of unease. After 10 minutes of suppressing it, the voice reached such a maddening crescendo in my head that I just had to consider, could it be some form of intuition? *I'll put this to bed once and for all,* I thought. It was dark now; and with a mere 35 minutes remaining, I made my way down the aisle to the driver, who did possess a basic grasp of English. Just as he began pulling off the motorway onto a slip road, I leaned forward and asked,

"Excuse me – this bus *is* going to Treviso Airport isn't it?"

The three words uttered by this man in his unfazed Mediterranean accent; and the resulting chaos that ensued, are seared forever into my psyche:

"Treviso Airport – NO."

It's funny enough now in the re-telling, but I cannot *begin* to put into words the panic I felt at that moment, all the blood draining from my face. I was going to miss my flight, let down my Principal and prove my word couldn't be trusted; worse than that, I'd be stranded, a stranger in a strange land, with insufficient resources to get home.

"WHAT?" I gaped in horror, as he stopped outside his final destination; a glass-fronted building resembling a shopping mall. To my incredible luck, directly facing us was a full taxi rank. With the concertina door barely open, I leapt off the bus and raced down to the first driver, shouting,

"Treviso Airport! Treviso Airport! How much?"

"290,000 Lira" he answered.

"How long?" I insisted touching my wrist to indicate a watch.

"30, 40 minutes" he estimated flatly. "Traffic, you know…"

"Okay – hurry!" I urged him, yanking the back door open and jumping in. Heart pounding, I reached into my rucksack and tore the cashbag open, still knotted. Frantically, I rifled through the contents, adding up my remaining coins and banknotes: 210,000 Lira – I was 80,000 (around £35) short.

"No-no-o-o!" – I cried. " I only have 210,000!"

"Not enough," answered the driver.

"Please," I said; in desperation reverting to my old New Orleans strategy from eight years earlier: "Me, artist – Leonardo, Michelangelo, Mona Lisa – I give all I got *and* do portrait!" He wasn't happy, but his fee was vastly overpriced and I guess he enjoyed the time challenge and drama of the moment enough to nod agreement. Unwinding the paper from a chinagraph pencil, I pulled out my trusty sketchbook, ripped out a page and in the juddering cab, managed a passable sketch of the driver in his seat; just as – remarkably – he got me to the plane with five minutes to spare.

It was the strangest airport I have ever seen; only one visible plane, there in the dark, jets roaring – and he seemed to be able to park directly alongside its steps. I spotted an emergency telephone on a post; and with enough shrapnel left for a lightning-fast call home, just had time to shout out:

"Listen – I can't explain now, but I'm in trouble... I've got the plane, but don't have a single penny left to get the car back – please try and do something..." before the air hostess cajoled me aboard. The *shame* of having to fall back on my mum and dad like that as an adult... Exhausted from the ordeal, not to mention starving, I had to eat my heart out watching all the other passengers filling their faces and drinking to their hearts' content the whole flight back – my just deserts for congratulating myself as a smooth operator... Once we touched down, I immediately sought out the airport police, who passed me the £50 my parents had wired over – just sufficient for the car park fee and enough petrol to get me home. I have an awful feeling all these years later that I never paid them back... Nonetheless, as promised, there I was at my desk first thing on Monday morning – and never did I breathe a word to a soul at work about how close-run it had been...

NESCAFÉ AND WEBSTER

"We don't want to go!" moaned my brother and I; complaints falling on deaf ears as we were motioned back into the car one day after school by our no-nonsense mum. She had to visit an ungrateful, not even remotely child-friendly old lady, who had her shopping delivered as part of a weekly care plan; however, it did turn out to be a worthwhile trip for us. On the way over, we spotted an intriguing-looking pet shop on the corner nearby; and were given permission to look inside while the old dear was seen to. Immediately, the most entrancing, tiny mice seized our attention; they were surprisingly affordable at around 75p each; and we just had to get our hands on a pair. No way would a request for them ever have been granted, for our mother had a lifelong phobia of rodents; but we had set our hearts on securing one each; and soon developed a plan...

There was no groaning the following week when the trip to the old lady came around; both my brother and I had pocket money grasped tightly in our fists, deceitfully promising to wait in the car while the sour old duck had her shopping delivered. No sooner was the coast clear than the pair of us burst out and into the pet shop across the road; knowing we had five minutes at most to get the clandestine transaction accomplished. In an uncanny match for our first Labradors a few years further down the line, I chose a long-whiskered little jet-black mouse I named Nescafé, while my brother picked an enticing yellow one he called Webster. Within their glass-fronted container, each was skilfully isolated, then pulled from its siblings into the air by its wriggling tail; before being placed by the shopkeeper into separate small cardboard boxes, along with a token handful of shredded paper and sawdust. With our precious live contraband hidden in our jackets, we rushed back through the drizzle and into the back seat; sitting there as meek as… never mind – just as our oblivious mum reappeared, car key in hand, pulling her now-empty shopping basket.

Acting as nonchalantly as we could, we made it up to our shared bedroom undetected. Where on earth were we going to keep the mice hidden, though? There was only one obvious choice: a battered white chest of drawers between our two beds. A receptacle for all kinds of junk; it hid a myriad of clutter which we removed from the second drawer down. Then, gingerly, we transferred the little furballs into their new environment. They really were the most engaging little creatures, rather timid and very tolerant of being handled; although we had to learn fast to move each hand repeatedly over the other as they climbed rapidly in search of food and new stimuli. At the ages of 11 and 12, we really didn't have a clue how to take care of them: it wasn't long before they escaped almost in unison the following Saturday into the tiniest gap behind a wall-mounted ornamental desk. With visiting grandparents requiring our attention downstairs, we were panic-stricken: cheese was about the sum total of our knowledge with which to lure the mice back out; but they were too clever: no sooner would one quivering snout reappear than it darted back out of sight. Eventually, though, with the use of a Lego-built ramp, each of them crept down towards the bait stolen from the fridge; and after a couple of well-timed finger-flips of the plastic, followed by frenzied rugby tackles, we recaught them both and, in relief, got them safely back in the drawer.

Given the unmistakable aroma of mouse urine and droppings, it didn't take long for our secret to be found out. Next morning, in came our mum to wake us up. All it took her was a single sniff and,

"You've got mice in here."

It was a statement, not a question. My brother and I exchanged guilty looks: clearly the game was up: we had no option but to confess and reveal all. But so winning and unthreatening were these little souls that soon we were allowed to keep them – provided we got a proper, secure cage, wheel and water dispenser and kept them outside. The next few weeks of ownership passed relatively uneventfully, until, one summer afternoon, a distraught wail went up. Webster had escaped! – leaving my brother in floods of tears. Curiously though, the *level* of his distress did seem somewhat disproportionate to the loss – I had never seen him quite like that – but who were we to judge? The entire family was roped in to look for the cheery little yellow mouse: high and low we searched, every inch of the garden, through the flower beds, across the lawn, in the garage, the greenhouse – we combed the entire property as meticulously as a police operation – but all our efforts yielded nothing; and, as darkness fell, the search was finally called off – it had to be accepted that Webster had gone forever. As time went by, though, the pain of the loss gradually subsided. With Nescafé's unfortunate demise in his cage at the hands of the family cat a month later, the status quo was restored; and, in our fickle way, we moved on to the twin fascinations of tropical, red-eared terrapins and treefrogs; the mice all but a distant memory.

Then – one day, the family car began to *smell*... At first, it didn't really bother me and my brother; something like that just wasn't on our radar – but over subsequent weeks, it became a stench unlike anything else, driving our house-proud mother almost mad in the process. In vain she bought air fresheners, vacuumed the interior from top to bottom, even washed down the seat fabric with car shampoo – but to no avail – the smell persisted. Finally, at her wits' end, she released a pair of seldom-used catches and hauled the entire back seat upwards – only to discover, among the fallen sweet wrappers, hardened chewing gum, half-eaten toffees, tissue and other debris in the hull, the suppurating, rotting body of – you guessed it – a tiny, yellow mouse. That stench had been the smell of Death itself. Having endured weeks feeling too embarrassed to give anyone beyond immediate family lifts in the car, she tore back into the house, shrieking my brother's name in an incandescent fury. Down he came to face the music; and faced with the irrefutable evidence, promptly burst into tears.

What had happened was this: months previously, a school friend of his had come over to play on that sunny weekend. Having fussed over Webster and played with him a while, my brother had asked our mum to drive them both up to the local Woolco in pursuit of sweets and other entertainment. Captivated with his furry companion, he had rashly brought Webster along on the trip to show him off. The little mouse was either in his pocket or clambering around adventurously from hand to hand in the usual way – I forget which; but our mother, never the gentlest of drivers, suddenly rounded a sharp bend and braked hard. He was thrown sideways by the jolt; the weight of his body instantly crushing Webster against the side of the car. The very air was squashed out of the tiny creature; and when my brother picked him up, to his shock, he found the tiny mouse dead. Consumed with guilt, he concealed the evidence by shoving the corpse out of sight down the back seat of the car. The knowledge, however, was too traumatic: he needed an outlet for his grief; and found it by pretending his beloved pet had escaped; leading all of us, through his sobs, on a fruitless search around the garden – when all the time, he knew *exactly* where Webster lay.

The tale has passed into legend in our family; and whenever recounted, never fails to raise a smile. Who knows? If indeed such a thing as the Hereafter exists, perhaps, in the long-distant future, my brother will have a glorious reunion with that lost, spirited little yellow mouse of his childhood…

GIRAFFE EPITAPH

In 1988, I had a beautiful new Italian friend, Rosanna, at art college. With not one, but *two* middle names, she was in the year below me, and I was nuts about her – but she already had a boyfriend back in Italy. I had met her the previous autumn whilst queuing in the Polytechnic refectory for lunch. Desperately in love with a girl in my own year who had 'friend-zoned' me, I had become very introverted and virtually ceased to communicate with most people at that point; when, out of the blue, I felt a tap on my shoulder and heard this earnest little voice asking, "Excuse me – are you a Second Year by any chance?" I looked up from my tray to see an absolute *vision*: a stunning, impeccably tanned blonde around five foot three inches tall, dressed from head to foot in brilliant white – it was truly as if she were a rescuing angel... One of the new First Year intake, she asked if she could see my portfolio; of course, I fell over backwards to oblige. She had the most incredible innocence; asking extraordinary questions like, "Oh Guy – *why* do people go to war?" or if I mentioned something dodgy I'd seen, she would say, "Oh no: do you think you should *report* him?"

I took her to see one of the earlier *Nightmare On Elm Street* films (which scared her) but, a staunch Catholic, each time I tried to put my arm around her, she firmly rebuffed all romantic advances. I couldn't get her out of my head, however – Rosanna had given me something fresh to live for. While my parents were away on holiday, I brought her back to our house; and there she stood, frying onions in our kitchen – I was so thrilled just to have her there... And when my 22nd birthday came around, I just knew I had to spend it with her. She lived in a nearby student hall, and although I didn't divulge the birthday element, she agreed I could take her out to Twycross Zoo for the day. The animals weren't my agenda at all: I took my faithful 35mm camera along expressly to capture *her* beauty; and I particularly recall taking a stunning shot of her in my jacket near the flamingo pool, with her long, slender legs and high heels – I couldn't wait to see how it came out.

She was particularly fascinated by the giraffes. In their own separate hangar with a corrugated iron ceiling, they were quite remarkably tall, with a loping, almost slow-motion gait. A large, unmissable sign was on the wall: "Please Do Not Touch The Giraffes." The message couldn't have been clearer. "Oh no, Guy – I *really* want to touch one," she said in her plaintive, little girl voice. I would have robbed a bank for her I think at that point; so agreed to stand guard at the entrance and look out for any officer or warden while she went over to the railings, climbed up and reached in to stroke the animal's hide. "Oh – it feels *really* nice!" she exclaimed. Well, I just had to get the sensory experience myself then. So Rosanna went to be lookout and foolishly, up I climbed. My fingers had barely touched the animal's flank than its head *shot* down towards me from the rarified upper atmosphere; exposing a piercingly blue tongue. I'm not sure what harm giraffes are capable of, but anyway, I only just leapt back in time: a staunch reminder to heed warning signs...

We spent most of the afternoon at the zoo; then the girl suggested going shopping in Nottingham. So I drove there and we parked in an NCP car park. I don't recall much of what we did now, aside from messing with a piano keyboard in a shopping mall; but later we went for something to eat, then saw another film. It ended quite late and we headed back to the car park only to find the shutters down barring all access: it had closed at 11 p.m. and my car was locked in – a disastrous end to the day. Stuck in the centre of Nottingham, which at the time was a city with possibly the worst crime statistics in the UK, it just so happened that a police car approached us. I flagged it down, explaining our predicament. The officers tried in vain to contact Security to release the car; but at least gave us a lift to the train station. They didn't take us directly there, however; midway, we had to sit in the panda while they drove into a muddy field to confront a group of angry travellers, ordering them to get off the site! We finally made it back to Leicester in the early hours and I saw Rosanna back to her student hall in a cab before walking the last couple of miles home. "You know, I didn't tell you – but it's my birthday," I confessed a little glumly, "I guess I just wanted to spend it with you." Which did at least make her tearful and won me *half* a kiss goodbye – half lips, half cheek, if you understand.

The following morning, I trained it back up to Nottingham, paid the full overnight penalty fee and retrieved the car from the car park. Several days later, I left it outside the Polytechnic's Fine Art building on the narrowest little slip road, where I was using the facilities to make a screen print. After meeting a friend for lunch at the famous Magazine pub nearby, I headed back towards the workshop, vaguely registering someone in the distance stooping down and peering into my car's rear window. Suddenly, I saw their arm hammer inwards as, simultaneously, there was a loud smash of glass. "Oi!" I yelled – and, throwing caution to the wind, began racing towards the car – only to spot a white Transit van tearing in from an adjacent private car park. The fella leapt on board and, with a screech of burning rubber, they were gone. By the time I reached the spot, gasping and out of breath, all there was in evidence was a gaping hole in the glass – and my camera, containing all those priceless shots of a day out with that beautiful girl, was gone forever. According to the police, an organized crime gang had been "doing" Leicester that morning and I had naively put temptation in their path by leaving the camera visible on the back seat – it was just one of many targeted that afternoon. I doubt the thief even bothered developing the film; odds are he just ripped it out; so all that remain now are my own enduring memories of the day. But at least, decades on, I'm still good friends with that loveliest of girls: the one and only Rosanna.

FUNGUS THE GUYMAN

I once inherited a memory foam mattress from my late grandfather, who had been an intrepid explorer in the jungles of Borneo shortly before his death. When the time came to wash my sheets for the first time, underneath them I found, to my disgust, a dark grey stain extending like sinister fingers all over that mattress. Whether he'd brought back some nasty tropical spore, I don't know, but after researching fungal remedies, I did all I could to treat it, spraying the affected areas with vinegar and pure alcohol and leaving it in direct sunlight for hours. Memory foam does *not* allow moisture through it; something most people don't know. Living at home then, I had to take much mocking from my parents giggling *"Fungus the Bogeyman"* at me. No one took it seriously. I hated still sleeping on the mattress, but with the only alternative a hard single bed, I hadn't much choice.

It wasn't until I woke in stiffness and discomfort in the early hours that my fingers felt something strange beneath them… Switching on the light, I discovered to my horror that my whole *chest* was now covered in jutting, solid spikes of a spiny black fungus: it had grown and spread at terrifying speed. I've always found body horror and possession the scariest of concepts; as one's most intimate cosmos, it really is an unspeakably frightening experience to feel you are quite literally being taken over; becoming a monster. I should really have gone to A&E immediately, but couldn't bear that expanding, sentient invasion on me a moment longer. While I did have the foresight to put some scrapings in a specimen jar, I went and shaved my chest there and then in the bathroom.

My parents were abroad, but I texted a shot of the by then, far lessened condition to my dad, a respected consultant. So shocked was he, he insisted I took the day off and sought an urgent GP's consultation. After all, a whole chestful had grown on me in just a few hours: thank God I caught it before it penetrated under the skin's surface – or entered the bloodstream! I did take the sample in to my GP that day – but the tests came back negative. However, as he remarked incredulously,

"It most definitely *was* a fungus – the labs often make mistakes."

The mattress itself had to be sealed in plastic bin liners and left on the street as bulk waste for council collection. I hope they incinerated it: the idea of it going on to infect others is unthinkable. But in any event, *neve*r could I be persuaded to sleep on anything made of memory foam again!

THE TRANSFORMATION EDIT

Back in the days of good old VHS off-air recordings, I was once compelled to compile my own "Incredible Hulk Transformation Edit" – every single Hulk transformation in the '70s TV series in chronological order; from initial provocation, when the angered scientist's irises went white, to the monster's eventual return to normal. Why? I can't even tell you – there *had* to be an obsessive element at play. There were at least two transformations per episode, and 89 episodes in total over five seasons – plus several TV movies, the last of which had the monster fall from a plane and, reverting to human form, die for good. Recording each sequence as it screened took a lot of commitment to the broadcasts over many months. At the time, that wasn't illegal; plus it was for solely domestic use. The Edit filled two 4-hour videotapes on Long Play mode; running to 16 hours. One weekend, I made a friend sit through the whole thing in what were then regular "subjections" between us. 240-minute tapes, though, were way more susceptible to damage than standard 180s. The Transformation Edit finally got chewed by the VCR; and all that precious work was lost. While it remains a fond memory, the whole enterprise was, of course, a ridiculous waste of time.

AN EVENING WITH THE FREAK

In the summer of 1992, my parents kindly offered to pay me to redecorate their entire house. It was a long job, but one I was up for, having been out of work for some time; and one evening, whilst taking a break, an advert in the local newspaper caught my eye. "AN EVENING WITH THE FREAK!" screamed the headline in bold, uppercase letters; below which was a black-and-white photo of the giant prison guard, Joan Ferguson – sadistic former corrections officer at Wentworth Detention Centre in the Australian TV show *Prisoner: Cell Block H*... The actress who played the corrupt Ferguson (referred to by the other inmates as "The Freak") was appearing live, right here, in a run-down area of the City Centre known as Lee Circle. Now *Prisoner* was something of a cult here in the UK. Given the nature of the content, it was on last thing at night and I was a relatively late convert to the show; but like many, soon found it compulsive viewing; the notorious Freak being the main draw – a villain everyone loved to hate. I rang up my best friend and insisted he come along to witness the spectacle. He didn't really want to, having never seen the show; but intrigued by the ghoulish nickname, was sufficiently curious to agree.

On the Saturday in question, I was busy painting a room and cut it too fine timewise. I did my best to wash the paint off, but with such hairy hands, each individual one was covered. I didn't have time to scrub them clean; so had to set out looking fairly freakish myself, hands still plastered in brilliant white emulsion. The venue was a now vanished nightspot – Granty's – whose clientele that evening were *horrid*. You just know you don't fit in when you overhear exchanges like this:

"'Ere Dave, your missus lookin' good tonight..."

"*Take* 'er mate! F**k her!"

Whole families had come out together for this must-see event; and a smarmy entertainer was perched on a stool playing *"Can't Smile Without You"* on a particular brand of twee-sounding plastic organ that was all the rage back in the '70s. Feeling out of place, I didn't know what to do with myself and unconsciously began picking paint flakes nervously off my hands until the carpet around my chair was covered in white. The £7 entry price included food, but it was a set menu: plates of vile mutton curry were dumped in front of us. The music descended into Victorian music hall as we watched in disbelief: the audience *lapping* it up, giving a powerful impression they came *every* Saturday; with one bespectacled lad punching the air as he jumped in and out of his seat, crying:

"'Oo were ya wiv last noight? Out in the pay-ul moon-loight; It wasn't yer sistah, it wasn't yer mah, AR, AR, AR, AR, AH-AH-AH ARRRR!"

Finally, the music subsided, plates were cleared, and with the crowd craning their necks in excitement, a big welcome was extended to – The Freak! I had really bigged Ferguson up to my friend, how huge and formidable she was, with her savage, unsmiling manner and butch, cropped hair. Expecting her to appear in her stark, grey prison uniform, perhaps even doing a mini-act in character, we were to be sorely disappointed. Here instead was a smiling, softly-spoken, really rather presentable actress appearing as herself in a flame-red ballgown and shoulder-length permed hair. The UK, you see, were way behind the Australian screenings; and the lady in question had left the infamous role years ago. We only stayed for part of the intimate "audience with"; then slunk rather guiltily away, feeling not a million miles from the base 17th-century crowds who revelled in public executions. That would teach us to be such vultures drawn towards the freakish!

THE ALIEN ABDUCTION

I was sleeping soundly one night, when *something* made me wake up abruptly. I hadn't even opened my eyes, but still, with a sixth sense, perceived a tangible presence in my room. I was in my youth then; and at the time, an avid viewer of horror films — I'm way too much of a wuss these days to watch them alone now — but in those days, I was bolder. A number of the films shared the same unsettling theme of alien abduction: films such as *Communion* or *Fire In The Sky*; even more tame sci-fi fodder like *Close Encounters Of The Third Kind* or *E.T: The Extra Terrestrial* touched on similar themes. So however illogical it was, I guess the fear of falling victim to such a kidnapping was lodged somewhere deep in my subconscious; and the first suspicion to come to mind when awoken at such an ungodly hour. Knowing I was being ridiculous, I knew I could swiftly put the unease to rest just by opening my eyes; so, taking a deep breath in from under the duvet, I did so.

I found the room in pitch blackness: not a thing could I see; but, peering into the murkiness, as my eyes became accustomed to the gloom, a vague shape began to form at my bedside. I could distinguish no detail, but could make out just enough to identify, at waist-level, the silhouette of a large, triangular head tapering down onto a long, stick-thin neck – the archetypal profile of a *'Grey'*... Gripped by raw terror, I froze: this phenomenon was *real*: a hostile creature of infinitely superior power had come to investigate me while I slept. It could only be the beginning of a nightmarish ordeal, the kind I had heard reported on numerous documentaries about the unexplained: ordinary civilians spirited away from their normal lives onto a disorientating alien spacecraft where, utterly immobilised, they were subjected to agonising medical examinations...

Rigid with horror, I was unable even to scream. I had not imagined a thing; what I had seen was corporeal, solid and right at my bedside, looking directly at me in the darkness. It was only a matter of time before spindly alien fingers reached out to drag me into an unearthly, out-of-body experience; from which, should I survive, I would be forever traumatized. Frozen solid with fear and without daring even to breathe, infinitesimally slowly, I peeled the outer edge of the duvet up over my head; lying motionless beneath it for what felt like hours, trembling with trepidation. *Why* had it not taken any action? Was I just being monitored in the first instance? Maybe I'd even been lucky enough for it to have left! I had to know: it was time to stare my tormentor in the face.

Moving not a muscle, a millimetre at a time I peeled back the corner of the duvet with a single finger until enough of my head was exposed to slowly raise my eyelids. I hadn't imagined it. *There* was the black silhouette exactly as before, entirely static; however, the darkness around it had marginally lightened as daybreak approached. I lay there, unmoving, gazing at the stark triangular outline, hunting out the facial features I knew must be there: enormous eyes, a tiny protuberance of a mouth – but neither of these could I yet discern. There had to be a logical explanation.

"If you eat yer carrots, you'll see in the dark!" That was the old wives' tale the school dinner ladies used to tell us. Right then, I wished I had listened. I looked harder, eyes straining into the fading gloom – until finally, as dawn broke, the full spectacle of my night-time assailant was revealed...

It was the inverted shade and uppermost arm segment of an ordinary, white Anglepoise lamp.

ROUGH SLEEPING

In the summer of 1988, a college friend and I signed up for a French exchange offered by the Polytechnic: a rare liaison between the Fine Art and Graphics faculties. It was an irresistible opportunity to immerse ourselves in a different culture and be inspired by new surroundings in which to draw and paint. The agreement was that the incoming French students would get to live in our rooms in Leicester; but our own experience was split in half. First, we would occupy their lodgings in Paris; after which a contact on the French Fine Art side would arrange further placements for us in Orléans, a medieval town in north-central France.

On the night before we left, a pretty blonde girl called Marie-France arrived to take over my bedroom. She turned out to be quite naughty, smuggling in her boyfriend before my assertive mum stamped out any hanky-panky (or so she chose to believe...). I, meanwhile, went to stay in Paris with the girl's equally fair-haired sister, aptly named Blondina. A very chic, sassy character, she gave me a key and didn't really have much to do with me after that. The two girls shared a rather swanky upstairs flat; and although I was just assigned a small box room under the rafters, all I really needed was a base in which to crash at night; as I was out all day drawing. I spent many evenings up into the early hours riveted to MTV, which I had heard of, but up to then never seen: one of the French promo videos screening in rotation was extraordinary, featuring the band's upside-down chins painted with eyes and wearing hats…

As fascinated by the faces and activities of tramps as I was at that time, I got to see all the usual tourist sights as well in between painting and sketching: the Mona Lisa at the Louvre, the Eiffel Tower, a dine-in bar called Le Piano Vache and, after a worthwhile climb, the amazing artists' village in Montmartre. I even caught a long-anticipated, crackly screening of Stanley Kubrick's at-that-time banned film, *A Clockwork Orange*, at the Studio Galande – a champion of underground cinema close to Notre Dame. But my friend and I were also to discover a truly creepy area, the Bois de Boulogne: a huge, remote area of parkland on the west side of Paris, which could be quite dangerous to venture into at night. The woodland was riddled with transvestites touting for business: cars full of German tourists cruising by in search of sex. As I watched, one of the drivers called to a six-foot tall, wildly extrovert specimen prancing up and down in fishnets, heels and a billowing gold cloak; he leaned over the open window agreeing a fee, then got in. As I watched: the car turned into a dirt track, went about 50 yards down and stopped – then the lights went out.

In Paris, you hardly needed to speak any French – the place was so cosmopolitan that just about everyone spoke English. Things could not have been more different in Orléans: you *had* to talk in French to get by! Having not used it since 'O' Level days, that was very good for me; I came back to England speaking the language almost fluently. Judging from the graffiti, it seemed many of the locals were fed up to the back teeth of the city's connection to Joan of Arc; longing to disengage from the lady who famously saved it from the English in 1429 and was burned at the stake. This, I felt, was the *real* France; breathtaking, inspiring rural scenery and endless, winding stone streets; a *tabac* on just about every corner and a hatch in the wall serving a delicious hot potato pancake (*galette de pommes de terre*…) Although not quite Arles, you could just imagine Vincent

Van Gogh occupying street corners with his easel around a century before; similarly tortured internally at that time, I identified with him more and more; with many of my paintings done there reflecting a very real private turmoil, plagued by frenetic brushstrokes.

I wasn't quite as lucky with my lodgings there; one of the hosts, a thin, pained-looking girl, Valerie, was friendly enough; but coiled up with tension. The other girl, Laurence, wasn't nice at all. Chubby as a beachball, she made no attempt to speak English; and left me only a thin mattress up in her loft. It didn't feel healthy at all – I was convinced I was breathing in toxic roofing materials.

"*Aimez-vous les tripes?*" she asked me one day. Thinking she was asking me if I was enjoying my trip, I gushed, "*Oui! Oui!*" – only to find she was asking me if I liked eating the stomach lining of a pig. The penny only finally dropped when she served me a huge fried plateful of the stuff – tripe...

"*Tu es bête!*" she said, not realising I *did* understand that – but I let her think she'd got one over on me: at least I had a roof over my head. Whilst sketching outside a café, I did draw one adorable, sweet-natured brunette, Lorraine, who sat down and wrote her home address in my sketchbook; inviting me back to her student commune. She introduced me to all her welcoming housemates and shared her food; we ate together in a circle, then went to see *The Unbearable Lightness of Being* at the local cinema. She was the exception, though: in general, I found French girls to have a rather twee sense of humour; often finding things side-splittingly hilarious when they weren't. For instance, in my pal's lodging was a girl who called her cat Ventolin; then, when she was genuinely stressed, needing her asthma inhaler, she would gasp, "*Où est le chat? Où est le chat?*" To her friends, this was hysterically intellectual – but they didn't 'get' our English humour at all...

After around eight weeks, my college friend and I had virtually run out of money and paint; and had finally had our fill of France. Bearing our open-return tickets, we headed back to Paris to collect our luggage from the previous hosts; making a plan to meet the following day and get the ferry back to the UK. Unfortunately, after saying our goodbyes, we discovered that the port was closed: it turned out to be a national holiday, with no route of any kind out of the country until the following day! We hung out until nightfall, then my companion got fed up of walking the streets and told me he was going to eat humble pie and return for one more night to his lodgings.

I was too proud to do the same, having handed back my key; so with little spare cash, had no other choice but to stay out. Somehow, I ended up on the Rue Saint-Denis, one of the oldest streets in Paris; notorious since the Middle Ages as a place of prostitution. Though I had no idea of its credentials at the time, I very quickly put two and two together, passing girls at the roadside dressed to cater for every possible fantasy; from psychedelic hippies, brides or cowgirls to leather-clad dominatrices with whips, chains and handcuffs; some of them looking quite shockingly young.

Still carrying my luggage with me, I was very tired now and needed a place to rest. I suddenly came across an abandoned three-piece suite sitting incongruously on the kerb. A moth-eaten, rat-infested thing it was; God knows what nameless acts had been performed upon it – but I just had to lie down. It wasn't the safest place, I knew, but it was a lovely warm night and I had a fool's confidence in my early 20s. I did at least have the sense to protect my cylindrical duffel bag, using it as a pillow and holding its handles firmly as I fell asleep. At around 1.30 a.m. I was abruptly awoken by torchlight beaming directly into my face, like the infamous 'third degree'. Two seven-foot-tall gendarmes were leaning over me asking to see my passport; while I couldn't understand their French, the gist of it was that I had to move on. Luckily, I wasn't hauled to the commissariat, for we had been warned that the civilian police had more than a passing reputation for brutality.

I still had time to kill until morning; and with all the night cafés closed, the only place I felt might be open was the Gare du Nord, one of the largest mainline stations in Paris. More or less asleep on my feet, I headed for it; but upon arrival, found the iron portcullises down, barring access to the platforms until 5.30 a.m. when the Métro opened. There was, however, an illuminated empty photo booth in front of the gates. I staggered inside with my bag and pulled the curtain across. Sitting on the hard, unyielding circular stool and resting my head on the only firm purchase – a metal shelf in front of the screen – I dozed on and off until then, before heading down to the now open tube station. There was a particular line of the Métro which I had learned just went up and down endlessly in a repeat cycle: that was the one I chose, curling up on the soft fabric until a guard passing through the carriage kicked my feet off the seat. By then, though, it had finally become daylight – and thus concluded, thankfully, the only night of my life spent rough sleeping.

THE RAT DISSECTION

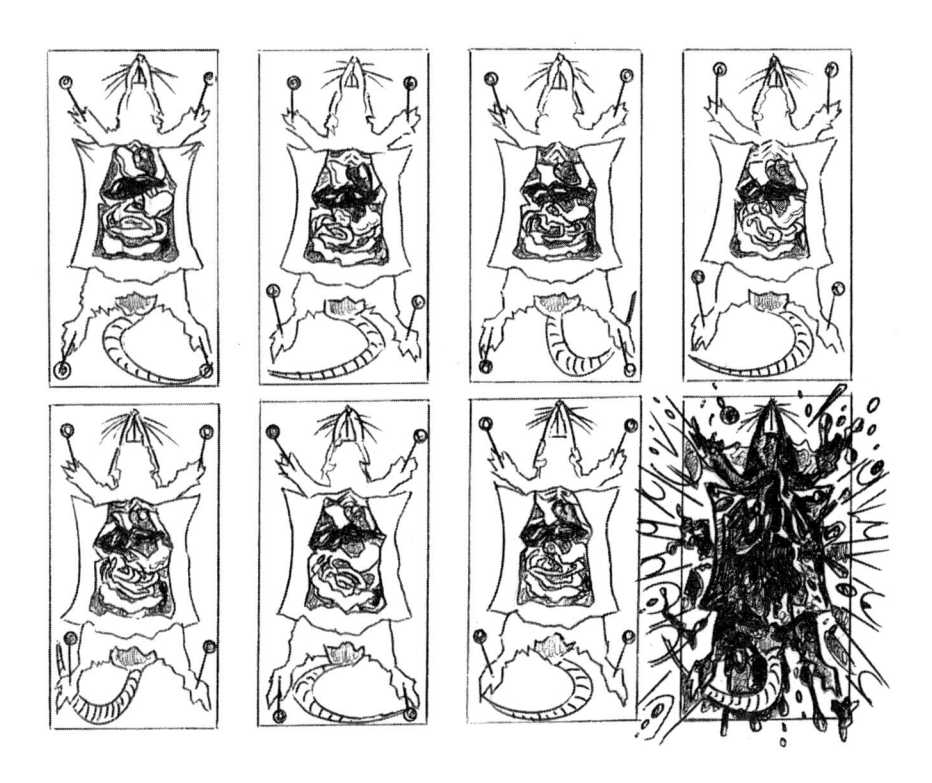

At the age of sixteen, I really didn't have a clue what I wanted to do with my life. Unlike most of my peers, who seemed to have their entire futures all mapped out, I was completely unworldly...

"*COME* and sit here by me... You've always got that *IDIOT* grin on your face!" came the words of one exasperated teacher – and I knew the time was fast approaching when I would have to make a choice. Sure, I had vague, half-baked, pie-in-the-sky ideas about becoming a naturalist, wandering through the rainforest peeling up verdant leaves to uncover red-eyed treefrogs, etc. I also dreamed of being a practising artist, although my skills really hadn't developed far at that point; my mother's constant fear ringing in my ears: "You'll end up starving in a garret..." The unspoken, ever-present suggestion was that I might follow in my father's footsteps and go into Medicine; but I certainly wasn't focused; having chosen an odd mix of 'A' Level options: Biology, English and Art, rather than the three sciences. I was also squeamish about blood and guts and massively needle-phobic, so the idea was a non-starter – yet I'd still picked Biology, just in case...

The 'A' Level Biology syllabus, however, turned out to be a far cry from the richly varied 'O' Level course I had enjoyed. Immediately, we were plunged into intense cell-structure work, with a cytology textbook of such ferocious complexity even my dad struggled to decipher the language used. I was completely out of my depth, grades plummeting; and wasn't helped by the constant presence of a friend who maliciously enjoyed making me have hysterics; dropping me in it at every opportunity. The subject teacher was a humourless, gowned academic who didn't suffer fools lightly; he would ask me a question at the very second I was being made to laugh at something lewd my pal had written about erectile tissue. I would look up in time to see the teacher sneering,

"You're not listening, are you?" and, by way of a helpful clue, my friend would whisper the answer "Osmosis" to me. Gullibly, I would repeat his suggestion, only to find he had betrayed me totally; the question relating to a different sphere of Biology entirely. It wasn't long before the frustrated tutor referred the pair of us to the Head, wanting us both to drop the subject before his pass-rate was affected. Tiptoeing nervously up the stairs to his office, I could hear my bullish friend inside spouting a mouthful of backchat; and the Head saying, "Now I know why people say the things they do about you..." I was far more contrite, telling him I was really trying hard, pleading to continue the course and promising to knuckle down. In the end, both of us were allowed to stay.

A major practical exam at the end of the whole course was going to involve a rat dissection; in which we would each have to expose and label certain internal organs with delicate paper flags on pins. We had all been required to invest in a rolled-up cloth dissection pouch with compartments full of precision instruments: scalpels and razor-sharp blades in foil, blunt and sharp-tip scissors, lancets, tweezers, nails and forceps. After just one teacher-led demo, we were each given our first, freshly killed, fully grown white rat to work on in the next lesson; my friend having already upset the lab technician deeply by asking her what it was like to be a murderer. I really hadn't got the first idea what I was doing: sure, I had watched the demo intently, but that still didn't give you direct experience of how deep to cut through the fur; and where the key blood vessels were to avoid. After we had all crucified our rats, gruesomely stretching out their four paws to the max and pinning them to the boards, I had made a relatively good job of cutting through and opening up the outer skin layer, when the group's attention was suddenly drawn to one poor bespectacled, whiskery lad with a harshly protruding Adam's apple; who, at age 14, had once been the tallest in our tutor-group; but had ceased to grow ever since and been overtaken in height by all the rest of us. You may think it's impossible for a person to actually turn green with nausea; and that the phrase is just a colloquialism: trust me – it's not. This fella's face had turned the colour of a greengage; he was unsteady on his feet, on the verge of fainting and had to use the rear exit into the fresh air to recover; all his plans to become a doctor requiring a rapid rethink!

Returning to the task in hand, I was in the process of removing a layer of surplus fat to reveal the internal organs, when, in my typically unco-ordinated, hamfisted way, I must have nicked one of the rat's major cables... Instantly, the entire internal cavity was flooded with blood, overflowing from the rat itself onto the very dissection board and desk. It was a scene of utter disaster, making any further work out of the question. All the internal organs were completely submerged, and with only a small handful of paper towels each, mine were hopelessly covered in the red, red "claret" before I knew it... Heart sinking, I looked surreptitiously around at the rest of my peer group; all of whom were thoroughly engrossed in pristine dissections. I dared not say a thing, but *imagine* that awful feeling of dread; knowing it's only a matter of time before someone sees what you've done. I didn't have long to wait.

*"F****N' HELL!"* exclaimed my neighbour, incredulous at the horrific sight; and making sure (with the teacher temporarily out of the room) that he drew everyone else's attention. "Uhh! (with a chuckle) – you've surpassed yourself this time, Goblin..." (I was known by a variety of nicknames for being the smallest.) "What the *hell* have you done?" The contrast between the obscene spectacle on my desk and all the others could not have been more

pronounced: my rat's internal viscera looked like the aftermath of some bloodthirsty Aztec sacrifice. I had to endure choruses of "You flippin' numbskull, Bonsai..." and "Oh – you *idiot*, Studs!" from the merciless throng; as one-by-one, they became aware of my dissecting catastrophe. I was of course, last to leave the lab, late for my next lesson due to the extent of the clean-up required – and the day wasn't through with rats yet. My villainous pal had managed to smuggle something out from the lesson unseen. Seated at the dining hall table that lunchtime, he waited until the student to his left was diverted momentarily; then surreptitiously deposited the grisly object he'd stashed away onto the unwitting lad's plate. You can imagine the reaction when the unfortunate victim looked down to see a rat's tail in the middle of his Egg Mornay. Seriously, the stuff that went on beggared belief.

    The sad thing is, I got really rather good at rat dissection in the weeks prior to the Biology exam; succeeding, on the day itself, in flagging every required organ correctly with no bloodshed at all. I still only ended up, though, with a Grade 'O,' which was useless, as I'd already passed the 'O' Level two years previously. Just before we went in for the exam, my so-called buddy had handed me a green "Keep Britain Tidy" charm for good-luck, which, whether you believe it had influence or not, he later admitted he had "cursed." With friends like that, hey... To this day, he remains convinced our papers got mixed up during the marking process. I had reams of self-created 'crib' cards all fully memorized, he had nothing – yet still managed to secure a 'D.' I was the only student *ever* to fail in that teacher's subject; meaning that while I had an excellent reputation on the Art front, I left one hell of a bad legacy behind in Biology for my brother, a genuine aspiring medic, to endure. It was never my intention, but tarred with the same "prankster" brush, he had to fight hard to escape my bad reputation and be taken seriously in a subject which really mattered to his future.

THE WHIRLING DERVISHES

Ever since seeing a late-night programme about this mystic, seldom-seen Turkish-Islamic order, I was fascinated by them. Their spinning dance and ever-rising and falling white robes represent the sphere of the divine, acting as a bridge from God to Earth; indeed, it has been claimed that these are the holiest people in the world... Specifically referred to in the lyrics of Kate Bush; with derivatives of them even glimpsed in one of her videos, the Whirling Dervishes inhabit a remote citadel in the high-altitude, mountainous region of Konya, the burial place and former home of Rumi, an esteemed poet and philosopher who established the Mevlevi order of Sufis in central Turkey. In the documentary I saw, the presenter described how, while most members are celibate, expected to forsake marriage and devote their entire lives to prayer; there are some who do have families and go home at weekends. In 1925, the Whirling Dervishes were banned in the country for several decades due to their religious associations; but the presenter discovered where a clandestine underground gathering was occurring, deep in a crypt. There in the dark, he found, in the midst of worship, two Needle Dervishes in an ecstatic trance, their cheeks ritually pierced with long, exposed "zarf"; and just one, extraordinary, *Whirling* Dervish...

Out of the blue, in the autumn of 2002, I heard to my astonishment that the Whirling Dervishes – the real deal – were making an ultra-rare, one-off appearance at Cambridge Corn Exchange; the first time they had ever been permitted to enter the UK. I just *had* to go... I tried to persuade my brother and a couple of other friends to come, but they were all too busy and couldn't spare the time; so after work that evening, I drove down on my own, selecting a multi-storey car park opposite the venue itself. The space I chose in the furthermost corner was notable for an enormous silver duct stretching from floor to ceiling adjacent to it. A good thing, for I couldn't miss a monstrosity like that when returning to my car!

The first half's entertainment was a Turkish music ensemble performing rather brooding unmelodic tunes I didn't enjoy at all. Strangely, the major draw of the night had second billing: in tiny type on the ticket; you could easily have missed it! But finally, there came an announcement:

"There will now be a 20-minute interval, after which the Whirling Dervishes will perform in total silence. They have requested no flash photography; and we ask the audience to respectfully comply." *Oh no*, I thought: *I've not come all this way to see them without getting any pictures... besides, my brother won't accept I've even been if I don't come back with proof!* We had a rather competitive thing about this between us at the time; he had beaten me to be first to meet a distant uncle we'd built up into a legend: a notoriously rich jeweller whom we'd never met, but heard had a harem of stunning air-hostess girlfriends, gambled extravagantly, served drinks with gold leaf floating in them and lived in luxury in San Francisco. Gallingly, my brother served me "The Evidence!" that Christmastime, standing victoriously next to the man in a candid photograph.

Now this was the era before camera-phones had become

mainstream in the UK – I didn't even own a mobile. All I had with me was a rarely used, rather oddball tube SLR I was given in 1990. Using standard 35mm film and looking more like a video camera, it had a 'fixed' lens cap which you flipped open to turn on the power. I wouldn't have *dreamed* of disrespecting the stars of the evening, but I honestly believed there was a way to compromise. The camera had a "Disable Flash" setting, activated by selecting a lightning icon with a line through it. As the returning crowds filed back to their places, I thought, *I'll get ready ahead of time, so I don't disturb anyone.* I flipped open the lens cap and zoomed in to the stage as far as I could, then pressed my way through the drop-down menu until I had highlighted the "no-flash" icon. So readers, please bear in mind that I did make a genuine effort to observe the "no flash photography" request...

As the lights in the auditorium went down, you could have heard a pin drop as I leaned forward in eager anticipation. Onto the stage came a large group of figures – but where were the dazzling white robes? This gathering did indeed have the familiar long, elongated hats I knew, but aside from white leggings just visible under their outer garments, all were clad in what looked like heavy brown dressing gowns! A pelt was spread out at one side of the stage, which one of the men, clearly the *Sheyh* – head or elder of the order – knelt on in front of the group. After kissing the ground and rising to their feet, the acolytes slowly began spreading out; parading in a respectful, repeating circle past him and around the perimeter of the stage; arms crossed over their chests. A 'deputy' of sorts whom I later found out was known as the "*Semazen Bashu*" walked slowly among them, as if inspecting the quality of proceedings; then, on their third cycle, as they passed the *Sheyh* sitting on his pelt, infinitesimally slowly, each of the figures opened their crossed arms, the brown overcoats dropping away to reveal the brilliant-white of the Whirling Dervishes – their skirts billowing outward like the plumes of a peacock. It was breathtaking – and deeply spiritual...

Each figure's head was tilted at exactly the same angle, slightly up and to the right, as they whirled as if in a trance; left hand up to receive the blessings from God; right one out, to give the received blessings away. I snapped off a couple of discreet photos; but unfortunately, was seated close to the back. Even with the zoom on, the figures were tiny dots. So engrossed in the performance was I that, out of habit, I *closed* the lens cap to preserve power; forgetting that in so doing, I lost all previous settings, including 'Disable Flash...' For some forty minutes, the Dervishes whirled in utter silence; then, towards the end, some came closer to the front of the stage. *That'll make a cracking shot,* I thought, flipped open the lens cap, zoomed in to the max – and pressed 'Take.' To my horror, there came a loud, *"wuh-wuh-RRRR!"* sound as the entire auditorium was bathed in the brilliant light of my camera's flash: closing the lens cap had reset it by default. I was *mortified* – and, consumed with guilt, slid down my chair like a worm, concealing my face; as the lady in front gave a disgusted "Uhh!" – tut-tutting in disapproval. I wanted the ground to swallow me up; and can only imagine what the Whiring Dervishes thought: *These English peasants have no respect...* In front of the impressed audience, they concluded their performance; after which I couldn't get away fast enough. Slinking out in disgrace, I headed for my car, hoping they wouldn't turn the full force of their mystical power on me. As it turned out, it almost seemed that they had.

Reaching the dimly lit car park, I crossed the bleak concrete floor to the corner where I had left my vehicle; fumbling for the keys while still beating myself up for the faux pas. Then, for the first time, I looked up – freezing in disbelief. The car was gone; its space totally empty. Had I come to the wrong place? No! There was that monstrous duct – how could I be wrong? I could've sworn I'd locked the car; and besides, it was hardly a 'babe magnet' worth stealing. Experience has taught me always to question myself before raising accusations of theft; as 99 times out of 100, the apparent disappearance of anything is down to oneself. Although I sought a logical explanation, this situation really did confound me. It was that flaming *duct*: I had to be in the right place. With no staff in sight, I began looking for a telephone to call for assistance. There were none visible in the immediate vicinity, so I took the stairs down to the basement to hunt one out. Still no phone – but then, my eyes fell on a familiar object. There, in the exact same far corner, was the *duct*! Was I losing my mind? Could a solid object move? Had I come through some bizarre wormhole in space? Or was this all simply karma – a punishment meted out by the Whirling Dervishes to teach me greater respect?

All at once, a thought struck me. No – it was ridiculous. But could it actually be possible? Come to think of it, it could... For the first time, I realised that this giant duct, vast as it was, might not be limited to one floor, but may extend to others. Retracing my footsteps, I went back up the ramp – and yes, there on that floor, in the exact same corner, stood the duct: the *same* duct, continuing through the ceiling! And – following that line of reasoning, was it not also possible that it continued even further, up to the floor above? With increasing certainty, I pursued my train of thought, vaulting up the staircase to the Second Floor above. And sure enough, there in its corner stood the duct, alongside which – was my *car* – having never, of course, moved at all. I hadn't gone mad; I had simply re-entered the car-park on a lower level than the one from which I'd initially exited!

The weirdness of the night wasn't over yet though… Heading towards the sliproad to the Leicester-bound M1, to my shock, I found the entire *North* cordoned off. I'm not the superstitious type, but this was too much: it *had* to be the revenge of the Whirling Dervishes, pooling their collective wills together into a force punishing me for taking flash photos. With my battered Road Atlas having vanished somewhere into the bowels of the vehicle, I had to pull into a petrol station and ask to look at one of theirs to work out an alternative route home. The soft kiosk manager let me do so without charging for the book itself; after making scrawled notes and buying an energy-boosting supply of junk food, I found my way back along a succession of winding 'A'-roads; finally reaching familiar territory at around 3 a.m. My sinful snaps of the event, once developed, left much to be desired; most of the figures either blurred or tiny white dots in the distance; but nonetheless, I had secured the essential evidence and finally *seen* the elusive Whirling Dervishes.

GET AN EYEFUL

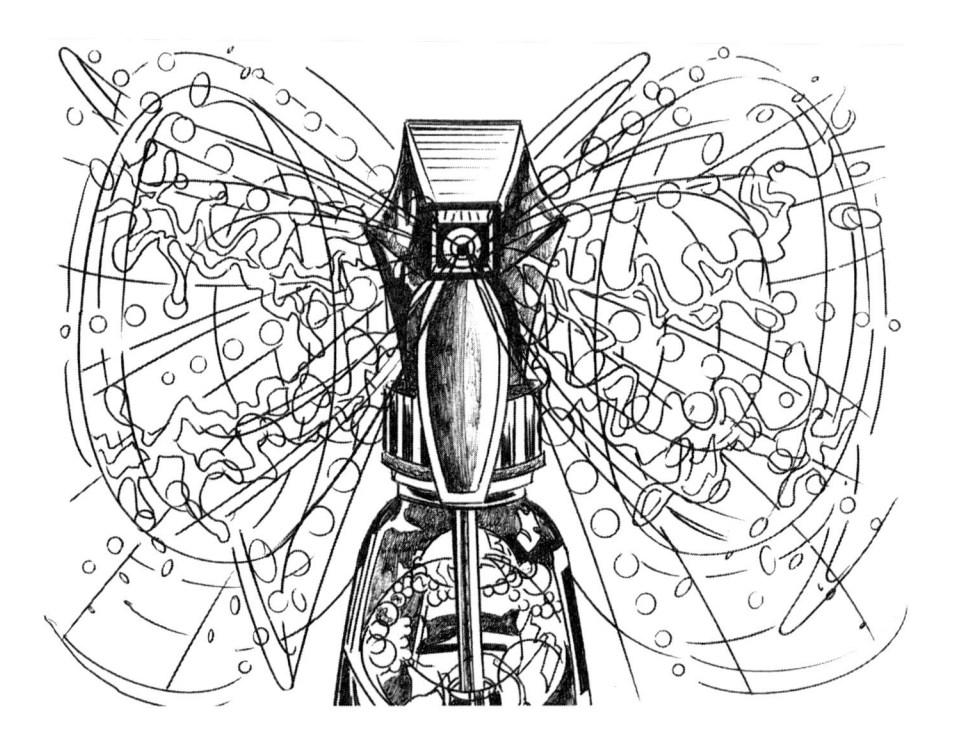

Shortly after buying my first property, I was cleaning the bathroom one day in preparation for a friend's arrival. I genuinely thank the Lord for such visits; for living on my own, I lack the motivation to deep-clean for my own sake. I always have better things to do, especially when in the middle of something creative; meaning my place alternates between being a horrendous mess, then tidy for a short spell, before descending back into its default chaos. Living in this cycle means I dread the idea of impromptu, unannounced visits; lest those unfortunate people get to see the *real* me at a less disciplined time; with the residue of dog everywhere. On this occasion, cloth at the ready, I picked up a new, unopened bottle of a well-known bathroom cleaner spray, all set to polish the sink bowl to perfection. Aiming it at the dirty porcelain, I squeezed the trigger, but nothing came out. What was I doing wrong?

I turned the bottle, rotating it around in my hand to look at the directions for use on the back. "Turn the spray nozzle to the 'On' position." Right... I guessed because it was a new bottle, that was what I must have forgotten. I gave the plastic block on the tip of the spray-point a 90° twist, aimed it confidently at the sink and squeezed the trigger again several times. Still nothing. Getting a bit miffed now, I reached for the old, empty bottle of the same spray I had just used up and tried a few test shots with it. No problem with the action at all: even though there was only the tiniest pool of liquid remaining at its base, I still got a weak spray. So what was the issue with the new one, then? Perhaps the twist of the nozzle needed to be 180° rather than a mere 90°: the instructions didn't actually specify which. If this didn't work, I thought, giving the square tip a further turn, I would just untwist the entire top section and switch it for the old bottle's. Perhaps now? I squeezed the trigger multiple times. Still nothing – plus I could feel what I thought was almost a resistance in the mechanism. *Hey, perhaps I'm turning it in the wrong direction,* I thought; *I know, I'll just try it the other way before giving up...* Uhh, the flaming thing – what was it? *Okay – well, how do I unscrew it from the neck then?*

Turning the bottle back towards me, I put my finger and thumb firmly on either side of the ergonomically ridged cap, to twist it anticlockwise. It was only at *that* moment that the nozzle, which, purely by chance, I had the misfortune to have rotated in line with my face, decided to come to life... My repeated, unsuccessful squeezes must have caused a bottleneck of pressure to build up inside the plastic container – and all of a sudden, the most almighty jet of spray shot out of the tiny nozzle. Had I actively tried, I could not have got a fuller dose in *both* eyes...

Recoiling from the impact, gasping in shock, I felt the corrosive chemical sensation instantly. Imagine the chlorine burn in a swimming pool multiplied several times... Fortunately, I was in exactly the right place; and, in – *literally* – blind panic, stumbled for the cold tap right in front of me. Throwing it on full force, I plunged my entire face into the sink... There was a degree of relief, but not nearly enough; so in desperation I raised each individual eye in turn right up to the running faucet, flushing them directly... I couldn't afford to risk not rinsing them enough: doing what I did for a living, my sight was essential… Torn as I was between calling for help and taking immediate action; I decided the latter took priority; spending no less than 25 minutes alternating the flooding of each eye. Only then did I call **NHS 111** for advice, telling the advisor the active ingredient, potassium stearate, which, through the blur, I could just make out on the back of the bottle. It was compound $C18H35K2$ – a metallic soap; in other words, a metal derivative of a fatty acid; and an "anionic surfactant" known to cause serious eye irritation… Fortunately, I had done the exact course of action advised on the bottle: "flush with water; and if symptoms persist, seek medical advice." The advisor was actually reassuring; opinion is divided as to exactly how many layers the cornea is made up of; but the general consensus seems to be anywhere between four to seven layers thick. He said that, as I had been able to act very fast indeed, I had hopefully only burned off, say, one or two outermost layers; but should the discomfort persist, I must go to A&E. As it was, my sight had more or less fully recovered within 48 hours.

If I'd wanted to be vindictive, I could have raised hell with the manufacturer for not indicating on the package the direction in which the nozzle turned; and for not stating the bottle's capacity to build up internal pressure whilst refusing to squirt – but I blamed myself for not taking sufficient avoiding action. In any event, as time went on to prove, there were no lasting long-term side-effects. I would urge everyone to avoid the same mistake: don't think your squeezes on any cleaning spray are having no effect – and whatever you do, before trying to remove the lid, it's common sense (of which I have little!) to check the nozzle is angled firmly away from your eyes…

FREE ADS

With many gaps in employment during my working years, at a time before today's big online selling sites, I had become wily at making spare cash by selling my own collectables through the local rag's Free Ads service. I would resort to this route whenever my normal powers of persuasion failed to impress my well-off medic brother, who occasionally showed pity and bought my wares.

"I've got a *SALE* on!" I would announce; waiting for his inevitable entertained reaction:

"Oh aye? What you got this time then?" he would say with a smirk. He loved the power to reject all my items as I became increasingly eager, dropping the price steadily. The most notorious thing I ever offered him was an unused ACME Army bog: a rough wooden toilet seat and lid hinged on a hollow galvanised metal base, which I used as a waste bin. The price began at £15 and there was a point when I could see he was seriously toying with the idea. He and his girlfriend were soon due to leave for Glastonbury where the toilets were barely more than festering, overflowing cess-pits; so the idea of a personal facility did actually have some merit. But he resisted; and eventually when I lowered the price to £5, my old mum kindly bought the bog as a seat for her greenhouse; embellished as it was on the inside lid with a photo of the local Tory candidate and his domineering-looking wife, crudely cut out for my own amusement from a junk mail manifesto.

It's all online now, but back when the free ads were only newspaper-based, they allowed just 15 words for anything under £100. I would renew my ads by telephone after they expired; and must have sold dozens of things over those years: from a Michael Jackson *Thriller* jacket, collectable figures and numerous Sci-Fi-related memorabilia, to my dad's gym bench, a beautiful laptop VCR which took full-size VHS videotapes; even a couple of unwanted genuine Gucci suits! Someone did well there... While I had a fair measure of success over those years, what confounded me most was the behaviour of some of the locals responding to the ads. "There's nowt so queer as folk" goes the oft-quoted saying; whether it's a manner particular to Leicester people, or a reflection of wider society as a whole I can't say – but this is what would happen – on *numerous* occasions...

The landline phone would ring and I would pick it up to hear:

"Oh hi mate... that (*whatever it was*) you've got advertised in the papers, where are you mate?"

I would give them full directions to the house and take their name, just in case.

"Okay, buddy," they would reply. "I'll just 'ave me lunch, then I'll be over, shouldn't be more than an hour..."

So I would wait in, put whatever I had planned on hold – then they wouldn't show up. Two or three hours later, thoroughly vexed, I would telephone the caller back.

"Oh hi mate," I would ask, "I thought you were on your way to see that item you wanted?"

There would then be a pause before the stranger replied in a "couldn't care less" Leicester accent:

"No... I decided to leave it..." Imagine the pronunciation, though, like this:

"Neeahhr – Aww dih-sword-id ter lay-vit…"

Well, cheers for letting *me* know, I would fume inwardly. Am I supposed to have inferred that by telepathy? Thanks for messing my whole day up! I mean, are these just professional jerk-arounds, like those semi-professional "carpet-treaders" who waste stressed house-sellers' time viewing properties they have no intention of buying? Pah!

WORLD WAR ONE IN WAPPING

In early 1985, whilst visiting London, I was tempted by a magazine ad to seek out the world's first-ever, recently-opened shop specifically devoted to my favourite TV show – *Dr. Who*... At that time, in its very first incarnation, the shop was situated in Wapping, an area of far East London I was completely unfamiliar with. I took a long train journey out there, changing tube lines several times until reaching the final leg, the East London Line. The moment I got off the train at the stop, I was struck by how primitive the whole station was. There were no lifts, just a steep, rickety spiral staircase with no one around except a poor old lady some way up ahead. Bent double, her legs wrapped in bandages as she struggled up the metal steps with her shopping bag, I had the impression this was where her home was; and that she probably did that arduous journey every day. My heart went out to her – what a life of hardship. Never had I seen a tube exit so minute: it had the familiar Underground logo, but was a far cry from the bustling West End versions with their wide openings: this one seemed barely larger than a pair of front doors! As I passed through the exit, I was busy fumbling with change, my ticket and journey-planner; so it was actually some moments before I looked up at the surroundings. When I finally did, I couldn't believe what I saw...

It was a scene of *utter* devastation... I had expected at the worst, unsightly docks and warehouses; yet, for as far as the eye could see, all that was visible was rubble: not a single building standing. Everything had been razed to the ground; complete desolation stretching to the very horizon itself; just an *ocean* of demolition... You could have been forgiven for thinking an atomic bomb had been dropped on the area; so total was the destruction. It was really shocking to witness, to the extent I almost doubted the evidence of my own eyes: how *could* such a vast area of ruin exist in the very capital itself without more people being aware of it? The bleakness of the scene was deeply troubling; evoking Wilfred Owen's nightmarish accounts of World War 1; or the front lines of Flanders Fields – yet somewhere here was meant to be the shop I sought. I turned to see what lay behind me; and spotted there, standing alone, the crumbling ruins of a building and staircase; the last vestiges of white paint peeling away from the brickwork. That had to be my destination...

While it's possible the memory can deceive, my recollections of the destroyed Wapping have proven far more enduring than those of the shop itself, which was a far cry from its impressive form today, complete with a screen-used props museum on the premises. Most of the things they sold back then I already had; so, for all the effort of travelling out there, I only ended up buying the tiniest, unpainted, die-cast metal figure barely an inch high! With the passing of time, there did come eventually, an explanation for what I had witnessed on that fateful visit. The whole derelict, poverty-ridden area, part of what was once the biggest port in the world; had, at that time, been completely levelled to make way for its imminent redevelopment into the glittering metropolis of Docklands and Canary Wharf; a major business centre and one of Europe's biggest clusters of luxury double skyscrapers. Just five years on, I went to meet a friend who worked there for lunch; again, my jaw dropped at what I beheld; but this time, I was infinitely more impressed!

THE RUNNING AWAY KIT

In my angst-ridden teenage years, when friction with my parents was at its peak, I had gone as far as to put together in my lowest desk drawer, a secret 'kit' for running away. I don't think I would have lasted long out there; for all there was in it was a £10 note, a bar of Kendal Mint Cake for energy and – bizarrely – "a string long enough to cross the River Thames..." Why this last item seemed even remotely necessary, I haven't the faintest idea. It probably wouldn't have traversed even the narrowest stretch of the Thames; but the point is academic now – I never did run away.

VOGON BILL

The first property I ever owned was a little two-bed detached bungalow in a quiet cul-de-sac. It had been newly built just nine years previously; and I was the youngest resident in the close; the rest being mostly retired pensioners with perfectly manicured gardens they took the greatest pride in. My next-door neighbour came over to introduce himself a day after I had moved in. The first thing that came to mind when I saw him was Douglas Adams' alien Vogon from the celebrated *Hitch-Hiker's Guide To The Galaxy*... A Welshman by the name of Bill, he was an absolute *block* of a man, built like a brick sh* – (well, you know what). In my mind, from then on, I always thought of him as Vogon Bill. He was a good soul and I got quite fond of him over the years; but in the first instance, his aim, I think, was to show me he was not to be messed with. Looking at me intently as if sizing up the challenge I might pose, he pointed to the ordinary concrete lamp post lodged some way into the gravel of his front drive; then, taking his huge forefinger (which trembled continuously whenever he raised it to make a point), he began in his slow, 'R'-rolling Welsh accent,

"You see that lamppost over there? That fell down on yer 'ouse a few years ago... I rang the Council. I said, 'There's a bloody lamppost fallen down on the house next door.' Well, they send out this daft young whipper-snapper in a nasty little suit, wet behind the ears he was, fresh out of college – I didn't like the look of him at all. And he's treading all over my garden making notes on his stupid clipboard. I said to him, 'You needn't come traipsing all over *my* garden... you can do that from the bloody road!'"

I could feel my mouth starting to twitch; a sure sign I wasn't far from an attack of laughter. But I kept a straight face as he went on:

"So – this young buck's umming and ahh-ing like an idiot; I could see he didn't know first thing about how to deal with the situation. I look him straight in the eye; and I say to him, 'Yer not a trained engineer, are ya?' Well, he splutters, 'I've got this qualification and that' – but I wasn't having any of it. I ring the Council back and I say to them, 'That young numbskull you sent me... 'e's not a trained engineer!'" (And then, with his finger still quivering in triumph) "They fired him..."

I couldn't hold it in any longer – and burst out laughing.

"Bill," I said, "remind me not to get on the wrong side of you!"

"Nah, nah..." he chuckled reassuringly, pleased with the reaction to his story.

"Now don't you listen to any of his nonsense – he talks a lot of rubbish!" his wife said to me; but it was the first of many classic nuggets I heard from him over the years. Another old man who lived in the corner of the close died a few weeks later. Finger wagging as ever, Vogon Bill reflected:

"I knew it wouldn't be long before his relatives showed up, sniffing around even before he died. I said to them, 'Don't you let me see you tryin' to get your hands on his bloody place before he's even in his grave... he *lived* with us – and 'e told us *everything* about you... every... *mortal* thing...'"

In the summer of 1999, whilst converting my front lawn into rockeries, I happened to have four tonnes of prime quality topsoil being poured onto my front lawn by a delivery lorry just coinciding with the most viewed Total Solar Eclipse in human history. The Moon's shadow seemed to race along the tarmac of the cul-de-sac, swallowing up all in its wake as the close was plunged into blackness in the middle of broad daylight. It really was a very weird experience… Some of us were armed with orange perspex, through which it was safe to view the spectacle; and although in our region, there was too much cloud cover to see the key moment of Totality, I called to Vogon Bill,

"Hey Bill – come and have a look through this – you can see the eclipse happening in the darkness!" But with eternally wagging finger, the old fella shook his head, smiling dryly,

"I've got too many years of darkness…"

Sadly, Bill fell ill a couple of years later; and, in the last stages of cancer, was too much for his wife to lift. I went in one night to help her hoist him up to a more comfortable position on the pillow. There he lay, as strong a presence as ever in his stripy pyjamas; still conveying a sense of dignity.

"There you go, Bill!" I said, trying to sound cheerful. "Does that feel any better?"

"*Much* better!" he said decisively; closing his eyes in satisfaction.

It was the last time I ever saw him.

TESTING THE BOUNDARIES

I was actually a good lad at school most of the time. In hindsight, I almost wish I'd messed around a little *more* – though I did commit a few minor transgressions. In our Junior school in Leicester, the dining hall, a large, separate building in the centre of the concrete playground, with an ugly corrugated iron roof, was referred to as "The Canteen." You had to leave it from the back and were expected to walk all the way around the edge of a large rectangle of grass to return to the classrooms. I didn't want to; and thought I would take a shortcut across the grass.

"Oi!" cried a playground supervisor. "You go round!" Back I went, but once her head was turned, I tried the shortcut across the grass again.

"I said *don't* do that!" she snapped. "Go *round* – and if you do that once more, you're on the Stairs."

Pretending to walk meekly around the outside, I waited until she was gone – then, quick as I could, tore across the grass, thinking I could make it to the other side before she saw me. But that lady *knew* I would try it. I was no more than midway across when out she sprang, having lain in wait just out of sight; her voice, cracking like a rifle-shot, stopping me in my tracks with a chill of fear.

"*ON* the Stairs!"

Bang-to-rights, there was nothing I could say; it was a *literal* example of "testing the boundaries;" and a true anecdote I used often in the classroom as a supply teacher. The Stairs was an effective punishment: it was a landing just below the Staffroom at the top; which meant as each teacher headed back downstairs, they couldn't fail to spot you; and would ask you in a disapproving tone,

"Have you been *naughty?*" They knew full well you had – or you wouldn't be there.

Only twice in Secondary school did I ever get a Detention – but I never had to sit through either. The first was when I was singled out for whispering to a friend in a History lesson, while the teacher, who had a speech impediment, was speaking.

"Wight! You can have a Detention!" he shouted. I was actually quite upset; saying not a word in his lesson the rest of the week. When it came to Friday afternoon, he must have realised he'd be inconveniencing himself more than me, as I wasn't a troublemaker. Calling out my name, he said:

"Due to your excellent conduct for the west of the week, I've decided to wevoke your detention."

"You flukey git!" marveled my friend, as I grinned wickedly from ear to ear.

The second offence was more deliberate. For some reason I decided I didn't want to go to Assembly; and hid inside a big walk-in cupboard with a sliding door in our Form Room. Our tutor must have realised, as I was there when he took the Register minutes earlier. A gowned Monitor (like a lesser Prefect) was despatched to look for me; he drew the cupboard door open and found me crouching inside. Not only did he give me lines, which I had to go and push through a box outside the Sixth Form Centre, labelled tauntingly, *"'Tis better to give than to receive;"* he also wrote out for me an after-school Detention Card – which, crumpled and worn as it is – I still have.

Offence: "Missing Assembly: Hiding in the 'P' Block."

I did attend, but nobody showed up to supervise the session; so after 20 minutes, I left. I was hauled up for my absence next day; and said I had in fact gone. As in the US "double jeopardy" rule, it seemed you couldn't be tried for the same offence twice – and I was let off that one too!

UN-GREEN FINGERS

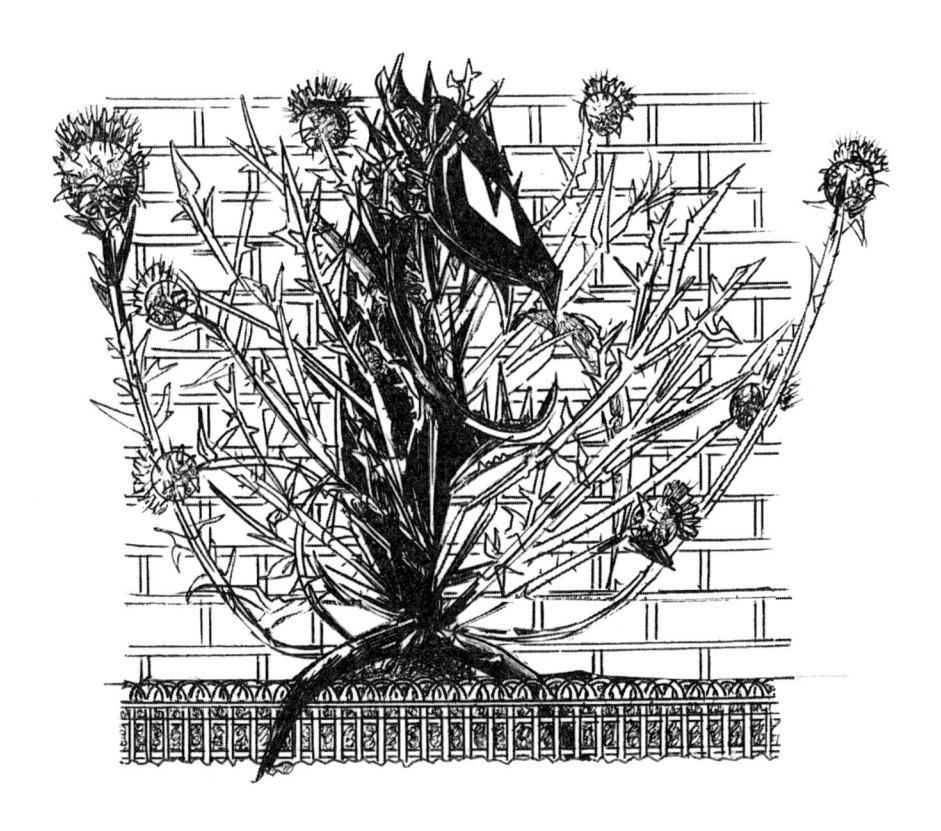

Having never been much of a gardener, I have learned that I need plants which survive *despite* me; not because of me. It's pretty hard to kill a cactus – but I managed it. Mine stood on a window sill for a year, until I realised it was just an outer husk, killed by over-enthusiastic watering. Venus fly-traps have captivated me since childhood; but never could I resist feeding them flies before the traps were mature, just to see them snap shut. The insects didn't nourish the traps; always, after killing their prey, they turned black, withered and died. Once, a tall, furry-leaved plant with delicate blue flowers grew in my garden. I was proud, cultivating it carefully until a neighbour said,

"You do know that's a *weed*, don't you?"

And I bought 'dwarf' variety trees for my rockeries which were supposed to be very slow-growing. Within five years, they had turned into monsters, obscuring all light through the windows. To make way for a builders' skip, I was ordered to dig them up during a house extension. I felt awful doing it, but despite lengthy advertising, offering them for free, I couldn't *pay* people to take them: nor would any park have them either; because as conifers, they weren't indigenous species.

Shortly after I moved into my first property, an enormous thistle grew. It looked so formidable I didn't dare touch it; so prickly were its thorns and stalk. Eventually, I couldn't stand the sight of it; it was the subject of gossip the whole close over; as the other neighbours didn't want its seed spreading; and with yellow petals sprouting from the top, I knew its days were numbered. Finally, one Saturday, I decided to tackle it. That thistle was a true survivor: the previous owner had installed a white picket fence with loops perhaps 20cm high. To maximise its chances of staying firmly tethered, the monster thistle had grown a *double* root, each fork plunging either side of that fence! I got a spade and began digging, as the old folk gathered around in a gossiping semi-circle to watch my progress. That root seemed never-ending – but after digging and levering, yanking and cajoling for what seemed an eternity, up it came, to the cheers of the spectators. I enjoy embellishing the story, saying it *screamed* like a mandrake when it came out of the ground... My friend persuaded me to bring the whole uprooted thing over to his parents' house in a dustbin liner. At midnight, we crept out and re-planted the giant thistle in the middle of his dad's most prized flower bed. Without a word to anyone, the man dug it up and disposed of it the next day...

My pride and joy was a six-foot-tall Yukka plant I bought for £24 from a nearby garden centre. I had this in a huge pot in my lounge corner, watering it only occasionally. All was well for a few years; then suddenly, one Sunday, whilst relaxing on the couch watching TV, I heard an ominous cracking noise. Before my eyes, *every* leafy branch fell away one by one from the main stem, leaving nothing but the tiniest green shoot at soil level. I couldn't believe it: it was as if the plant had made an active decision to die there and then! I was really disappointed, but replanted the remaining shoot. Believe it or not, over 25 years later, it still survives; and has formed a thin, woody stem of its own. But it stopped at two feet and never grows higher. I hoped it might be an aerial root, which would become as big as the original – but it just refuses to grow. The *only* long-term success I have ever had with plants is with heathers. They need little maintenance and seem to come back repeatedly from the dead. So, if you're anything like me, useless at growing anything, go for them.

VOLUNTARY SERVICE UNION

Once you reached the Fourth Year of our grammar school, if you wanted to be a conscientious objector and avoid square-bashing with the Army, RAF or Navy via the Combined Cadet Force (CCF), your only choice was to opt for VSU – Voluntary Service Union. This involved doing odd jobs every Thursday afternoon around the homes of elderly residents who lived nearby. If we were lucky, we got a lift part of the way by minibus, but always, it was a long walk back. You didn't get much say in who you were allocated each week; and it could make the difference between a cushy afternoon and hard labour. It's probably okay to name the old folk now at least by their surnames; all must be long gone – as even the youngest were well into their 70s in the early 1980s.

The toughest person to be sent to was Miss Tindall; a humourless, well-off, smartly-dressed woman who lived up a flight of steps in a large detached house set back from the road. She never let us inside, which meant staying out in freezing weather for a good two hours; sweeping up an enormous mountain of leaves which always seemed to gather within the bounds of her property. Never once did she offer us a brew or thank us for the work. When we rang the doorbell at the end, she would come out with a sour, suspicious look, cast her gimlet eye over the job and say something critical, or at best, grudgingly accepting. That was it – we were just used as dogsbodies.

Then there were the types who had us there on the vague pretence that they needed work doing; but who, more than anything, were just lonely and craved a little human contact. Old Mr Oakes was one of these; my brother was assigned to him; but an artist friend and I got to hear about him and hijacked the placement; the main advantage being that this old man lived much nearer to the school and we could get ice-creams from the van along the way. He just sat there in his armchair; and after a few minutes' conversation and perhaps a cup of tea, said little, read his paper and simply seemed glad of the company. My friend and I were obsessed with Life Drawing at that time; and this wizened, bespectacled specimen was too good a subject to resist. We brought large wooden drawing boards with us on which we taped sheets of cartridge paper. Each of us began drawing him; we should have asked permission really, but I don't think the old man even got a say in it. In any event, it wasn't long before we all had an attack of laughter... I can't remember who started it – probably me – but in any event, it was contagious, spreading like wildfire. Soon, all three of our drawing boards were shaking visibly as we hid behind them, tears of mirth streaming down our cheeks. Poor Mr Oakes must have picked up on something; as the service manager received a complaint that all we did was draw him; and the three of us were swiftly re-allocated.

Looking back on it, it really was quite a leap of faith all those frail old folk took letting a group of strapping young lads, each infinitely larger and stronger than they were, into their homes. It was opening the door, potentially, to literally *anything* occurring; but thankfully, the hearts of our crowd were more-or-less in the right place; mild pranking around being the worst that occurred.

The most regular of all my visits over those four years was to the home of Miss Munton; a tiny 85 year-old lady with one eye, who lived in a one-bedroom bungalow sunk below street level. You had to descend a set of concrete steps to reach her front door; and her back garden was a veritable orchard of apple trees... The rooms were all minute and she had virtually *nothing* in the house, a small, framed sepia photograph of a relative in World War 1 uniform and a silver brush is all I can recall. I don't think she even had a TV... I went there with a combination of different friends over the years; although I'm sure I was the most consistent visitor for the old lady. One half-starved member of our group stole apples from her trees and ate them one after another while we waited for her to open the front door. At first, she would insist on making us tea; but her hand trembled so much as she brought in the cups on saucers that there would be a virtual fountain plopping out of each, leaving us in paroxysms of laughter. The three of us took it in turns from then on to make the tea; as there was only room for one in the minuscule kitchen – it was more of a cabin. We probably mistook Miss Munton as simpler than she was; for one day, the old dear felt the need to say, rather nervously,

"You know, I do enjoy having you all... as long as you're not making a monkey-puzzle out of me..."

It wasn't a phrase we had heard before, but we got the general gist of it; and, exchanging worried glances, thinking she may be on the verge of reporting us for misbehaviour, we fell over ourselves to assure her that, no, we weren't ridiculing her. It would have been a costly placement to lose, as we were always warm and dry there; in addition to which she hardly ever made us do any work!

After a few more visits, though, it was clear the old lady absolutely loved the youthful mischief and laughter we brought her each week. I'm not saying offences didn't occur: she once got me to open a new packet of biscuits saved especially for our visit. Eyeing us evilly behind her back, my villainous friend quite unforgivably slid one onto the floor behind her foot, so that with her next wholly predictable step backwards, she ground it deep into the carpet with her tartan slipper. I was simultaneously appalled, yet bent double in hysterics; my two friends quick to drop me in it:

"Miss Munton: Guy's making a monkey-puzzle out of you!" – which left me spluttering a vigorous denial as they sniggered conspiratorially. But always I felt the old lady cut me some slack; for I was by far the littlest and least intimidating of our group.

I don't think we ever found out how she came to lose the missing eye: it was both horrific yet fascinating at the same time; the top eyelid permanently sewn shut, the lower rim moist with a glistening layer of mucus. Somehow, it must have entered my subconscious; because one day, between visits, I had the most *awful* nightmare. It was so vivid, it seemed it was really happening. The group of us had gone as usual to visit Miss Munton, but when we knocked on the door, there was no answer... We pushed and it opened – but the house was empty. I walked right through to the back where there was a pair of patio doors; white curtains billowing open to the garden. With an increasing sense of foreboding, I passed through them and up the lawn, to an allotment at the far end. There, to my horror, I discovered Miss Munton lying on her back, half-buried among the vegetables; her abdominal cavity open, exposing all her internal viscera at soil-level – she had been murdered... While I would never have dreamed of upsetting the old lady with the details, I literally couldn't *wait* to visit her that week to see she was okay – and she was, of course, absolutely fine.

THE THREE PEAKS WALK

To complement the obligatory VSU, I also joined up for The Duke of Edinburgh's Award Scheme. In order to qualify for each of the Bronze, Silver and Gold badges, you had to fulfil the increasingly difficult requirements of four categories: Service, Expedition, Skills and Physical Recreation, with a Residential project added at Gold Level. The far-off Gold seemed a worthy long-term goal, with a chance for those rare few completing it to receive the award at Buckingham Palace, direct from the hand of Prince Philip, the Duke himself... The Award was also a qualification held in the highest regard when applying for this or that in later life; speaking volumes about the character and tenacity of those seeing it through to completion. You had a little dark green booklet to be signed by those in authority for each target completed; and I sailed relatively easily through the Bronze requirements, doing an old lady's shopping each week for Service and for the Expedition, a 15-mile camping trip through the Peak District in Derbyshire. This included crossing the village of Eyam, which famously quarantined itself off from the world during an outbreak of the Black Death in 1665. For Skills I did Aikido; and to satisfy the Physical Recreation aspect, the rather tenuous "Dog-walking" – something I had to do anyway! There were similar, more advanced tasks to satisfy all the Silver criteria too. The only target I had outstanding for that badge was the Expedition – which, unbeknown to me, was to prove an Achilles' heel of the worst kind...

The Expedition at Silver level had to be 30 miles long – a daunting prospect to say the least (50 miles for the Gold being quite unimaginable). Before going, we had to practise tent-pitching, plan a balanced diet and familiarise ourselves with compass and map-reading skills, plus the route itself. When the time arrived, we were driven over to the Yorkshire Dales National Park with heavy rucksacks and waterproof clothing; to tackle the infamous Three Peaks of the Pennine range. I was, I regret, something of a soft underbelly back then; inexperienced, insufficiently fit and wholly unprepared for such a test of endurance. We were to do one of the Peaks each day, pitching our tents on suitable fields after asking each farmer's permission.

"Aye," agreed one rough-ass example; pointing to a beaten-up wooden door in the stone wall. "There's the sh*t an' piss house; and don't you go buggering up them lasses neither!"

The first day's walk, up the peak named Pen-y-ghent, was by far the easiest, with even a little sunshine breaking through – but the second was an unmitigated nightmare. To say the weather was poor is an understatement: it rained the *whole* time; and the peak we were climbing, the tallest of the three – Whernside – seemed, at 736m, never-ending... No sooner would you reach what seemed the top than you discovered it was just a plateau, with an equal distance to go looming just on the horizon. My brother, also on the trip, was on the verge of feeling he couldn't continue; I did my best to encourage him by promising him we would do it together – but I was struggling myself. Always just above us were groups of mountain goats clinging effortlessly to the dangerous precipices and laughing down at us... I kid you not: anyone with first-hand experience of goats knows they enjoy taunting humans; and this particular strain seemed spawned by hell itself. Most infuriating of all, though, was an ultra-fit Chinese lad in our group who made no allowances for the slower pace of everyone else; ploughing on ahead like a super-efficient automaton. A fog came down so thickly you could barely see your hand in front of your face, let alone the person in front; and until it lifted, we were solely dependent on compass skills to keep us safe. The walk down was just as perilous, if not more so, than the ascent – you really felt the steepness in your calves; by the time we reached base camp, I had a mass of agonising blisters on which to face the final peak, Ingleborough. It was either do it or quit; that, for me, wasn't an option.

To my disbelief, upon our return to school, an ultra-keen student from the Expedition went behind our backs to the head of the Duke of Edinburgh's Award Scheme, asking him to fail the whole lot of us for low morale. That teacher only took up the plonker's suggestion and did so, refusing to pass us on the spurious grounds that there was "insufficient carbohydrate" in our provisions! I was *gutted*: the trip we had done was an enormous test of endurance – three days of real physical pain and sacrifice which, under the prevailing weather conditions, left us at genuine risk of hypothermia – all, now, for nothing...

This same teacher also happened to teach me 'A' Level English; he was a colossal egotist; with a mind-numbingly dull approach. I wasn't disruptive, but I was so bored, I ended up doodling through each lesson. One day, he got so exasperated, he jumped off his stool, raising it as if to throw it in my direction. Unfortunately, one of its legs struck the metal housing of a low neon light, bringing the entire frame down on his own head. He then erupted at me; but as a Sixth-Former, I was bolder than a couple of years previously: it remains the only time I ever talked back to a teacher.

"Perhaps if you didn't always take the lead role yourself, it might be more engaging!" I said, leaving him completely speechless. I was saved by the bell, but fearing repercussions, went and apologised a day or so later. In fairness to him, the teacher graciously conceded,

"I suppose I did rather fly off the handle myself..." It cleared the air; and a couple of months later, long after the dust had settled and we were getting on better, he raised the prospect of another 30-mile Expedition.

"Well, will this one actually *count* towards the Silver?" I asked.

"Uhhh – no," he murmured, "We're treating it as a practice run; a 'mock', if you like..."

"In that case," I said, "you know what you can do with your Expedition!" Which did result in an accepting, good-natured chuckle.

That pretty much marked the end of my involvement in the Duke of Edinburgh's Award Scheme. Everything except the Expedition was already signed off for my Silver badge; and I would have dearly loved to secure the coveted Gold Award. But the whole club was run so ineptly back then, its very existence seemed sporadic. Pressure from other subjects soon made further commitment impossible for me. It was difficult to get access to the Scheme outside of school; and back then, you were only permitted to participate until the age of 24; years when I was immersed in my degree. As someone who completes *everything*, it remains a galling flaw in my track record: a loose end and a lasting regret. But hey – nobody's perfect...

THE AWKWARD PREDICAMENT

One summer, a good schoolfriend and I went down to visit my tiny grandma for a week in Bournemouth. Using her flat as a base, we had an absolute blast: boating around the lake and playing crazy golf at Poole Park, competing on arcade machines, eating fish and chips and Indian food, having frenzied water fights on the beach, flirting with girls and going to the pictures. My grandma seized an immediate liking to my pal, even making him his own apple pie; even I didn't get one; and I was her grandson! But just as we were due to leave, she gestured animatedly for him to come into her bedroom. Taking my friend towards a wardrobe, she urged in a hushed tone:

"Listen, listen: you take these home..." – then pulled out a load of my late grandfather's off-white drawers: long underpants which looked as if they dated right back to the turn of the century...

"Oh no, really – I couldn't!" he spluttered, trying to extricate himself from the awkward situation.

But my grandma was having none of it.

"You *will* have them!" she cried. "They'll suit a nice young man like you!"

And because he didn't want to upset her, he had to accept a whole bagful of the unwanted kecks. It was so funny: you could see the poor lad's predicament; but there was nothing he could do to dissuade my grandma – she had made up her mind they were to be his. So he took them home – where he and his dad burnt them on the fire.

OUTDOOR ANTICS

As children, my brother and I were obsessed by frogs and toads and the thrill of catching them. There was no shortage of amphibians in the rural countryside of Bucklebury, where we spent three idyllic years growing up. At the bottom of our close lay the foundations of a housing project which was begun without planning permission and abandoned when consent was refused. All the shallow brickwork, left open to the elements, had filled up with rainwater and became known to us as "The Bog" – an overgrown mass of individual ponds teeming with caddis fly and dragonfly larvae, water boatmen, frogs, toads and newts. Unaware of the toilet connotations of the name, my little brother was even sent to the Head one day for innocently writing in his News journal:

"I went to the bog; and there was a frog in the bog and I caught it."

An older girl and boy from up the road introduced us to the site; impressing us with their daring. Lighting individual blades of wheat with a match, they puffed on them in semi-awareness of "smoking grass." I once saw a metre-high, green shoot burst out of that marshland, shrieking upward before my eyes. As far as any eight-year-old might interpret it, I had witnessed a miracle and never told a living soul; although the weight of my boot on soggy ground may have forced something up from beneath. There were frogs of every shape and size; and we learned the hard way how *not* to treat them: a whole bucketful we caught boiled alive in their water one awful, scorching lunchtime. We still beat ourselves up for that as adults; but I suppose it's how kids learn.

Animal life was less easy to find once we moved to the vastly more urban city of Leicester; but it wasn't long before we found out about "Beaumont Hall" – a stately home in a setting commonly known as The Botanic Gardens. In the grounds of this paradise of flora and fauna was a long stone pond; although having arrived in November, we couldn't fully explore it until the spring. As soon as the amphibious mating season arrived in what must have been around late February or early March 1976, my brother and I were raring to go in pursuit of our prey; persuading our mother to take us up there in the car. He was the real animal enthusiast, but his excitement was contagious. Up and down he ran with a net in his baggy coat, marvelling in excitement. We had never seen anything like it: the stagnant green water was *heaving* with mating frogs; the males gripping the females' backs so tightly whilst fertilising the eggs, they were in real danger of suffocation; in some cases, several males fighting to mount the *same* female. Masses of cold, jellyish frog spawn clung to the sides of the pond; the occasional long strings of rarer toad spawn visible also in the murky depths. Obviously we couldn't take mating pairs home, only singletons; and within minutes, I had caught "Superfrog:" a dark, slimy specimen who looked more like a toad. Well, of course, my brother *had* to get one himself then. Impeded a little by his glasses, he stretched out for a fine example swimming alone, misjudged the distance – and lost his balance...

With an almighty splash, he plunged head-first into the freezing, filthy water. I like saying there was actually *ice* on the pond's surface to add dramatic emphasis, but that's an exaggeration. Nevertheless, it must have been hideously cold and deep; and the following minutes were high drama; my mother, who couldn't swim, gasped in horror as he flailed, coughing and spluttering in the water, coat billowing out around him as it filled with liquid. Luckily, he wasn't far from the side and managed to reach her outstretched hand. Out she hauled him, his teeth chattering uncontrollably, all his clothes dripping with teeming rivulets of water. He was in real danger of catching hypothermia and she had to run full-pelt for the car to bring it to the nearest exit as I guided my shivering brother towards it.

"I'm gonna die, I'm gonna die," he wailed in panic, but luckily, we were only minutes from home; after rushing him into a hot bath, all was well — bar the fact that, for all his efforts, he'd failed to catch a frog of his own! Had I been a nicer older brother, I would have given him mine; but I didn't.

The Botanic Gardens was also connected to another pond site, which we learned about from schoolfriends later in the year. It was off a narrow dirt track called Blackthorn Lane, part of which remained unadopted in the 1970s. There, in addition to frogs and toads, was the added lure of an elusive, protected species: the Great Crested Newt. At six inches long, much larger than their plain, beige, common or palmate cousins, these magnificent creatures were like glossy, black salamanders, with a livid orange fire pattern on their bellies. Only the males had the crest on their back; they were stunning creatures; and the lad next door even put an inflatable swimming pool on his balcony in which to keep several pairs. Of course they escaped; some plunging over the side and a couple getting into his bedroom. It was the now-legendary hottest summer in 200 years — and six of us kids headed down to Blackthorn Lane in pursuit of that famous newt. Chattering excitedly, it never occurred to us that we might be trespassing, so intent were we on our objective.

All of a sudden, there came a roaring *"OI!!!"*

We swung around in terror to find ourselves faced with an enormous, double-barrelled shotgun aimed directly at us; at the other end of which was an incandescent, old-school groundsman dressed in breeches, with the most fearsome handlebar moustache imaginable. In my mind's eye, I can still see him now: you just knew he was the type to have a shedful of blasting gelignite, rabbits and pheasants killed in snares and an aggressive ferret in a cage.

"WHAT THE *HELL* ARE YOU LOT DOING IN HERE?" he growled belligerently. "THIS IS *PRIVATE* LAND!"

"W-we, we just, just wanted to catch some newts..." we spluttered ridiculously.

"*GET* OUT OF HERE – *ALL* OF YOU – BEFORE I BLOW YOUR *HEADS* OFF!" he bellowed, brandishing the gun menacingly. We couldn't get out of there fast enough; stumbling over each other in our panic to get out of the line of fire – we really thought we were going to be shot. Years later, I found out the fella's name: Sid Fritter. One of my next-door neighbours, himself a more recent worker for the Botanic Gardens, remembered that fearsome groundsman *solely* from my description: they don't make them like that anymore; and apparently he was a legendary local character. Our parents were genuinely alarmed when they heard about the incident, although I think they only semi-believed us – it must have sounded a tall story! He would be hauled over the coals if he ever traumatised children like that now; but then, this was the 1970s; a different world entirely.

Frogging wasn't the only illicit outdoor activity in our youth. Scrumping for plums aside, there was also a night-time craze for "garden creeping" through residential land. I was never that physically inclined; but many of my teenage peers were raving about their antics; some not such a nice lot. *"Guy is fat, Guy is slim, that's why we call him Slim Jim,"* they wrote on our form-room board... To see if their boasts were genuine, I dared a pair of them to come to my parents' garden dead on 10 o'clock one evening. On the promise I too received some form of trophy marking the occasion, I agreed to bring them a plateful of biscuits and drinks as a reward. I never expected the two of them to make it, as the task not only involved climbing over a series of adjacent fences, but also counting correctly in odd numbers; identifying, in full darkness, the correct garden to stop in! But I got the agreed supplies ready, looking out for them at the designated hour. To my amazement, dead on 10 p.m., I spotted a flurry of torchlit activity around our garden pond. Although it was relatively harmless, the intrusion wasn't something my parents would have welcomed; so I snuck out of the back door, bringing the pair their refreshments. In return, one of them fumbled in his pocket and brought out my "gift": a grimacing black and white passport photo of himself, eyelids turned inside out. Unbelievably, I still have it; and often wonder what happened to that lad: reportedly, he went off the rails a few years later, getting expelled and sent to Borstal after a 'dirty protest' at his community college. Anyway, suddenly there was a noise which alarmed the pair of them. Scaling the fence with a splintering of wood, the pair of them scarpered away into the night.

THE CABBAGE INCIDENT

Dinner-ladies, now known as Lunchtime Supervisors, were a different breed in my childhood. Armed with their little bit of power, they could be truly vindictive – some, I don't think, liked children at all. There were three dinner-ladies at our village primary school; and the boniest example had a horrid habit of sticking her finger in your mouth when she was telling you off. The Cook was the last word in authority to them; they were forever threatening to report you to her for misbehaviour in the dining hall. She was quite old, a heavily built lady in an all-white outfit, lips permanently twisted as if she had just swallowed a stinging nettle. Every day you would see her squidge a sample of each dish into a jar and screw the lid tight on the repulsive mix, obliged to retain small portions for testing in case there was a spate of food poisoning... One day, I heard the dinner-ladies asking a gentle giant in the top year why he wasn't eating as much as previously.

"I'm on a diet," he said.

"'EE'S ON A *DIET!*" they cackled cruelly at the top of their voices, so that the whole Hall fell apart at him. I can still see the metallic water jugs and cups on those tables, garishly-coloured in red, green, blue, silver or gold. Whether you got a decent drink depended on whose turn it was to be in charge of dispensing it: if it was one of the nastier lads, they would soon contaminate the jug, leaving blobs of bread or other horrors floating inside which then got poured into your own cup.

There was one nice lady behind the hatch, a brunette with loud, vermillion, over-painted lips. But all she ever did was extend a loaded tablespoon, asking brightly in her ascending, soprano pitch:

"Salad cream?" and looking terribly crestfallen when you refused. But there she was, bouncing back like a jack-in-the-box the next day and the next, with the same hopeful spoon full of gloop:

"Salad cream? Salad cream?" – like one of those talking dolls with a string on a plastic loop pulled in and out to make it speak. For three and a half years I refused the stuff: there were only 100 kids in that school, and you'd think she'd learn who liked it – but no: right to the end, there she was: "Salad cream? Salad cream?" (the same disapppointed look on her face whenever you refused it).

At least on Fridays they served chips, and there were some good sweets like jam roly-poly or treacle pudding in wide-rimmed, white bowls. Occasionally, the call "Seconds!" would go up – and there would be a free-for-all to be first in line.

"Massive!" this one obese boy in my class used to demand.

"Andrew – you'll get fat!" the Cook warned him sternly – but he was already fat.

Mostly, disgusting desserts were served: semolina, rice pudding with a gob of jam in it, or translucent tapioca: "frogs' eggs" we used to call it. In those days it was less than thirty years after World War 2 and you *had* to eat what you were given: if you didn't like something and there was too much left on your plate when you went up to scrape it away into the pig-slop bucket, the lady in charge of it would send you back to your table to eat more. By far the worst day was Thursday.

"What's for lunch?" we would ask excitedly, the dinner-lady squawking one awful, minimal word:

"ROAST!"

'Roast' consisted of one meagre hemisphere of mashed potato, a couple of slices of grey-brown beef in watery gravy and a heap of revolting, overcooked mush which was once cabbage. It *stank* before you even reached the serving hatch; and was put on your plate whether you liked it or not.

Now one lunchtime, the dish for the day happened to be salad. Working through it, I came to an unfamiliar mass of pale green, evil tasting, raw, grated *cabbage*. That's a dirty trick, I thought; they'll not get it down me that way either! I knew I'd get sent back if I tried to clear it into the swill; so although it was naughty, I scraped as much as possible into my metal cup; hiding the rest in a pocket to bin once safely in the playground. Triumphantly, I headed outside; but someone must have "snitched" on me; for up stalked the bony dinner-lady, clear relish in her croaking voice:

"Oi! The Cook heard what you did today; and she says tomorrow, you're gonna have a whole plateful of hot cabbage!" The ground tilted before my eyes and I felt sick, thinking about it all night, and next morning; hoping the Cook would forget. But no sooner was I up at the hatch than...

"*OH* yes! Maybe this'll teach you not to waste good food..." To my disbelief, she dumped the most colossal pile of steaming hot cabbage onto my plate – there was nothing else. An 'example' was being made of me, everyone in the Hall was staring. Word had got around: I was a public spectacle.

Sitting down at my table, it wasn't long before I began to cry. It's actually a *huge* thing, as a child, being made to eat something you don't like. Of course I couldn't eat that cabbage; couldn't even begin to... One by one, everyone finished and got up to leave, until there was just me sitting there.

"If you're going to keep crying, you can go and sit on the babies' table!" said another dinner-lady sharply; then a few moments later, "RIGHT! Go and sit there!" I found myself alongside the youngest 4+ Reception children, food dripping down their bibs as they were wiped down roughly; smiling and looking at me curiously as if I was a novelty... Even they were taken out; until I was the very last child in the dinner-hall. The tables were all being wiped down and stacked;

and still, there I sat. It wouldn't be long until afternoon lessons commenced: I knew I had to do something.

I waited until I was sure no one was looking in my direction; then taking my knife, placed it in the centre of the cabbage heap, pushing the contents to the periphery until it formed a 'moat' with a large, clear space in the centre. Then, with just five minutes to spare, I took my plate up to the slops bin, lying blatantly:

"Look – I *have* eaten some!"

Thankfully the lady 'bought' what was, in hindsight, a rather enterprising ruse for an eight year-old to devise; and I was free to go. But as soon as she heard about it, in went my mum like a bull:

"Don't you *EVER* force my child to eat something he doesn't want to!" Clearly she rattled the Cook enough for her to complain to the Head; for next day I got called out of my lesson into the corridor.

"What's all this nonsense, boy?" he barked; slack jowls vibrating. "The Cook's very unhappy with you. Never in all my born days..." But I said nothing, just hung my head silently – and he could only huff and puff for so long before he had to let me go. And never again was I made to eat cabbage.

THE HAVE-A-GO HERO

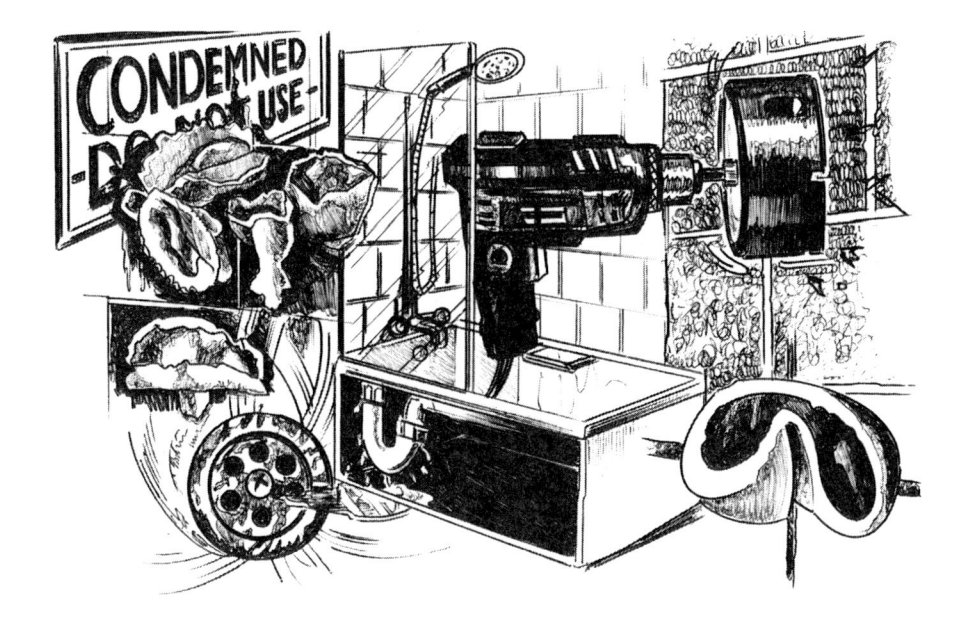

One day, I went into my bathroom to find the carpet soaking wet. I'm not a huge fan of carpet in the bathroom anyway, but it was already fitted when I moved in. Anyway, I dried the damp area with towels; but next day, found it soaked again, with no indication as to how. At that time there was a seldom-used bath in there, with a shower and screen I favoured more. I decided to investigate, reaching under the rim of the bath and pulling back the front panel to discover, on the far wall, these weird, semi-translucent mushrooms growing on the plaster: peziza fungi; which only flourishes in the presence of moisture: a sure sign there was a leak. It had to come from the plughole. I felt around the rough fibreglass mould until I got the right area: sure enough, it was wet underneath. Perhaps the seal had gone. I wondered if I might be able to tighten the connection by dismantling and reassembling the plug, which is what I decided to do. I had no training or competence whatsoever in plumbing, so was going in blind, trying to be Mr Fix-it. I took the entire mechanism apart; but it wasn't quite as easy as I'd imagined to reassemble. The task made me contort like a sloth: in order to tighten the seal, I had to have one hand inside the bath while the other was underneath. Anyway, I hoped I'd done an okay job; only time would tell.

Alas, within a couple of days, the carpet was soaked again. I'd had enough of pulling it up and drying it out – it was time to defer to a professional. You learn, once you find a good, honest and reliable tradesperson, to stick to them like glue. They're a rare breed, and although I would never let any of them go without at least *some* money, a few seem not to care for it at all: just grateful to be working, they seem to do the job almost for the love of it. My plumber was one of those; if you gave him a tenner and a bottle of plonk to take away with him, he was more than happy...

"John, mate!" I said to him, trying to get him on side; "I did have a crack at it myself; I took the panel off, you know; had a little go at retightening it – I mean you gotta have a try, haven't you...?" Although my brother and he didn't get on, he did like me: and I hoped he'd approve of my efforts.

"Yeah, it dun't hurt to try," he conceded gruffly.

"I don't know how good a job I did, though," I went on. "Chances are I didn't do it tight enough, so you might feel a couple of drops escaping..."

John crouched down, natal cleft exposed in the way of so many workmen; and ran the bath tap, putting his hand under the housing again and feeling for the plug. Turning around with an incredulous expression, he snorted derisively,

"A coupla' drops? It's *PISSIN'* it down!"

"Oh no!" I said, having a job keeping my face straight. "That'll be down to my meddling then..."

"*YEAH!*" he growled emphatically.

Of course the problem was resolved quickly with a full replacement plug mechanism from the D.I.Y. store, a bead of silicone sealant to keep it in place and the use of some powerful glowing bar heaters left on to dry out the plaster. Happy with his bottle of red wine and £10 note, John went on his way. But it wasn't long before I had to call him out again.

All the bungalows in the close had been built together, with the same boiler installed in each. Although I did have mine serviced each year, it was the first time I had seen *real* soot before – vile stuff: even a small amount can make a horrendous mess. I'd been warned that a couple of the other bungalow owners in the close had had near-misses in the past; one even carried out with carbon monoxide poisoning; which didn't exactly fill me with confidence. And then one winter's night, I was awoken at 2.30 a.m. by the most violent metallic banging. To my astonishment, the noise was emanating from the boiler: it's no stretching of the truth to say it sounded as if a *man* was inside it, kicking it... Frightened it was going to explode, I immediatedly switched everything off and called out an engineer first thing in the morning. A nasty little fella he was, with a little brown moustache; clearly suffering from short-man syndrome, he wielded his power ruthlessly.

"Whaddayou expect?" he said. "It's 14 years old!" And with that, he slapped a "CONDEMNED" sticker on the front. It was only a few days until Christmas.

"I'll consult the trade and get back to you," he promised. I never heard from him again. That's how old people can die... By December 23rd, I was freezing; and, with no hot water or central heating, was absolutely livid. Finally, the elusive engineer chose to answer his phone and I challenged him.

"Err, excuse me?" he said; "Excuse me? I am entitled to a holiday, you know..." I couldn't hold back any more; and throwing caution to the wind, unleashed a torrent of verbal abuse at him – after which he hung up. It made me feel better, but I knew I had now burned that bridge entirely.

"I'll have a look round and see what I can get you," said John, knowing my income wasn't great. Until he put me in the picture, I had no idea that the trade shuts down completely over the festive season; not re-starting until around a week into January! That truly *was* a chilled Christmas – just me and my faithful black Labrador huddled shivering in only a metre of warmth from the lounge fire... But good ol' John showed up with a brand new combi-boiler within days of the New Year. I'd never seen a drill-bit so gigantic: 12 inches in diameter with a diamond tip; the grizzled old chap went straight through the breeze blocks with it. Showering him with excess praise, I said,

"You're a true craftsman, John." He flushed the system and removed my old cylinder; along with labour, the total job cost £1200 – nothing by today's standards – but a lot then. There's always a silver lining, though. I was about to try something entirely different from Teaching, but the necessity to recoup those funds steered me into supply instead – where I stayed another 16 years!

THE HOSPITAL BREAK-IN

Why I was part of this I really can't tell you; the only possible explanation being an excess of energy and susceptibility to peer pressure. I had taken the train to Liverpool in April 1989 to visit an ex-school buddy, my best friend back then. His body-clock had gone rather haywire, as he'd hired studio space in an abandoned sweet factory; in which he would paint feverishly through the night, sleeping most of the next day. His state of mind couldn't have been aided by the fact that sugar from decades of confectionery production had impregnated the very walls of the building; an overpowering, cloying sweetness hitting you as soon as you entered. Imagine spending months in that environment! Because I was visiting, my friend suspended his normal routine to show me his favourite haunts.

I particularly recall the abandoned docks, relics of a once thriving cargo and shipyard trade; and an absolutely historic announcement before the curtain rose at a stage play:

"Following the tragedy at Hillsborough today, we'd like everyone to observe a one minute silence in memory of the victims..." The pair of us exchanged bewildered glances; neither of us had seen the news. I'd been in transit on the journey up and he was busy with other stuff. What on earth had happened? It was only afterwards that we heard about the dreadful crushing of Liverpool and Nottingham Forest fans at the Sheffield football stadium; the highest death toll in British sporting history; spawning legal action running on for decades and a major inquiry into police misconduct.

The next day, my friend was eager to show me the site of a derelict hospital he was curious about. It did seem interesting to explore; however, the building was locked within a barrier of rusty green iron railings, bisected only by a crumbling, standalone toilet block. If we could get through that, we were in. There was only the narrowest of windows, but we managed to squeeze through; and, dusting off the cobwebs and flaking plaster, found we had secured the coveted access. True, it wasn't anyone's house, but in hindsight, it was at best trespassing; and (although we never stole a thing or committed any other offence), technically 'breaking and entering'; even though the window was open. It was also a highly dangerous act: the place was deserted; and structurally, we had no idea how hazardous it was; much of it in a state of partial demolition. But back in our early 20s, perhaps having been influenced by seeing Tucker and his mates break into a building site on the kids' TV show *Grange Hill,* we had a similar devil-may-care sense of being indestructible.

The hospital itself was one vast, open block. We had brought torches; and made our way gingerly through what seemed a mass of fibreglass loft insulation, each step we took raising dust clouds up to our knees in the darkness. The place was *ancient*, almost certainly Victorian; at one point, we came to a foreboding-looking, wrought iron spiral staircase leading down to a basement. We couldn't even begin to imagine the horrors performed down there; it conjured up stories my cockney grandfather used to tell of his younger days in quarantine with tuberculosis; worst, the time he was moved downstairs to a level from which, it was murmured in hushed voices, no one returned. Down there, we found the hidden remains of former operating theatres, some with the most hideous-looking surgical tables and archaic medical equipment, not to mention syringes with terrifying needles over a foot-and-a-half long. The ground beneath our feet on the level above didn't feel all that stable; we took each step with care, lest we fell through the very ceiling. After a good hour, having progressed deep into the bowels of the old hospital, we began to hear a searing, high-pitched rasp, increasing in volume as we approached. Some form of construction or cutting work was under way: the place wasn't as isolated as we'd assumed! Careful not to draw attention to ourselves; upon reaching a corner at the end of a corridor, we peered tentatively around it towards the source of the noise. There, in the eerie blackness, was a bizarre sight: what appeared to be an illuminated tent, incandescent with light. Three figures, encased in what looked like white welders' suits with heavy visors obscuring their faces and oxygen cylinders on their backs, were entering and leaving, wielding strange tools and passing artefacts to each other we couldn't identify. What *were* they up to? It was pretty unnerving – and certainly our cue to leave.

We were about to exit through a side door at the outer shell of the building when I spotted an old wall-mounted Bakelite telephone. Was the line still connected? Our curiosity got the better of us and I lifted the receiver... At first there was deathly silence; then a staccato voice suddenly barked *"HELLO?"*

It was the *last* thing either of us expected – and that was it – we lost our nerve. I slammed down the receiver and we legged it out of that godforsaken place, back to the railings, back through the toilet block, up through the tiny window to freedom and the sunlight of the familiar world beyond.

The experience did leave me quite troubled for some time after; a vestige of unease persisting even to the present day; for I realized it was almost certain that the work being done in such protective gear by those illuminated figures (in breathing apparatus) was the removal of some hazardous material; the most likely being asbestos. For all we know, the dust clouds raised by every step we took was that very substance becoming airborne: whatever it was, we breathed it in. The most toxic form of asbestos, once inhaled, stays dormant for decades, symptoms of asbestosis only presenting themselves 20 to 30 years after exposure. Once it does manifest, you're pretty much done for; although hopefully we're in the clear by now. But please – *don't* do it, kids.

SLUG

Our grandparents lived on the first floor of a scenic block of flats. You could get to their apartment either via the stairs or in a shiny, sickly-brown lift; which operated with a droning hum. On the floor above them lived this unctuous, rather suspect bloke, known only by his surname – Taylor – a tall, lanky, bespectacled retiree with an over-toothy grin. Always in a black suit, he had no empathy for children whatsoever. Our grandma detested him, only ever referring to him as "Slug." Opposite Slug lived his 90-year-old mother, "Mrs Taylor". Betwixt the two of them, they owned that entire floor. We kids got up to all manner of mischief; our older cousin's favourite prank being to press *all* the outside intercom buttons together, so we heard every confused resident calling, "Hello? Hello?" out of the grille. We often took a short cut to the toyshop, bursting through the foliage in the long back garden to the road on the other side. It hardly endeared us to the residents basking in stripy deckchairs on their balconies; they were forever shouting out, trying to intercept us; our grandpa getting the backlash when our conduct was raised at the next committee meeting. Once, we snuck out of bed with pre-prepared thermos flasks, meeting friends in a bus shelter for a midnight feast of baked beans. We even got into a famous floral garden, Compton Acres, running amok in the early morning mist. Given today's security, you couldn't get away with it now.

The most amusing trick of all though, was to send the lift up to Slug's floor with no one in it. Taylor, you see, had a reputation for being incredibly nosy, wanting to know all the goings-on in the building. The moment he heard the lift, he would shoot out of his flat to see who it was. It must have been infuriating to find nobody inside… Even the green woodpecker, eternally at work on the trees opposite, knew it was us; without doubt, so did Slug: we played an eternal game of cat-and-mouse with him. Sometimes, we would even travel up to the floor above his, then send the lift down one floor, peering over the balcony to watch his torment as he burst out, braces hanging down as if he'd just got off the toilet. By the time we had been there a week or so, he must have been going spare with frayed nerves. Once, our little cousin, a few years younger, but equally full of mischief, wasn't quiet or quick enough getting away. Taylor caught him and began shaking him. "Get off me, Slug!" our cousin shouted in his rough Croydon accent, breaking free and escaping…

We certainly brought youth, vigour and a breath of fresh air to what was an over-sedate building. At least, that's how we saw it. Our proud grandma, forever showing us off, would telephone Mrs Taylor, never failing to mention each of our imminent visits. Always, the old dear would respond,

"Oh, you *must* bring them over for tea." We hated it: not only did we have to be on our best behaviour, but old Mrs Taylor insisted on preparing the cups of tea herself. She had the most horrible 'dewdrop' building almost constantly on the end of her nose; no sooner had one fallen than the next was forming: you just knew you'd get at least one drop of nasal mucus in your tea…

But one day, our grandpa, a successful furniture salesman in his former days, was heading down the corridor to his office at home, to read his "Pink Paper", more commonly known as the *Financial Times*. In a tiny ledger, he always kept a close eye on his stocks and shares, noting their progress up or down in the most minute handwriting. To his astonishment, on that particular morning, he caught Taylor there, *in* his office, blatantly trespassing and rooting through his private papers. Slug must have tried the front door, found it unlocked and seized the opportunity to ooze inside.

"Oi!" our Cockney grandad shouted in fury. "*Whadda* you think you're doing in 'ere? *GET* outa my 'ouse!" He really should have called the police. Taylor slunk out like the dodgy geezer he was: whatever information he was hoping to discover amid his crooked foraging, we shall never know.

LEARNING – THE ROUNDABOUT WAY

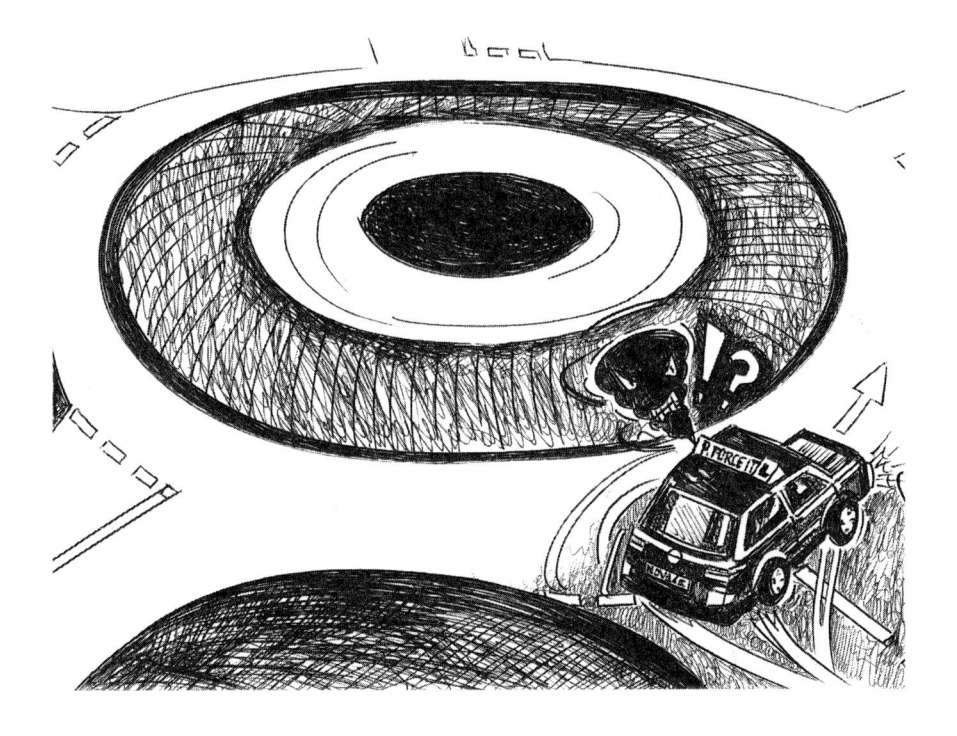

Soon after a lad on my school bus mentioned an ex-police driving instructor he'd done well with, my parents paid for me to have lessons once I turned 17. A huge bloke, this instructor was; with a flat, peaked cap, obviously winding down in his working years. I think his prostate was playing up, or at very least, his bladder; for without fail, he made me stop outside the same park every lesson so he could go and use the Gents. That wasn't as bad as the experience of a friend, who noticed his instructor's stick had white on its tip; by his second lesson, the white had gone all the way up the stick – the poor old fella was near-blind! It soon became apparent that my own instructor had no patience whatsoever, nor was he a good teacher. One minute he'd be fine; the next, totally lose his rag. Clearly he had assumed all trainee coppers were blockheads he had to yell at to drill anything into their skulls; and had become accustomed to behaving like that. I don't know why; he had dual control and could take over whenever he chose; but he would let his attention span drop; then only notice a near-disaster at the last minute. I didn't last long with him.

"Tight in! Tight in! Follow the bend of the road," he would bark. "Give it some gas!" – then, "You're going *too... FAST!*" He would take his eye off the road, engaging you in stupid chatter about his little brown and white mongrel dog – then suddenly go ballistic at something you'd done. People go for lessons because they *don't* know how to drive – they're there to make mistakes and learn!

My finest hour, clanger-wise, was an absolute flippin' *corker*. He said to me one peaceful Sunday,

"At the roundabout, turn right." Well we'd never done islands before; and, never having been all that observant when other people drove (I mean, why would anyone until the need arose for *them* to drive?) I didn't know how to use roundabouts; or that the procedure in order to go right was to go left around them. He'd said "turn right" and I took his instruction literally. *Right* I went...

"BLEEDIN' HELLFIRE!" he screamed, grabbing the wheel and twisting the car violently to safety. Luckily no other vehicles were passing around it at the time or we'd have been in major trouble...

"Do you know what'd 'appen if you did that on yer drivin' test?" he challenged me officiously: "This is what'd happen. The Examiner would make you pull over. 'Get out of the car,' he'd order ya, 'Oi... am... *terminatin'* this test in the *interests* of road safety.' And he'd leave you there by the roadside – he would; and you'd 'ave to wait there 'til your instructor came and picked you up."

After countless more of his outbursts I wrote a letter sacking him; although gallingly, my brother did go on to pass with the same bloke. My test was already imminent, however; and I failed for "over-confidence". A car was approaching in the distance at a 'T'-junction and I judged that I had time to go: I mean, some are also failed for being *over*-cautious. The Examiner felt differently, slammed on the brakes and I knew the game was up there and then. But I got a younger, infinitely calmer instructor, who instantly booked me a retake. After each manouevre, he would inform me if it was Pass or Fail standard – and two weeks later, his tuition had done the trick. The best people pass second time. Which was far better than my brother's friend, who failed on no less than *six* different occasions – the last, reputedly, for "swerving about in the road..." His Examiner told him,

"I'm sorry, but you've failed..." In absolute exasperation, the poor lad burst out:

"Yer not sorry – yer not sorry at *all!*"

THE PLASTER DISASTER

I am still in regular contact with my old grammar school Art teacher, whose room back then was a creative refuge from the pressurised drudgery of the rest of the curriculum. That easy-going teacher made me welcome even though I was notoriously untidy, to a point where he used to verbalise that, were he ever granted a brand new facility, he would get me back in to "mess it up" for him and make it feel more lived-in. My worst-ever offence took place in a back room reserved for ceramic work. The project in question never got beyond the "head" phase; but I had brought in the *Radio Times* blueprints for how to build a Dalek; an ambitious plan which would take months. The aliens were surprisingly large in size, well over five feet tall. I had already created the domed head out of clay; but in order to cast it, it first had to be covered in plaster of Paris to form a mould into which liquid fibreglass, plus a catalyst, could be poured. I had the head all ready on the work surface; apron on in preparation for the messy activity to follow. The Art teacher was committed elsewhere that afternoon overseeing the painting of Hall sets for a performance of Shakespeare's *Macbeth*; he couldn't be there to oversee things; however, as I was now a Sixth-Former, he was happy to leave me to it; warning I'd have to be fast, as plaster of Paris set quickly.

Excitedly, I set to work, covering the desks with a protective layer of newspaper and lubricating the clay to facilitate its easy removal from the plaster cast. I then began pouring the powder sachets into a large metal bucket, following the prescribed ratio of water to powder and stirring it constantly. After several minutes, nothing seemed to be happening; the mixture was way too thin and drippy to apply and I was getting fed up, so added a couple more sachets. All of a sudden, it began to thicken noticeably. Here we go, I thought, and began to lift big dollops of it; slapping it onto the clay. Not having planned sufficiently, though, I had left the bucket on the other side of the room, meaning crucial seconds were wasted crossing over and back; not to mention the plaster dripping from my hands onto the floor, desk legs and my own trousers. To my alarm, I could see the plaster in the bucket getting too thick now; I had no idea that when the reaction kicked in it would accelerate so fast; I now had to to wrench chunks out; and when I went to apply it, it broke apart, crumbling onto the floor and desk. In an attempt to soften up the remainder, I filled the top of the pail with water, adding another sachet and stirring; but the exothermic reaction was well out of control now; before I knew it the bucket was boiling hot and set solid, right to the brim. The fallout from my ineptitude was disastrous: not only had I utterly *nuked* the room, with every surface and myself covered with white dust, dribble and crumbs, but the clay itself was barely covered; the mould meant to be at least two inches thick. In hindsight, I was lucky worse didn't happen: plaster of Paris is now banned from many schools: pupils have lost *fingers* in it – and I had made a whole bucketful...

There was no one around to ask for help; and with the situation beyond me, I had to swallow my pride and run over to the Hall, confessing I was in trouble. A white-coated assistant took pity on me and came back over to the Ceramics room to survey the devastation. I thought I was going to get it in the neck, but she was wonderfully calm; while I cleared the mess as best I could, she made up more of the mixture a small amount at a time (which of course is what *I* should have done!) and we got the clay covered by the end of the afternoon. My own teacher did grumble somewhat about the state of the room, but that was it.

There was, however, another member of staff freshly recruited to the Art Department. To most of us, deprived of all female contact in a boys-only environment, a physical barrier between us and the girls' high school up the road, this new teacher was breathtakingly beautiful; dressing in what was really quite a provocative style, with cascading shoulder-length permed hair, flame-red lipstick, skirt revealingly above the knee, blue stockings and high-heels. In comparison to the few matronly women already on the staff, her figure was sheer dynamite, embodying our wildest fantasies; several of us had a real crush on her. If she as much as walked past the dinner queue, a collective gasp went up, not to mention some highly colourful sexist language muttered by the cruder lads under their breath. She happened to be there when I returned to the Ceramics room a few days later to see if the mould had dried out, remarking with concern about a prominent new double 'dent' I could see in the hardened plaster.

"Oh – that was me, Guy," confessed this utter vision with a teasingly saucy giggle. "I'm afraid I *sat* on it by accident! I hope I've not caused too much damage?" Caught between highly conflicting emotions, I didn't know whether to be flattered or furious. Ultimately, due to time constraints, I ended up abandoning the project; but it did get as far as the casting stage. And with the mixture having set in the mould, when the resulting dome was pulled out, there was the unmistakable bulge of her shapely rear end protruding from the fibreglass; preserved in its prime for all eternity.

MR B

I had a reputation at Secondary school as a notorious giggler. Whenever I was asked to read aloud, the room would become electric with anticipation: the whole class willing me, it seemed, to break down in nervous laughter. I seldom let them down. It took until I was around 14 to outgrow the habit; but footage still exists in outakes of student films when even then, I couldn't keep a straight face. Although I do laugh a great deal, I've always thought it's one of the rudest acts anyone can do to laugh directly in someone's face. Never would I *ever* have intended to do it – but it happened.

My brother and I had gone on a blissfully remembered holiday to Barbados in the West Indies. Staying in a relatively basic beach apartment, we found it riddled with monster cockroaches and had to have it treated on the first day. But it was just a base: we were out for most of the time in a canary yellow, 'mini-moke' buggy, travelling the length and breadth of the island. The hotel was run by a very big momma indeed: a lovely, charismatic lady who would go out every night, gambling simultaneously on a whole row of one-armed bandits. Her husband, known only as "Mr B," who must have been well into his 80s, spoke only in a *pidgin* English virtually indecipherable to our ears. Baked to the deepest brown after decades in the sun, he was stick thin; and appeared suddenly at the foot of the white stone stairs just as we were halfway up, holding an absolutely *rotten* black mango in each hand and gurgling in a gravelly voice something that sounded like this:

"ORIEURI-OM-UNI... GIWULASHI OMORGAW!!!"

"I'm sorry?" we asked; but Mr B just pushed the mangoes further forward, uttering the same line:

"ORIEURI-OM-UNI... GIWULASHI OMORGAW!!!"

Although we didn't understand the words, we could tell that he was offering us the mangoes as a welcome gift it would have been rude not to accept. Now don't get me wrong, I love mangoes; but I like them slightly *under*-ripe, if anything. These were just revolting and completely inedible – just vile brown mush inside – but I guess that's how Mr B enjoyed eating them.

The next day, the same thing happened. We were halfway up the stairs after our day out – and suddenly heard below us,

"ORIEURI-OM-UNI... GIWULASHI OMORGAW!!!"

We turned around to see Mr B at the foot of the stairs, again holding out two rotten mangoes.

"No – no thank you," we said, politely but firmly, heading upstairs; agreeing it was a little awkward. I had barely kept my face straight; and whilst driving home the following day, said to my brother,

"I don't know what i'm gonna do if Mr B's there waiting for us again with those rotten mangoes..." But to our relief, he was nowhere in sight.

"Let's go up really quietly," I whispered; and with the lightest footsteps, we began tiptoeing up the white stone steps.

"ORIEURI-OM-UNI!!! GIWULASHI OMORGAW!!!" came the now-familiar voice; even louder and more insistent. I turned around to see Mr B proffering a pair of even more foul, blackened mangoes than before – and that was *it*... any fight not to laugh was over. I was on the floor, doubled up right there in the proud old gentleman's face – I couldn't help myself. I think it was partly because we'd anticipated it: he was like a cuckoo emerging from a clock right on cue each day; as if we stepped on some invisible sensor alerting him exactly when to come out of his room.

I tried to apologise, but was completely inarticulate; leaving my brother to take over. He was laughing too, but at least managed to get me upstairs. That was the last time Mr B offered us mangoes; the poor bloke got the message, but I always felt bad for it: he was such a nice old fella...

THE SPACE INVADERS MACHINE

It's fairly common knowledge what a phenomenon the original Space Invaders was when it first appeared in UK arcades at the tail-end of Punk in 1979. Having been so popular in Japan that it actually caused a shortage in the Yen, it was a real cult thing; a craze adults almost universally disapproved of. The machines, rumoured to have been adapted from old crane cabins, were huge, frighteningly loud but nonetheless utterly compelling; with the increasing tempo of an alien heartbeat giving it a hypnotic allure as you fired at the staccato monsters nearing touchdown. The roughest lads at our comprehensive school raved about the game; forever nicking cash from their mothers' purses and skiving off school to spend the whole day playing it. "Gamble! Gamble!" one of them would shout inanely... Without question it was addictive; at only 10p a go, my brother and I secretly devoted many afternoons to frenzied tournaments on it; catching the bus into town specifically for that purpose.

In Leicester, the first examples appeared next to the old ABC Cinema in the long-since vanished Tivoli arcade, which was always full of choking cigarette smoke. The 'King' of Tivoli at that time was an older, massively tall African-Caribbean lad with long, plaited locks who would play the game endlessly. He had a scary violent streak; and whenever he lost a "life" would swear and kick the cabinet... in hindsight I realise that, given the fact he was in there every day, he was almost certainly long-term unemployed; but he was still undisputed ruler of the arcade; and players moved aside if he wanted to go on the machine. Later, slick table-top versions of the game were added, along with many other alternatives: Pac-Man, Galaxians, Frogger, Phoenix, Asteroids, Red Tank; though none had the iconic status of Space Invaders – it was that title alone which spearheaded the explosion in popularity of arcade and console games in general.

I was in no way an expert, although I was familiar with the hushed "23:15 rule": a trick enabling you to score the maximum 300 points from the overhead spaceship (by saving the 23rd shot for it, then every subsequent 15th on the same 'sheet'). The highest I ever scored, clearing some 25 screens of aliens, was 27,950; I left with a pain behind my eyes. It was always a dream of mine, though, to secure a full-size Space Invaders of my own. I narrowly missed out on a Bally version sold at a street auction near the student house I was living in, but I had a limit of £30 and the bids went too high. A year later, though, as a student in London, I spotted one of the original Taito models covered in spiders' webs, authentic cigarette-stub marks and dust at the back of a long-since defunct Deptford Sci-Fi shop, The Dark Side of the Moon. The owner wanted £150 for it but I managed to talk him down to £70. In the end, it actually cost more to have the machine driven to Leicester than the game itself! Its delivery was a logistical nightmare. I had to return to live with my parents for a while and there was no way they would allow that enormous thing into the house: it had to *be* there, installed before my old mum could stop it. I deliberately arranged the Space Invaders' journey up at a time I knew she would be out having her hair done. The delivery man & I nearly broke our backs getting it upstairs to my room, and as expected, she wasn't happy; but once there, it stayed until I moved out. Always a talking point for friends, few of them could resist the opportunity to "defeat the alien spawn". To increase the eye-candy of the game, I took the back off and overlaid different acetate gels over the black-and-white monitor, which made the monochrome aliens look multicoloured, just as they were in later deluxe versions of the game.

I got around 15 years' pleasure out of my Space Invaders, but gradually used it less and less. Sadly, the screen began developing glitches: the program started to blip and diagonal lines appeared across it; then the image became more and more faint until it all but fizzled out completely. I did a lot of research, but it was beyond economic repair. All the specialist companies in the trade wanted £300 just to transport the machine to their premises, let alone service it or address the faults. It was taking up too much space; and after fruitless months trying to sell it, to my lasting regret, I stripped it down completely over a period of weeks, disposing of the smaller parts in my wheelie bin and taking those that were too large to the local tip. There were literally *hundreds* of nuts, bolts and screws inside holding the circuitry together, not to mention two large spiders; but I couldn't part with the prized thing altogether, keeping a tall side panel with the evocative logo and screen-printed artwork of a monster striding over the cratered planet's surface; spaceships overhead. It was way too heavy and irregular in shape to display on a wall, so I took it first to a carpenter's shop, where the elderly owner trimmed it into a neat rectangle; then to a sawmill where it was passed several times through an industrial plane, thinning the wood as much as they dared without risking the image. At least then it could be neatly framed; and has since hung on my lounge wall right up to the present – a nostalgic reminder of the glory days of Space Invaders.

ADULT SWIM

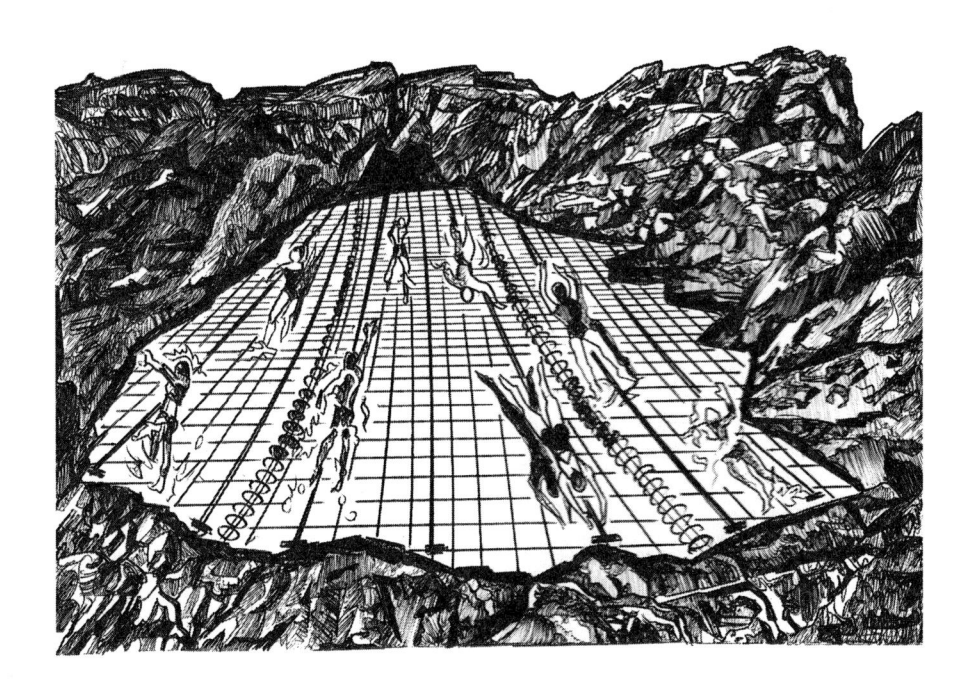

Much as it is in a classroom, the swimming pool community tends to be very much a microcosm of wider society, with every type of humankind present: your shy folk, loudmouths, ultra-competitives, bullies, diplomats – you name it, they are there... It really is fascinating to me how any environment, no matter how large or small, always seems to fill with a representative sample of each kind of person. Before Covid restrictions closed swimming pools entirely for the best part of a year, we were free to swim in any direction: widths, lengths, diagonally, whatever you wanted (within reason); but since ours re-opened, we are now in lanes cordoned off to a choice between Slow, Medium or Fast. You do feel rather like a goldfish in a bowl, the swimmers all looping around behind each other like an outstretched elastic band... The old folk used to gather in a gossiping huddle on the right-hand side. I had my own private nickname for them: *The Gaggle of Geese*... Utterly preoccupied with their health, you couldn't fail to hear the words "hospital appointment" when you swam past. God forbid I end up like that...

There was a frenzied front crawler, a tall, Swiss gentleman who thrashed through the water giving you a faceful: once confronted, he did apologise, saying he had no idea it was a problem as no one had ever told him. He hasn't changed his ways though; I simply take a deep breath and go underwater whenever he passes. One notoriously aggressive, white-haired swimmer I call *The Silver Surfer* has clashed with several people, including me. As strident as a Union rep, she thinks she owns the pool and can order anyone already in the Fast Lane to move elsewhere as soon as she arrives. The open-mouthed grimace on her face as she smashes her way through the water is fearsome to behold. My pal likes to call her *"Your Nemesis"*, just because once, I obeyed her order to move over. I'm not scared of her; but as a general rule, avoid confrontation! That rival acquaintance, however, is predictable to the *nth* degree. Eating hot cross buns all year round, he is constantly trying to sue his next-door neighbour for something or other. On Monday nights, he visits his daughter, whose boyfriend cooks a jacket potato for him; on Tuesday, to his Rock 'n' Roll class; on Wednesday, he sits in his conservatory; on Thursday it's The Whitehouse for a lunchtime curry; and on Friday, The Whitehouse again, for a child's portion of fish and chips. At weekends, he's back to Rock 'n' Roll. *Never* does he deviate from this routine – all of which of course makes him perfect for a wind-up...

"Mate!" I call to him every Monday as he swims by, "Are you going up your daughters for your tea?"

"Yeah," he replies; then every Thursday,

"Mate! Are you going up the Whitehouse for your curry?"

"Yeah," he replies; then, on a Friday,

"Mate: Are you going up the Whitehouse for your fish and chips?"

"Yeah."

"Child's portion?"

"Yeah."

"Hey mate, what would you do if you arrived at The Whitehouse and found someone sitting at your table?"

"They can't – I book it."

"Okay– but you can't reserve that *specific* table: let's say there was someone sitting there…"

"Well they'll 'ave to move."

"Well, what if they refuse, though – what would you do?"

"I'd make them get off."

"And if they stay put?"

"You ain't seen *me* mate, once I get mad… I'd *make* 'em get off."

"What if it was an alien, though?"

"I don't care who it is – they'll 'ave to go!"

"Yeah, but what if the alien's got a ray gun in his hand? You wouldn't touch him then…"

(I can see the eavesdropping lifeguard laughing at this.)

"Yeah I would, you *d*ckhead*…" It doesn't take much for him to resort to abuse.

"Don't wind 'im up!" grins the swimming-capped lady from the slow lane; but I find it amusing to go through this ritual every week; just as he likes to tell me, as he passes, exactly how many partners he danced with on a Monday or Tuesday.

"Twelve partners last night," or "Only eight partners; there were no atmosphere…"

Then when he enters the changing room, he announces his arrival with his usual victory call:

"*HoOo!… HoOo!*" (my cue to ask, "How many lengths, mate?")

"54," he'll say, or something close.

"Not bad, mate," I'll reply. "Start of the week, you know; you'll do better tomorrow…"

In the process of completing a mile, the water tends to loosen my trunks. "Time for a *pit-stop*, mate!" I announce as I complete my 44th length. "Sort my *drawstring* out…"

"Yeah – adjust yer fat," he says (despite having a persistent tyre of gristle himself).

Then, once my trunks are firmly tied, I tell him, "All set for my final Top 20; perfect physical specimen…"

But what makes him most livid of all is my insistence that a true mile in a 25-metre pool is not 64 lengths, but 64.4; which he refuses to recognise – which accounts for why I get out at the *middle* steps. There are no steps at 0.4, so I treat the extra 1/10 of a mile as a "baker's dozen" – doing 64.5 lengths instead, just to make sure. Now, this fella prides himself on his thrice-weekly front crawl. I do front crawl one way, breast-stroke the other. But for the last half-length, I *always* do the crawl, like a lap of honour. The lifeguards know it's a signal I'm about to get out after an hour-plus in the water. I say to my pal,

"Time for your free tuition in the crawl (rolling the 'R')... Learn: watch and learn from the master."

"Yeah — and how many of the crawl do you do?" he ridicules. It's all banter.

I've been steadily doing biro portraits of all the swimmers: one old fella's had eight of his family drawn. The staff themselves are a nice lot. It's tradition on your birthday to get a powerful, invigorating dousing from the lifeguard with the firehose they use to fill the pool. When that jet hits you full force, you feel it — but like an initiation, it must be endured. The ribbing you get in the 7 a.m. queue is merciless... Gives you a thick skin, though. There was an L-shaped privet hedge on the path outside the Leisure Centre which reeked with a vomit-like smell especially after it had rained. Apparently it was caused by the saliva of a ravaging insect reacting with the wet leaves; anyway, the queue were often remarking on the unpleasant aroma; finally, I wrote a series of e-mails to the manager of the whole group of leisure centres, entitled *"Unsurpassable Stench Part 1, Unsurpassable Stench Part 2, Unsurpassable Stench Part 3,"* and, once the year-long campaign led to the hedge being cut down, *"Unsurpassable Stench Part 4: The Finale!"* My pal promptly cut his own hedge into a bizarre 'L' shape — inspiring me to give it its own mocking nickname: "Tufty".

I love it when a topic of conversation spreads across the entire population of the pool, dividing opinion. One of the best ever came about when I asked Matey how many chips he got at the Whitehouse (part of a chain notoriously mean with their portions).

"About 15," he answered.

"Fifteen?" I echoed, incredulous. "No wonder they've got a reputation for being tight!"

"That's enough for me," he argues. "I 'ave a child's portion."

"Call yourself a *man*!" I chuckle. "You should get at least 80."

"No I shouldn't, cos then I'd be as fat as you!" he retorts. (But now he counts them every time.)

Gradually I quiz everyone as they swim by on what they think is the optimum amount of chips. Answers vary between 20 and 45. The next day, a new subject: how many baked beans are there in a typical can...? (I counted them, so I know.)

"You need to *get a life...*" one sensible woman growls scornfully, delighting me with the reaction.

Different coloured shards of foam, eroded from the floats, often appear in the pool. I noticed this several years ago and began to collect them, gaining me the nickname FBI – "Foreign Body Inspector." I now have a giant jarful, why I can't explain – but it's an amusing diversion. Other swimmers now point me to these floaters, even placing them on the poolside for me. When he can, my pal maliciously hides the larger ones. I'd like to design and display a 'Keep Calm' Ministry-style portcullis all over the premises, with the words, *"If you see a Foreign Body, ask for Guy: FBI."*

BUNGALOW CAKES

For most people, it would be a comedown. Going from an extended five-bed detached bungalow tucked away in a leafy cul-de-sac to a tiny, one-bedroom version of the same on a busy main road. My reasons for moving, though, were two-fold. The first place had been a blissful home to share with an adorable working PAT Therapy dog; but at almost 17 years old, his time to cross the Rainbow Bridge eventually approached. There were too many memories; it could never be the same without him. Secondly, supply work had declined to such an extent I was struggling not to get into debt. Seeing the writing on the wall, I put the house up for sale before that happened.

Downsizing left me with a lump sum on which to get through similar periods when work was scarce: it was also an exercise in minimalism, ensuring my footprint on this Earth would now, by necessity, be the smallest possible, shackled by fewest possessions. This new place really was an extreme in terms of size: it looked more like *Play School*, effectively a garage with a pointed roof! Visitors drove past, it was so minute; and when the smallest house in the UK sold to great media coverage, I measured the width only to find mine six inches *smaller*. Yet to my disbelief, it was still rated Band 'C' for Council Tax – same as the five-bed. I wasn't having it and began doing research.

What I discovered was nothing short of astonishing. It was of course former Prime Minister Margaret Thatcher's government who brought in, and were largely defeated by, the massively unpopular Poll Tax bill. The way individual properties were valued and banded the year after was not only mind-blowingly arbitrary, but also highly subjective. A vehicle was driven past every dwelling in the country, with the banding judgment, from what I could glean, made seemingly on a throwaway "Oh – I'll call that one a 'C;' I'll give that an 'E'..." basis: A simplification perhaps, but not an enormous one. Those bands, fixed back in 1991, have applied *ever since*; unless you challenge the verdict, you could, in some circumstances, have paid thousands more than you should have. I filled in a preliminary appeal form and quickly got a call from a local Council official.

"I agree that, given your property's size, 'C' seems a little high," he said. "I'd be happy to lower it to a 'B' if you like." It was a gesture in the right direction, but one that didn't go nearly far enough.

"Have you *seen* this property?" I asked, incredulous. "Quite aside from the cold problem, it's the size of a postage stamp! If this isn't a Band 'A,' I don't know what is..."

We had reached an impasse.

"Well, your only option to contest it further is to take it to formal Tribunal," I was told flatly. I *had* to do it. Experience has taught me that to get anywhere against the unhearing face of authority, there's no point fighting procedure: you jump through *every* hoop, being as bloody-minded as they are. Red tape's there precisely to put off those lacking the stamina from pursuing a challenge.

That was where the learning curve began... The onus, I discovered, is very much on *you*, the homeowner, to put a case and prove that the value your property *would* have had (not now, but back in

1991) is commensurate with property values the lower Band covered *back then*; 'A' being the cheapest. It's not so easy. Perhaps there was no sale of your property in 1991; in which case you have to start with the sale *closest* to that date, arguing your case with that price. You must measure and work out the exact dimensions of your property in square metres, room by room, adding them up to find the total footprint; and most importantly, to justify a reduction in your own Council Tax, you must then find larger, better properties currently in *lower* Bands than yours! The way I did it was to visit the Council to get a list of all Band 'A' and 'B' houses in my postcode. When I did, I was told paper records were no longer made public and to try the local Valuation Office website. Via an Advanced Search I generated a list several hundred pages long of solely Band 'A' & 'B' houses in Leicester; but *not* a list specific just to my own postcode. I then had to spend hours going through every page, logging each Band 'B'or 'A' address which *was* in my area!

Although there are other factors to banding decisions, such as external property footprints and the general reputation, desirability and affluence of the area in question, as a layman in the field I decided to focus on the one measurable criterion I could use by way of comparison between my own property and others: *internal dimen*sions: the only finite data on other houses *already* in the public domain and available on well-known property databases. After all, the chances of people accepting a stranger's request to come in and measure every room in their home are slim: I did try; and you can bet I got short shrift! Next, I took my shortlist of Band 'B' and 'A' properties and grouped their street names in alphabetical order; then visited a famous property website seeking all dwellings on *sale* within my area; noting any whose street names matched those on my shortlist. But as a house number is often not visible or deliberately blurred out on the photos, the only way to be certain the properties on sale were the same numbers as the Band 'B' or 'A' houses I'd narrowed down was by actually going *past*, or calling the relevant estate agents for confirmation.

By painstakingly identifying and matching addresses for sale to the house numbers on my Valuation Office shortlist, I now had (via floorplans on the estate agent ads), internal dimensions of properties guaranteed not only to be Band 'B's & 'A's, but *also* in my postcode area, with which to compare my own house's dimensions. As bungalows are scarce and I struggled to find enough similar ones; the properties I chose as comparisons were mostly semis or townhouses. In my view, though, that added even more argument that a bungalow half their height shouldn't be banded similarly. I'd done my best; and just had to hope the panel treated the comparisons with fairness. The closest sale date to 1991 I could find for my property was 2004: not ideal at all. But using that 'sold' price, I was able to find its 1991 value via an online House Price Index Calculator created specifically for that purpose. It turned out, had it ever been sold exactly then, it would have been just £29,911. Quoting the Valuation Tribunal booklet, Band 'A' in 1991 covered houses up to £40,000. With my place valued £10,000+ below that, I'd made a case! *Quod erat demonstrandum.*

Fortunately, I had not long previously completed an ECDL course; a software training which included learning how to use a well-known Microsoft slideshow-creation application. Being all too aware via my Teaching experience of the power of visual aids in hooking an audience, I decided to present my entire argument and photographic evidence via such a slideshow; the advantage being that, whilst narrating it, I would be in full mouse-click control; certain they only saw each piece of evidence exactly *when* I wanted them to! In my spare time, it took a month to compile an elaborate 36-page slideshow, with everything from detailed step-by-step mathematical calculations that could be easily followed, to SFX and pictures of each comparison house along with the relevant dimensions. But something was missing. I wanted my presentation to be nothing short of *theatre*. I had to have a "gimmick" of some kind – something that would never be forgotten by the panel...

Idly channel-surfing that evening, I happened to flip past a regular TV cooking show; not my thing at all – but all at once, it hit me. *Bungalow cakes!* I would make a tray of miniature, edible bungalows and offer them to everyone at the end of my presentation. True, it was a mad gamble, but I felt sure it would work well in my favour... Inexperienced cook that I am, I know nothing about baking; so the night before, bought a large, plain sponge cake, icing sugar and pink food colouring from the supermarket, cut the sponge into regular blocks, and made triangular pieces for each side of the roof. You can be sure there were disasters along the way, not least of which was the roof icing refusing to set – I had to partially freeze it in the end. The procedure was not aided by my being in hysterics most of the way through anticipating the reaction; but it was better to get the laughter out of my system, as I wanted to present the tray with a completely deadpan expression. Finally, I had a cling-filmed tray of 20 crude and lumpy iced bungalows all ready to go.

My ex-girlfriend and a good pal of mine were both keen to witness this spectacle at the Tribunal. It had taken months to arrive; and on the day, I found myself surprisingly nervous. The venue was tricky to find, miles out in Beaumont Leys, tucked away behind an Industrial Estate (we'd have been done for without SatNav!) but I made sure we were there ahead of time in order to conceal the tray of cakes on a chair pushed in at the boardroom table. My greatest concern was that there might be compatibility problems between my laptop and their screen, but luckily, their technician had all the connectors we needed and soon I was ready. I'd realised I probably couldn't *actually* offer the panel the cakes, as it might have been seen as bribery; so I carefully primed my friends:

"*Just* in case, I'm going to offer one to each of you too; and I need you – please – to accept, *even* if you don't want to, just so it looks as if the gesture is appreciated and enjoyed by others at least."

The Tribunal was actually a very formal affair, conducted more or less like a legal courtroom. What I haven't mentioned yet is that, while the judging panel itself was guaranteed to be made up of unbiased, impartial and neutral members, I most definitely *did* have a rival, whom I believe heralded from the Valuation Office itself. A right humourless, silver-haired old grudge-bearer he looked, in a nasty business suit; and he was a slippery bloke as well; a big fella who had cunningly convinced me by mail that I was required to divulge to him details of all the properties I was going to present for comparison. I had no idea he was actually very much my opponent; who, armed with that advance information, would easily attempt to assemble targeted evidence of his own specifically against *those* particular properties – contradicting my own testimony! Suspicious, however, I'd done some digging and via a call to his department, found out in no uncertain terms from his colleague that the man most definitely *was* my rival, not harmless at all. When I came to present my evidence, I raised this grievance at the *start*, putting him instantly on the back foot. While efficient enough at what he did, giving the requisite paper copies of his material to each of the panel, he showed no imagination or creativity in his presentation, speaking in a wooden monotone and relying on a single sheaf of notes. He was done in five minutes. Now it was my turn.

There was no way I was going to blow this: I'd thought about nothing else for the past month; having practised my spiel to the nth degree. By way of copies, I simply passed to each of the panel a tiny memory stick containing my full presentation before beginning. The slideshow took 20 minutes to screen; during which I had the whole room in the palm of my hand, hanging on every word and even breaking into laughter at a 'gurgling' burglar visual I'd made to emphasize how requests to measure other people's properties had been responded to. My very last slide ended with the caption, *"Enjoy your cake!"* – my rival looking on in utter disbelief – as, managing to keep a straight face, I pulled the shmoozing trayful out from the chair under the table, saying apologetically, "Now I've made a little group of bungalow cakes to mark the occasion: I would *love* to offer the panel one each, but I'm aware I probably can't." (They nodded in confirmation.) "Perhaps, however, I can invite my opponent?" Sourly, the man shook his head in refusal, looking completely undone. Instead, I turned to my pre-primed buddies seated at the far end of the room; each of whom graciously took a sponge bungalow and began eating it, "mmm"-ing effusively in approval. The panel were smiling from ear to ear as we left: *never,* I was informed, had anyone presented their case in slideshow format, let alone with themed cakes: the whole experience was quite unprecedented and surreal for them all – but I sensed also that they found it rather sweet...

A week later, a letter arrived from the Valuation Office confirming I had won my appeal and that my property was being reduced from Band 'C' to Band 'A.' While certain of my claims were contested, my reliance on internal dimensions having been viewed as "irregular", they could see that in terms of "kerb appeal", my property was far inferior to all the others I'd compared it to – so my claim was upheld. Despite the fact that it was the previous owner who went on to gain the thousands of pounds in compensation for two-and-a-half decades of overpayment (as I had only just moved in), a win is a win – and I was absolutely jubilant with the victory, which lowered my monthly Council Tax bills substantially. Ironically, no more than a month later, I happened to do a day's supply teaching for a class in which there was a kindly old Teaching Assistant. We got on like a house on fire, but her surname rang an uncannily strong bell; and before I left, I just had to ask:

"You don't happen to know a Mr ...... who works in the Valuation Office?" (naming my opponent).

Her eyebrows shot up in surprise.

"That's my other half!" she exclaimed. "He's just retired, you know…"

"My goodness," I smirked somewhat guiltily, relating the "bungalow cakes" episode. "I hope it wasn't the final straw that finished him off… Send him my best: I doubt he'll forget me in a hurry."

THE BROWN DERBY

It was always a treat to be taken out to one of the best-known fast-food restaurants of the 1970s; a chain which is far more scarce these days. Competition from other high street giants has meant only a fraction of the branches it had in its heyday remain nationwide. I remember with fondness the uniformed waitresses taking our orders, table service being virtually non-existent in similar outlets now; and the large tomato-shaped dispensers housing a uniquely tangy brand of ketchup. Our mum never trusted the hygiene of those devices, squirting the topmost residue into a paper napkin before we could use them. But by far the most memorable thing about visiting was forever begging to be allowed the most tantalising item shown on the dessert menu: the 'Brown Derby'.

Roughly resembling that famous hat synonymous with the Golden Age of Hollywood, the Brown Derby was comprised of a doughnut heaped with a spiralling helter-skelter of vanilla ice cream, cascading down over which was a waterfall of the most delicious-looking chocolate sauce, topped with big, toffeeish fudge flakes. Making the banana longboats and knickerbocker glories of the day look pitiful in comparison, it was the most spectacularly sinful choice there was, its calorie count unimaginable; and it was also quite unattainably expensive, eternally lodged in my youthful psyche at the monstrous price of £9.99. But the memory deceives: research into vintage menus of the time reveals the Brown Derby was, in fact, only 17p… To my parents, the thing looked absolutely disgusting, massively unhealthy and over-indulgent: never was I permitted to have it.

Finally, though, one momentous day, we ended up there with a family's worth of other friends; and I seized the moment. Feigning ignorance of the disapproving adult frowns around me, I cheekily requested the Brown Derby, knowing it would make a scene if my folks refused – but in the end – *what* a disappointment. All we saw when it finally arrived at the table was a paltry, shrunken parody of the wonderful-looking dish in the picture; even to my uncultivated childhood palate, it was *repulsive*, tasting as if the doughnut had been deep-fried 100 times. Did serve that greedy little juvenile version of me right; but the Brown Derby remains an evocative childhood memory.

THE SUSPICIOUS HOUSE

A few years ago, whilst visiting my parents, my mother asked if, on my way home, I might drop a misdirected parcel left at theirs to the owner of a property a few doors down. The large white house, hidden behind overgrown foliage, was fairly dilapidated in appearance; it looked as if it may once have been a beautiful dwelling, but had since fallen into disrepair; white paint flaking and covered with abandoned cobwebs and ivy. I rang the doorbell, but there was no answer. I knocked; still no response. So I wandered curiously along the weed-invaded driveway to see if there was an alternative side entrance. As I did, I heard the sound of bolts unlocking back at the front door; it creaked open by degrees to reveal a tall, youngish lad looking distinctly zombified; possibly under the influence of a recreational high. He peered out warily as I explained my presence, holding out the parcel, which he finally accepted.

To my astonishment, when I turned to go, there, right in my face, was a grizzled, unshaven old man brandishing a hockey stick already swung out in the air above his head – literally seconds away from delivering a fatal blow. I was numb with shock... Maybe they had something suspect inside they feared being discovered and thought I was an undercover detective; so he had tiptoed up behind me to take me out. In any event, some discreet form of non-verbal communication – a negative shake of the head? – must have passed between the young man and the old to reassure him I was no threat, for the latter suddenly lowered his weapon and without a word, trudged sullenly past the youth into the house. No explanation was forthcoming; so I took my leave with some haste. When I mentioned the episode to my parents, they couldn't believe it, saying I should've called the police. I never did; but on the local news a few months later, there was a report of a massive haul of cannabis seized from *that* very property: a vast, hydroponic, soil-free indoor 'grow' under fluorescent lights had been intercepted. The police described this enormous factory as a professional set-up with specialist lamps and fans; the walls of the plant-growing room lined with a silver reflective material. Half the building has since been torn down, the development under wraps behind hoarding panels; diggers moving to and fro. For all I know, I may have been seconds away from being struck down and dragged inside, never to be seen again.

THE FURRY ASSAILANT

At the time of writing, I have been the owner of three successive black Labrador Retrievers; all of which have become the most adorable companions you could dream of. Although each has varied widely in terms of size, build and personality, the breed's general temperament is so placid, gentle and loving; their nature so noble and rewarding, that somehow they get through to me on a level no human being can: until you have lived with one yourself, you are on the outside of that bubble. Every owner is different; I'm not someone who 'overlaps' one dog with the next; there's only room in my heart for one; and although some feel it's excessive, I always take a gap of three years between dogs to ensure I have grieved fully for the previous occupant and am ready to welcome the next puppy. It's the least the newcomer deserves; and very necessary if the two of you are to bond successfully. As someone who never does anything by halves, I'm aware I tend to put my dog on a pedestal; but it means each one receives all the joy and celebration I have to give. The downside of course is that, as a result, each becomes almost the focus of worship rather than just a pet; leaving me feeling as if half of *me* is gone when I lose them. Yet the ride is so worth the fall.

The first of my dogs, Opal, was a stocky Labrador from the famous Lawnwood kennel in Markfield; generations of show champions in his pedigree. A giant; he was solid muscle, ate from a casserole-sized bowl and was so big, his paws reached your shoulders. At first he was a rather bullish, independent soul, leaving me rather lamenting the fact that he wasn't as demonstrative and accepting of love as my brother's yellow Labrador. Some family friends brought their toddler over one day; and even though the dogs were still little, my brother and I had been forewarned not to let them out into the garden where the baby girl was; as they were boisterous and could have done some damage. Somehow though, they *did* get out; and from inside the house, it wasn't long before we all heard a frightened wail. Dreading what had happened, we opened the side door only to find the toddler unhurt, flanked by both 12-week-old puppies, one either side, tails wagging as they guided her gently from the garden into the house, heads level with hers. With other breeds, it may have been a different matter, but even as babies themselves, these two had an innate understanding of the child's vulnerability; protecting her and bringing her in to safety...

As they got older though, the two could be quite a handful, working as a team, tearing and ripping things between them and escaping, only to be found on one occasion some seven miles away in a vicar's garden. After learning how to jump up and open the door to their room, wreaking havoc in the house while we were out, we had to have the door handle reversed, necessitating it being lifted up to open. Highly intelligent, they learned their way around that too; and a bolt had to be added. Opal even pulled a solid gold necklace from my mother's neck once and swallowed it, leading to a revolting surveillance task: my having to poke a stick through every poo he did in the hunt for it. After three days in transit through his gut, my efforts were finally rewarded by the glint of precious metal. The necklace had to be sterilized, though, before it could be worn again...

There's meant to be one devilish puppy in each litter; and I sure picked it for my latest – aptly named Budulinek. Originating in a Slovakian fairytale, the word means "naughty boy". Way smaller than the previous two; and a 'Drakeshead' Labrador from Aylesbury, famous for their uniquely domed craniums, he makes up for his diminutive size with a far more wilful personality. Despite coming top in two obedience trainings, he has zero recall outside, regardless of any treat offered. I had him neutered after he ran circles around an old lady who lost her balance and fell; she was okay, thank God, but could easily have broken her hip. Contrary to what I was led to believe, the operation did nothing to subdue him: on seeing any dog on the far side of the park, he got tunnel vision and vanished into a speck in the distance, unresponsive to shouts or bribery. It was when he made it through a small copse onto a busy carriageway where he could have either caused an accident, or been knocked down, that I vowed he would stay tethered for life; despite appeals from others to give off-lead walking another try. The buck stops with the owner at the end of the day: this one's unpredictable, a loose cannon; and it's the only responsible thing to do.

Never have I known a dog with a *will* like Budulinek: he knows exactly where he wants to go, yet would pull his own head off rather than be taken somewhere he isn't comfortable with. Planting his feet like a donkey, he has snapped multiple leads, destroyed entire rooms in separation anxiety; and as a puppy, his milk teeth, razor-sharp, drew blood from me every day. He went as far as eating the garden fence and even the bricks; *everything* goes in his mouth: grass, wood, acorns, berries; and most disgusting of all, he is an occasional coprophage (I'll let you look that up!). Mischief aside, though, this one is actually very needful, terrified of fireworks and craving physical contact. Being near you isn't enough; he must be physically *upon* you, which can be suffocating. But would I sell him? Not for a million: he was an absolute lifeline during Lockdown...

It is however my *second* dog – dhruvesh – that this tale centres on. Named after a tiny charismatic child in one of my first-ever classes, I used a lower-case 'd' to distinguish dog from boy to avoid offending his mother. To all who knew him, this particular Labrador (originating from a Melton Mowbray kennel, Lynquest) was an *angel*; not an ounce of malice or instability in his nature. He idolised me, following like a duckling if I took as much as a step. There wasn't a member of the family who didn't benefit from having him around; even one of the cleaners burst into tears whilst alone one morning following a relationship break-up. Putting her arms around dhruvesh, she wept openly; and he was just there for her: sat, nuzzled her and gave her the silent comfort she needed.

"*DON'T* kiss him!" my mum used to snap when dhruvesh first arrived, "he's an *animal!*" – yet within a few months, she was kissing him too; as with everyone, he just wove his way into her heart. I took him to Faculty parties and could let him off the lead without the slightest qualm; there he would be in the midst of ongoing cricket games, enthralled children crawling both under and over him – he had such tolerance and almost intuitive awareness of the need to be gentle. A perfect traveller on long car and train journeys, I could take him to public firework displays: rockets shooting up just metres from him; he didn't bat an eyelid. This was no ordinary family pet: dhruvesh was so special I couldn't keep him to myself; and had him endorsed as a PAT dog working for Pets As Therapy. In hi-vis uniforms, we did phobic work with children who had suffered bad experiences with dogs. Via gradual exposure, they became increasingly tactile with him until their fear evaporated. dhruvesh did over 100 visits, mainly to the Stroke Unit at Leicester General Hospital, literally pulling me up the stairs in his eagerness to reach the ward. Often, he met the most acute, newly admitted cases; then, a few weeks on, when the same patients had transferred to the less critical Rehabilitation ward, they would recall that at their worst moment, dhruvesh had been there. Out would come the affected limb; many people overcome with raw emotion...

After three years, the contagious MRSA became no longer confined to the odd side room, but rife in whole bays; and I began to feel it was unsafe to bring the dog in, lest he carried infection out into the community. I got a transfer for dhruvesh to a local residential care home, where the old folk were seated in the lounge sipping their morning sherry. I would bring him around them one by one; then, with an old piano in the corner, would secure the loop of his lead around one of the stool legs and hammer out a few golden oldies to which the residents would sing along. After a few months of such piano sessions, I looked down one day to find nothing under the chair leg – the lead must have worked loose; dhruvesh nowhere to be seen. Anxiously, I got up to find him – only to see him doing the work all by himself, moving to each resident one by one and laying his head in each of their laps. He just knew what was expected of him and was doing it independently.

Now one of dhruvesh's favourite walks was to Shady Lane Arboretum, up through Piggy's Hollow, former site of a 13th-century moated manor-house; and onto the adjoining Golf Course. Often on the arboretum was a dog which, due to its owner never having it on the lead, was a real nuisance. It was a beautiful Japanese Akita, a large, powerful example with a wolf-like head and looped tail forever curved up over its back. A breed which tends towards aggression and dominance with same-sex dogs, this one had something against dhruvesh. On several occasions, it had attempted to mount him; and each time I'd had to firmly order its owner, a wiry Asian youth, to pull it off. On this particular day, though, the owner had become separated from his dog and was nowhere in sight. The huge Akita looked especially stunning, almost certainly fresh from some expensive canine grooming salon. Primped and preened beyond belief, not a hair out of place, its fur was as brilliantly clean and white as freshly-fallen snow – but once it saw dhruvesh, in habitual manner, it mounted him; and gripping him firmly with its forepaws, began roughly humping him from behind. Several verbal admonitions proved ineffective; and although dhruvesh was reserved by nature, the noises emanating from his throat indicated that he wasn't happy. This attacker was essentially trying to rape him; and I wasn't having it. I looked around for a weapon to drive the Akita off with. There wasn't even a loose branch; and, short of actually kicking the dog, in desperation, I resorted to the only thing I had, a full poop-bag, decidedly loose in consistency. Troubled by dhruvesh's discomfort, I began whacking the Akita with the knotted bagful; becoming ever more frenzied in my swings, until, inevitably, the flimsy plastic bag gave out with a loud bang.

Picture the most violent mudburst, the pressurized contents erupting forth in a 360° wave, with that impeccably-groomed, pure-white Akita at its epicentre. A hot arc of brown fluid whizzed dangerously over my head, as the aggressor's pampered, pristine white coat was covered in liquid dogshit from head-to-toe – just as its bewildered keeper re-appeared, stumbling down the bank.

"You want to get that creature *DONE!*" I roared at him, as he regained ownership of his now filthy, soiled pet." It's a flaming menace!"

"'Ow would *you* loike to be done?" he retaliated in a textbook Leicester accent; leading the stricken Akita away over the brow of the hill.

FROM STUDENT RAGS TO A TASTE OF RICHES

In December 1987, to fulfil the requirements of a project set at Art College, I headed for London with a sketchbook and much of my creative kit in a rucksack. The opportunity to get away couldn't come fast enough: I was hopelessly in love with a girl on my course who already had a steady boyfriend; and I couldn't tell her, knowing the parameters of our relationship and the trust she had in me as a platonic friend. The need to keep my feelings secret was eating me up inside; it was affecting everything (my artwork included) and slowly but surely, I was headed for disaster. But that's another story. I wasn't running away; just needed some distance to get perspective on the situation. At the time I had an absolute fascination with tramps; it was something about their 'outsider' status in society and the vivid life experience writ large on their faces; I had even befriended one homeless man named Gordon in the City Centre, who had a leg riddled with gout; every now and then he would allow me to draw him for a small fee; and several years later, I became really quite pally with a larger-than-life, highly charismatic tramp in Deptford, who kept all his possessions (including golden goblets) in a hooded pram to which he'd tethered an enormous pair of German Shepherd dogs for protection. You couldn't miss him with his huge beard; he would push that pram through the streets, yelling *"GERONIMO!"* at the top of his growling voice. I even accompanied him once to a soup kitchen in a nearby church crypt where he got a week's supply of food for just a few pounds, had a hot lunch and told me how he lived in a squat. Whenever he wanted a wash, he would take a wheelie bin inside, fill it with cold water, stand it in front of the fire and when it was warm enough, climb inside for a stand-up bath... But in the West End, I discovered many more such characters, both men and women, some of whom could be unpredictable and aggressive, not just to me but to each other... There wasn't as much empathy towards the homeless then as there is now; on several occasions I witnessed the Transport Police being pretty callous towards them in the tunnels leading to the Tube; their sole agenda being to move them on from the London Underground to anywhere but there.

At an emotional level, at least, I was as lost as those tramps at that time, wandering aimlessly without focus; which is perhaps why I identified with them so much. One freezing night, I ended up crouching on the icy ground doing an oil-based monoprint on a sheet of plastic of an old-fashioned, bay-windowed shop-front in a strange, curved alley somewhere behind Piccadilly Circus. All the stores had closed and I was totally alone. Feeling flat as a pancake and having all but completely lost faith in myself in every respect, I was about to give up when out of the shadows appeared this equally ragged old bag-lady. Looking down at my recently-printed artwork, she exclaimed, in a distinctly German accent, "Vot an *amazing* talent you have!" – then, smiling benevolently, vanished into the darkness. She might just as well have been an angel – for at my lowest moment, she somehow gave me renewed self-belief and an extra boost. Half an hour or so later, having walked on into the Green Park area, I found myself quite literally busting bladder-wise; but there were no restaurants I could use anywhere in sight; just huge stone-fronted buildings on both sides. In the distance, just past the park itself, I spotted an official-looking attendant standing outside one of them and approached him seeking the nearest facilities. He turned out to be some kind of uniformed Commissionaire. "There's a public toilet just across the road there, Sir," he said; pointing to a small building jutting out onto the pavement a few yards further back. When I reached it though, it was all derelict and boarded up – so I went back to him seeking further directions. "Look – I never saw you, okay?" he said, "but see the outside staircase? Just use that..." Thanking him effusively, I headed up the steps, not knowing or caring where I was, such was my urgency. As it turned out, it was as if I had entered another world.

    I found myself in the most opulent WC I had ever seen, all the units constructed from the most beautifully polished marble, complete with gold-rimmed sinks, discreet ceiling lighting, piping hot water cascading from what looked like solid gold taps – and a host of complimentary bathroom items, from rolled hot towels to individually-wrapped soaps, matches, moisturisers and miniature bottled fragrances, all featuring a curious, distinctive logo of a rearing gold lion holding a royal orb in its paws above an ornate, cascading scroll. Wherever I was, it was the last word in luxury... *No way am I leaving down that same external staircase,* I thought; *I've got to find out where I am!* So now, much relieved, I took a cheeky alternative route out via a set of inner steps leading down into the main building proper. Barely seconds elapsed before I was overlooking the most extravagantly elaborate and tasteful interior I had ever seen, filled with twinkling chandeliers and the most pristine dining tables, each individual place-setting clad with multiple sets of cutlery, rolled napkins and the finest porcelain plates; the periphery decorated with delicately tapering marble columns and the most lush, verdant fronds of ferns and other exotic plant life in priceless-looking vases; a tuxedoed musician playing the most tasteful of melodies on an enormous white grand piano and the seated guests themselves immaculately turned out in the finest clothes; a number of them clearly proud fathers taking their beautiful young debutante daughters out for the swankiest of culinary experiences... In my rough Guernsey tunic, denim jeans and messy backpack, I stuck out like a sore thumb; sidling towards the exit as rapidly as I could! It wasn't until I passed safely through the purple exterior awning with its golden fringe and down the elegant steps back onto street level, that I was able to look back and finally discover where I had been. The nearby street sign 'Mayfair' should've been the giveaway: I'd only gone for a wee in The Ritz.